HELP YOURSELF

A Revolutionary Alternative Recovery Program

Dr. Joel C. Robertson

OLIVER
NELSON

A Division of Thomas Nelson Publishers
Nashville

PUBLISHER'S NOTE: This book is intended for general information only and is not intended to supplant medical advice, diagnosis, or treatment by a personal physician. Readers are urged to consult their personal physicians regarding addictions and recovery.

Published in Nashville, Tennessee, by Oliver-Nelson Books, a division of Thomas Nelson, Inc., Publishers, and distributed in Canada by Lawson Falle, Ltd., Cambridge, Ontario.

Unless otherwise noted, the Bible version used in this publication is THE NEW KING JAMES VERSION. Copyright © 1979, 1980, 1982, Thomas Nelson, Inc., Publishers. Scripture quotations noted TEV are from the *Good News Bible*—Old Testament: Copyright © American Bible Society 1976: New Testament: Copyright © American Bible Society 1966, 1971, 1976. Used by permission. Scripture quotations noted NIV are taken from the HOLY BIBLE: NEW INTERNATIONAL VERSION. Copyright © 1973, 1978, 1984 by the International Bible Society. Used by permission of Zondervan Bible Publishers.

Printed in the United States.

ISBN 0-8407-9132-1

To Vickie, my wife,
for patience, understanding, love, and support
as I did things differently from my peers.

To Nicole, my daughter,
for inspiring me to mature,
and to help and understand others.

To Heidi, my daughter,
for inspiring me to ask questions, seek answers,
and then ask why.

To Brooke, my daughter,
for inspiring me to work diligently and hard
on developing a system to help others.

To my parents
for allowing me to always challenge the system,
but respect people.

Without the four women in my life, I would never have learned to see through sensitive, caring, and emotional eyes. Mom and Dad, thanks for the challenging and inquisitive spirit. I love you all.

Contents

Acknowledgments

No book, especially this book, is entirely the creation of the author who receives the credit. This book was inspired by and written by the many patients I have met who suffer from and overcome addictions. I thank them for giving me the answers to share with others.

Thanks to *Victor Oliver*, publisher, the man who understood how to take a clinician's view of life to people. I can never thank him enough for his patience, insight, wisdom, and prayers. *Cecil Murphey*, a special writer, for his insight, love, and care for people, which are manifested in his writing and, especially, in the way he took my final draft on this complex subject and skillfully revised it to make it work. *Lila Empson*, an editor who tops them all. I appreciate her hours of time and incredible talent. *Bruce Barbour*, publisher, for his enthusiasm and interest in seeking new and effective information. *Robert Zaloba*, marketing executive, for his knowledge of knowing what people need to understand and knowing how they listen.

This book is the combined effort of those above. Although I may have the credit on the cover, the credit will always be theirs. Many clinicians have good concepts, but only a few have the people to make those concepts affect the world.

Foreword

by James D. Mallory, Jr., M.D.

Director of the Atlanta Counselling Center

This book is for the thousands of people suffering from various addictions who need alternative treatment. Many people cannot afford traditional inpatient or outpatient programs, and many don't need them. Dr. Robertson presents various treatment plans that attempt to tailor-make the recovery process to fit the individual. He makes a strong point, with which I agree, that there is no single treatment approach that helps all people. He has avoided an elitist attitude of having *the* answer. He does not detract from traditional treatments but simply points out they will not work for all people.

Dr. Robertson's treatment process helps individuals identify specific features of their nervous system and personality and then guides them into the type of recovery program that will most likely work for them. Diet, exercise, and support-system recommendations vary depending on which one of eight different types of people he describes. His dietary recommendations involve some concepts that are not proven, but his position is if they help, use them, and if they don't, use other aspects of the recovery program. At the very least, the dietary guidelines are healthier than those that most people follow and represent a step toward new, more positive behavior.

He makes several points that I would like to underscore as being vital.

1. Addictions include all behaviors that are repeated despite destructive consequences.
2. Simply stopping a behavior will not result in recovery. The person must learn new patterns to get basic needs met; otherwise, relapse will occur or another destructive addiction will be substituted.
3. People are not likely to change because of a concept (you

don't talk or argue them out of it), but because of the benefit. The key is to find new, healthier rewards.

4. There is a spiritual element to recovery that is crucial. Dr. Robertson's steps to developing a functional faith can radically change a person's life.

5. The real battlefield is not the addictive behavior. Rather, it is a person's thoughts and concepts plus the psychological needs the behavior is meeting. It is likely that negative thoughts produce negative effects on neurotransmitters in the brain, which, in turn, promote more negative thinking. This cycle absolutely must be broken.

6. Entry points for breaking the cycle may be spiritual, physical, or emotional. Ultimately, all areas need to change for successful recovery to occur.

7. Family members are not the cause of the addiction; however, they are encouraged to be a part of the solution. This position helps alleviate much of the guilt that families have over a member's addiction.

In summary, this book presents a refreshing, flexible, comprehensive self-help program that has the potential to guide many people trapped in addictions to a new, happier, healthier life.

Preface

Whenever a new book or idea is presented, people need to understand the purpose and usefulness of the information. Since this book offers a new concept and approach, I would like to clarify its purpose and usefulness.

This book is about addictions, not just drug and alcohol addictions but behavior that is out of control. The traditional alcohol and drug definitions of addictions will not be used in this book. Individuals trained in the alcohol and drug field may be prejudiced in their view of how to treat addictions. For example, inpatient treatment or residential care is the usual approach to alcohol and drug addictions. This book is not geared toward individuals treated by present systems. It should provide insight to them, but its strength is for another population. That population includes the millions of people who are addicted but may never admit it or even seek help. The reasons are varied for not seeking help. They may not be able to afford the present system. They may have tried the present system and found it ineffective. They may not like the present system. Perhaps they don't want to admit their problems to others; perhaps they don't want anyone else to know. We can discuss denial, pride, and any number of reasons, but it doesn't matter. They will not seek help with the present system. This book provides an alternative method for those who choose it. At the best, their lives will be changed; at the least, they will be educated.

I've chosen to use reward centers and brain chemistry as the methodology to develop a "help yourself" approach. I'm assuming that the reader is motivated and doesn't want more motivational reading but desires a clear-cut method of change. Since brain chemistry relates to reward centers and compliance, I've developed a method to follow. Therapy is individualized, to say the least. By dividing a person's behavior into rewards, responses to thoughts and feelings, and baseline feelings, we can begin to tailor treatment. I am the last person to admit that we know enough about the brain to be able to precisely treat and change behavior by manipulating the brain. However, this book is the beginning of an ever-changing and expanding way of looking at human behavior.

I've chosen to make this book practical instead of research oriented. The reason is twofold. First, if it is only research oriented, it will be obsolete the day it is published. The research on brain chemistry and behavior is and will be explosive in the next few years. Second, research doesn't change lives; practical application of information does. Those of you who wish to look at this book as a research position paper will be disappointed since that book would best be published as a medical textbook. Those looking for practical and sensible guidelines for change will probably find the book most helpful.

I believe it is important for me to take a few positions in the areas of brain chemistry, genetics, diet, activity, and behavioral changes. I take these positions to make it clear that people looking for a key to their recovery will still be looking for a key after they have read this book *if they make no changes*. If they choose to make changes, this book will provide practical guidelines for them.

Brain Chemistry Technology

Brain chemistry technology is still in the investigative and developmental stage. The exact mechanisms for changes are not well understood. However, concepts don't have to be perfected to be useful. For example, we know that alcoholism has a genetic component to it. The exact mechanism may be an enzyme alteration, a dominant or recessive gene, or any number of causes. The concept that it is genetic is enough to be practical. I will use as much medically proven information that is available and rely on reasonable assumptions to connect the information. As time and research progress, the pieces of the puzzle will be identified and even changed. The concepts will probably be altered only slightly. I have included Appendix B for the "prove to me, or I won't accept it" population. This appendix is technical and not exceptionally practical but is the foundation for the assumptions made.

Brain chemistry technology will probably link our physiological, emotional, and spiritual parts. Thoughts will change biochemistry and biochemistry will change thoughts. All contribute to a unique spiritual view. The exact method is unclear, but the concepts are reasonable.

Genetics

Genetic or inherited addictions exist, probably in alcoholism and compulsive overeating. As genetic studies continue I suspect a few other behaviors will prove to have a genetic relationship. Whether an addiction is genetic or not is probably significant only if genetic depression or anxiety is causing it. For example, the old term for depression used to be called endogenous depression. This means brain chemicals will need to be altered to clear the depression before addiction can be eliminated. Addictions can be treated at the same time, but a replacement behavior will probably become addicting unless the brain chemistry alteration is resolved.

Diet Therapy

Diet therapy is a controversial approach. The majority of conservative medical practitioners will refer to diet therapy as quackery. Others will claim miraculous benefits from dietary manipulation. I take the position that whatever works for you is the best method. This book will provide the theories behind dietary manipulation. They will at least allow you as a reader to approach dietary manipulation from a semiscientific approach. At the present time, dietary manipulation of behavior is somewhat controversial and unproven, using traditional medical research. I believe a person can benefit from dietary manipulation in two ways. First, it is the beginning of changing a life-style; therefore, it is actually a behavioral modification step. Second, if it works for you, use it. If it doesn't, discard it. It may work, or it may be a small investment into learning what doesn't work. Scientifically, it can't be proven at this point, so don't look for a conservative medical practitioner to approve of the approach. A healthy, balanced diet is accepted by all, so I would encourage that to be the minimum commitment from you.

Activity/Exercise Therapy

Although not as controversial as diet, activity and exercise programs are usually suggested but not considered proven therapies. They are suggested because they are generally considered healthy. I will encourage them more vigorously than diet therapy, but I am aware of their unproven benefits in psychological issues. I view activity and exercise therapies as beneficial for four reasons. First, they are a change in behavior, which is essential to recover from addictions. Second, if used correctly, they are healthy to a person physically. Third, most people feel better emotionally through exercise. And finally, exercise and activity therapies are alternatives. We will all continue to get angry, depressed, and frustrated and experience any number of other emotions. Often the addicted person uses the addiction to respond to these emotions. Activity and exercise may provide an alternative approach to some.

Other Recovery Methods

All recovery methods work. However, not all people will recover with one method. I believe in anything that will work for you—if that be inpatient, outpatient, intensive outpatient, self-help groups, religious conversion, or a help yourself book. This book is not to replace any approach; it supplements and offers an additional approach. If you find it isn't working for you, please use another method but don't quit trying. If you suffer from severe psychiatric conditions or medical conditions or have long-standing addictions to alcohol and drugs, please consult your physician and/or a physician trained in addictions. They may not agree with this book because of its approach, but that's all right. You need their help more at this point. No person with these conditions can recover with this book; such conditions must be recognized and treated for this book to be helpful.

This book will use unique terminology to help you understand yourself. Since the approach is new, so are the terms and their meanings. Please pay attention to the terms and definitions in this book, and apply them to you as an individual.

In summary, this book is not to replace your physician, psychiatrist, psychologist, or others if you have them. It provides another approach to your problem. If you aren't in treatment and don't suffer from severe psychiatric or medical conditions or have long-standing alcohol and drug addiction, it may help you without your seeking professional services. Above all please remember, whatever approach you begin with may not be right for you. Don't think of yourself as failing. The treatment just wasn't right for you. Keep trying!

Introduction

Here is what happened to three different individuals on Wednesday of last week. Which of them would you call an addict?

Bill, an executive at a highly competitive company, has a demanding job. After an extremely difficult day at work—and each day seems to get worse—he came home. He was late. Immediately he noticed a fire in the grill when he pulled the car into the driveway. His wife had put the steaks on the grill an hour and a half earlier—the time Bill normally got home. Then she forgot about them. The two kids were screaming at the boy next door. Everyone was obviously in a bad mood.

"So much for a peaceful evening at home," he muttered as he got out of his car and slammed the door. Brushing past the kids, he turned off the grill but didn't even wave at his wife.

"I need a drink!" he announced to anyone who happened to be listening. To himself, he said, *I just need to unwind. After all that pressure, I don't need more of it at home.*

Bill didn't remind himself that this was becoming a daily pattern. He poured himself a drink of scotch and water. He gulped it down and waited for the calming effect. Soon he started to feel better and less stressed.

Sally had a miserable day involving a lot of conflict with an employee at the office. "Lately it seems as if every day is stressful," she said to her secretary. Before leaving, Sally, who is a single parent, called her twelve-year-old Nancy at home. She explained she had had a tough day at work and needed to go to the club to work out. She added, "I'm really very, very sorry I won't be home to tuck you in, darling. But I'll tiptoe into your room when I get home. Okay?"

"Again?" Nancy sighed, although she had come to accept the daily phone call. Each night she sits alone in front of the television, eating a TV dinner because she feels that no one really cares about her.

"Honey, I just have to go for my workout," Sally said. "Otherwise I'd be home with you. Honest."

Ann is a working mother, married, and a compulsive eater. Although not overweight, she constantly diets. She had been having a great day. She got a raise at work, the kids were cheerful when she got home, and her husband cooked dinner. Ann decided to celebrate her raise by eating more at dinner than she knew she should.

After dinner, she had a drink and then snacked on chips and dip. Before she went to bed, she had a piece of cake.

All evening, Ann kept thinking, *I shouldn't eat this.* But she seemed unable to help herself. She ate and ate. "Oh, well," she said to her husband before she went to bed, "I'll just not eat anything tomorrow."

Which one is the addict?

If you said Bill, you made a good choice.

If you chose Sally, you're correct.

If Ann was your choice, you picked an addict.

So the answer is ALL THREE. Let's see why.

Bill rewards himself with scotch and water to alter his mood. He does feel better after having a drink. This is the first step to developing an addiction.

Bill didn't really need a drink to calm down. He could have unwound by running or watching television. The choice of behavior will depend on the individual's personality. It doesn't matter what that activity is; if it removes the pain, it can become an addiction rather quickly. It becomes an addiction when the person *has* to do the behavior to feel better *and* when the behavior has a negative consequence for other people. That is addiction.

Sally *has* to exercise. She has to go through her fitness regime to get fixed (i.e., calm). Her behavior is destroying her daughter's life. That is addiction.

Ann may not seem like an addict. Addictions, however, don't always develop by a person trying to overcome the bad times. Often addictions result from celebrating good times. She wants to hold on to a good feeling. Her loss of control means she did what she really didn't want to do. She put her body at risk with unhealthy eating habits.

Ann ate because she felt she deserved a reward for such a good day. Her self-will was not enough to control her behavior. Even though everything seemed positive, she turned to food. She could have said something like, "I did it against my will," or "I failed because of lack of willpower." She took more food because the food rewarded her with a good feeling. That is addiction.

———————— ♦ ————————

Help Yourself offers something new. But before I explain my new concepts, let's look at the present system for the cure of addiction. Frankly, the present system is antiquated and ineffective for the majority of people who need treatment. The few who will recover through the present system will resist any other options.

This isn't a time to try to prove that one is right and all others are wrong. Or even that most others are wrong. Now is the time to be concerned for persons not being helped. Some of them are dying. Others live in torment each day.

For such individuals, we must provide alternatives. There is no choice but to change the system. The present system can't afford to treat all addictions. Nor does it have the human resources to treat the vast number of people who need and want treatment for their addictions.

Here's my position: I can help anyone determine the most appropriate method to recover from addiction. Most will recover using the principles in this book; others will at least learn how to use another method that will work for them. The least you will get from this book is an understanding of addictions.

Recovery can be accomplished in the home environment. How? Home recovery is possible using brain chemistry manipulation. Until now, the techniques were too complicated, too expensive, and too limited in their results. That's no longer true. *Recovery can now occur at home.*

This book also describes the strengths of the twelve-step fellowships and treatment programs, such as Alcoholics Anonymous. People can learn from individuals already in recovery. I commend such groups for their proven strong points. *But* such groups simply don't work for every person. According to *Newsweek* (July 8, 1991), the unofficial cure rate of AA is about 29 percent, much higher than any other program.

I specialize in the *pharmacology* (the study of the properties and reactions of drugs) of the brain, and I will show in this book how the chemistry of the brain affects addiction. I will also show you how your overeating, perfectionism, alcoholism, cocaine habit, etc., are directly linked to your personal chemistry. And I will teach you how to use nonmedication techniques to change brain chemistry.

Individuals serious about recovery can finally have a recovery program they can tolerate and actually enjoy—all within the privacy and support of the home environment. The real message of my home recovery system is a message of hope. It is a practical message that says, "Here is a plan that actually works." During the past sixteen years I have worked with more than ten thousand addicts around the country, and my methods have proven themselves effective with 85 percent of the addicts I have treated.

Help Yourself is arranged into three major sections. Part I is "The Issues," which discusses the problem of addiction and misunderstandings about recovery. Part II is "The System," which explains brain chemistry and addiction and the link between the two. I urge you to read these two sections thoroughly so that you are better equipped to implement "The Program" in Part III.

The exciting techniques described in *Help Yourself* will be your passport to an addiction-free life:

- You can be cured from addictions—once and for all.
- You won't go through a twelve-step program (unless you choose to).
- You won't have to be hospitalized (unless you are suffering from long-standing alcohol and drug addiction or medical or psychiatric complications from your addictions; you may require hospitalization to stabilize you or detoxify you to use the principles in this book).
- You won't need to blame anybody for a program that doesn't work.
- You won't have to live in hopelessness.
- You can be free.

Part I

———————— ◆ ————————

THE ISSUES

— 1 —

What Is Addiction Anyway?*

An addiction is a behavior that causes a reward and that you repeat often to feel better.

The word *addiction* can trigger many emotions, including anger, fear, hopelessness, and confusion.

Anger. To some people, addiction triggers anger because a person close to them is addicted. They're hurt by the effects of the compulsive behavior and because the addicted person won't change.

They don't understand *why* the person won't change.

"I've been tender and deeply caring. Or I was. Now the addiction has changed me, too," they sigh. For years, they've made excuses to children, friends, and employers for the behavior of the addicted person. "If only it could just be over," they declare. The problem has consumed their energies and stolen their hope for recovery.

Fear. Addiction triggers fear, a fear of losing control because of the addiction. They may be trying hard to recover in a recovery program. They seek a long-awaited peace. The fear of total relapse and the remembrance of the painful turmoil that addiction has caused in their lives haunt them every day. The last thing they want is to hurt the people they love all over again.

These individuals feel guilt-ridden. The fear of relapse affects their whole life. Sometimes they fear they may be going insane, and they may secretly wish they were dead.

Hopelessness. Addiction triggers hopelessness; they have tried many times to stop their addictions, but something happens to cause them to return to their overpowering habits. They're tired of talking about their

---

*If you haven't done so already, read the Preface before beginning this chapter.

situation, and they're weary of apologizing to those they have hurt and failed. Those close to them no longer believe in them. Whenever someone talks to them about trying again, the knot in their stomach tightens.

What kind of advice do they get?

- "You can stop anytime you want to. Just make up your mind. And do it."
- "If you really wanted to, you could stop."
- "You're just weak, that's all."

Confusion. Addiction triggers confusion. If pushed, most people can't explain addiction, and most do not know that addiction is a disease. "It's just something that weak and insecure people have," they may say.

Although public education has created an awareness of the problem, it hasn't added much to our understanding of the disease—and addiction *is* a disease. Our society doesn't understand the disease because few people actually understand the human mind and body. Instead, they get caught up in the politics, the partial understandings or repeated "truths," and the tragedies of addiction but never learn about addiction.

Physicians understand the complications of addictions such as alcoholism, drug and other substance abuse, and overeating. Psychologists, psychiatrists, and addiction specialists are aware of the personality and emotional needs; pastors and chaplains grasp that this is a spiritual illness. However, finding professionals who possess the combination of knowledge that includes the whole person is unusual.

The lack of understanding, coupled with personal anger and frustration with people who cannot change, has limited the number of professionals willing to work in the field. For years, the researchers were outside the addiction field, just looking in, and were not welcomed, either.

"You don't understand the real needs of people," they heard. "You can't study human needs under a microscopic lens."

Unless research supported the twelve-step recovery principles, the information, no matter how helpful, was ignored by those who believed there was only one way to cure addiction because they had been through it themselves.

Recently, I have seen more willingness to include new research techniques in treating addictions. The reason isn't only open-mindedness but necessity. "We have to do something," addiction experts have been saying to one another. "Our programs sound fine, but they don't work for large numbers of people."

The worldwide problem of addiction is worsening. Treatment has been successful only on a limited basis, and it has also been expensive.

"We don't know what more to do," some practitioners are saying. *Until now,* there has been no effective and inexpensive way to solve the tremendous problem of addiction.

Out of this concern I began to try new methods in the late 1970s. I worked mostly among medical doctors, wanting to prove my ideas and to get their feedback. Now, over ten thousand patients later, I'm ready to share the results of my work.

Let's start with a definition of addiction: **A behavior that is repeated in spite of consequences is an addiction.** The behavior is continued even though it is destructive to families, physical health, friends, spiritual health, vocations, or academic pursuits.

Addiction isn't limited to alcohol or drugs. Public awareness has centered on those two forms, however, since they're often associated with traffic fatalities, homicides, criminal activities, and other forms of behavior that get the attention of the public. Most television, news, and advertising awareness is alcohol and drug related because of the sensationalism and newsworthiness of their consequences.

Other addictions may not appear to have social consequences. These addictions, called *silent addictions,* are often less sensational. Yet just as many individuals and families are destroyed by silent addictions as by the publicized addictions. Here are some silent addictions:

- Compulsive eating
- Perfection
- Controlling behavior
- Smoking
- Compulsive sexual activities
- Gambling
- Media fascination
- Work
- Exercise
- Religion

Some disorders such as depression and anxiety can become addictions if they are voluntarily continued despite their consequences.

Behavior becomes addictive when it changes moods or emotions. Almost any form of behavior—even chewing gum or wearing makeup or working crossword puzzles—can become an addiction. Those things we do that consistently alter our moods become the stronger addictions. Of course, mood alterations vary from person to person. Some individuals become stressed by the same behavior that relaxes others. As I will point out later, something in our brains produces these different effects.

All Repeated Behaviors Aren't Bad

When an addiction is positive, we call it a habit. When a habit is negative, we call it an addiction. Most of us acknowledge our habits; however, we usually deny our addictions.

Generally, the less impact the addiction has on others, the easier it is to admit to the addiction. For instance, it is as rare to find cigarette smokers who *deny* the addiction as it is to find alcoholics who *admit* the addiction.

Habits can become addictions rather easily. *Exercise* to relieve stress isn't necessarily a problem. But if you *must* exercise to relieve stress, you no longer control the activity—it controls you. If exercise becomes excessive and interferes with your relationships, work, or health, that exercise has become a negative addiction for you.

Here's the story of Sam who works in a factory. The routine work stresses him. On top of that, the company is having financial problems; he faces the constant threat of being laid off. But Sam has found that he can work in the woodshop he set up in his basement and he relaxes.

Aware of the way he responds to his family under stress, Sam doesn't like what it does to him. So most evenings when he gets home, he spends an hour in his woodshop. He relaxes, and then he can interact with the family. Often he spends the rest of the evening playing games, taking drives, or doing other family-related activities.

Sam *is* addicted to his woodshop, but it isn't a problem. His family give him little projects to build; often they help him. Sam's habit hasn't consumed him. When a family matter takes priority, he handles that first. His habit hasn't created a conflict with him personally, with his spiritual life, or with his family life. In fact, this habit (or positive addiction) helps him to be more open and relaxed with the family.

Habits become addictions when they cause harm—whether mental, spiritual, or physical. The addicts themselves may be the only ones who realize the harm, even when denying effects to others.

Overeating, perfectionism, and hypochondria (imagining physical illnesses) are usually more destructive to persons who have them than they are to others. But gambling, alcoholism, and workaholism are as destructive to others as they are to the addicts.

Addictions, such as alcohol and drugs, can be inherited. Current research indicates that children of alcoholic parents have a higher incidence of alcoholism than do other children. This is true even in children of alcoholics not raised by their birth parents. They have as high a tendency to become alcoholics as those raised in the alcoholic environment.

An obvious factor of addiction, then, is genetics. One study of adolescents revealed that in homes where one or both parents are compulsive gamblers, 75 percent of the children have gambled for money before the age of eleven, compared to 34 percent of those raised in homes where compulsive gambling is not present.

Similar results come out of studies of families addicted to compulsive overeating. Although the research done on gambling and overeating doesn't rule out environmental factors, further research is expected to show a genetic correlation.

Washington

To show the role genetics can play, I'd like to tell you about Washington. He was born after his father left his mother. The boy and his father never met until Washington was sixteen. As the boy was growing up, friends and family members kept saying, "You're just like your father."

Washington was tall; he walked with the same swaying movements; and he had the same unusual lisp in his speech. Both father and son would respond with a haughty 'right' when confronted. Both had similar attitudes about the need to work hard to change the system. And strangely enough, both disliked mustard, beans, and pepperoni. Both enjoyed potatoes and considered shrimp their favorite food.

When the father returned, Washington was amazed by how similar they were. He looked like his father. He walked like him; he even used similar slang expressions. He had many likes and dislikes similar to those of his father, whom he had never seen. The only explanation is that genetics must have played a role in developing Washington's personality.

Washington is similar to scores of people in the world today. Studies now indicate that personality traits have genetic correlations. I believe that further studies will continue to reveal genetic components to all addictions.

When I was doing my research on genetic effects, I read a passage in the Bible that amazed me. It's about the sins of the people of Israel, yet it speaks of the effects on ongoing generations:

> The LORD, the LORD, the compassionate and gracious God, slow to anger, abounding in love and faithfulness, maintaining love to thousands, and forgiving wickedness, rebellion and sin. Yet he

does not leave the guilty unpunished; he punishes the children and their children for the sin of the fathers to the third and fourth generation (Exod. 34:6–7 NIV).

The Bible recognized this "passing on of traits" in one of the earliest records of the human race. This recognition may refer to setting examples to children or to genetic changes. Because it refers to third and fourth generations, I tend to surmise the reference is to genetics.

Brain Chemistry Changes Can Create Addictions

The release of Anafranil in December 1989 to treat compulsive disorders shocked the medical profession. The studies used to gain approval for the new drug stated that the drug alone was more effective than counseling in the curing of compulsive hand washing. The medication changed brain chemistry. This change of brain chemistry cured the compulsion without any psychotherapy.

Yet it's improper to assume that medication is the answer to all addictions. In fact, in some instances, medication is part of the addiction.

For years, a number of individuals with addictions have insisted that their brains were different, even though they knew nothing about brain chemicals (neurochemicals). One person could drink alcohol and never become alcoholic, while another could drink less alcohol and yet become addicted. Compulsive overeaters have known instinctively that something was different about them. The 1989 studies showed they were right: Their brain chemistry was different, and because of this neurochemical difference, they were addicted.

Perhaps an example will make this clearer. Although Gary had been in recovery from food addiction for fifteen years, it had been a struggle. He had dieted, been active in a twelve-step program, and received professional counseling. Nevertheless, every few months he went on eating binges. Then he would suffer from feelings of guilt for failing his program.

Gary came to us because he felt he had some kind of chemical imbalance in his brain. He said he had never felt normal, even as a child, long before he ever developed an eating disorder.

Extensive blood analyses showed that he did have a chemical imbalance. We treated Gary with what I call a prescribed behavior. For the past five years, he has not had a single eating binge, and he says, "For the first time in my life, I feel normal."

Gary is similar to thousands of addicted people whose addiction is caused by chemical imbalances in the brain. Their addictions are actually treating their chemical imbalances.

Addictions Change Brain Chemistry

Detoxification is the phase the body goes through after people discontinue alcohol or drugs. All but a few alcohol and drug treatment programs use medication to control withdrawal symptoms. Medication also manipulates (changes) brain chemistry. Physicians sometimes choose this method to change the brain chemicals back to normal.

Other addictions change brain chemistry. Long-distance runners develop a "runner's high." The brain releases certain chemicals that create a good feeling. A 1990 study with gambling addicts revealed neurochemical or brain chemistry changes with their addictions.

People change as their addictions progress. They view life differently; that is, they misperceive reality. We know that many diseases are caused by chemical imbalances in the brain. When people suffer from these diseases, they change. The brain interprets information differently with the altered brain chemicals.

Addictions affect brain chemistry, and brain chemistry affects addictions. These chemical changes in the brain provide positive changes in mood or emotions. When a behavior is performed long enough and feels good, it is reinforced in the brain. Eventually the need for the behavior is stronger than the consequences of the behavior. When this happens, the person has entered the addictive cycle.

Addictions Can Be Acquired

Addictions can be genetic, or they can be acquired. Individuals, if placed in a conflicting situation long enough, can become vulnerable to an addiction. Such long-term conflicts change the brain chemistry, bringing about alterations in thoughts and perceptions. These feelings and emotions cause the sufferers to self-medicate with compulsive or addictive behavior.

I think of Judy as someone with an acquired addiction. After fifteen years of marriage, she came to us for treatment. She had become a perfectionist. While she cleaned the house compulsively, her marriage fell into shambles. Finally her husband had had enough of hearing her say, "You can't do that. It will mess up the house."

"Judy, you're crazy, and you're driving me crazy. You need help," he insisted. It took a long time, but Judy eventually admitted that she had a problem.

During therapy, Judy recognized she had been a rather laid-back nonperfectionist before she was married. She described herself as insecure and said that she wanted people to like her. However, she didn't think that she had changed values or personal standards for approval.

After they were married, her husband didn't share financial information with her. He did all the "intellectual business," telling her, "You aren't smart enough to understand my work or finances."

His interest in sex decreased, and he told her, "You aren't sexy enough," or "You don't do things right when we make love."

Judy slowly realized he had been putting her down in almost every area of her life. Through long-term conflict (being put down by her husband), she gradually turned into a perfectionist around the house. Having a spotless house became her one source of identity and the place from which she measured her self-esteem.

It's not that unusual in unhappy relationships. Many develop into perfectionists or compulsive cleaners or take on other control characteristics after conflict in their marriages.

Who Wants to Be Addicted?

If you went to your physician and were told you had high blood pressure, your physician would probably prescribe a medication. If that medication didn't work, your physician would try a different method of treatment. Yet when a person seeks treatment for addiction and that treatment doesn't work, the person rather than the treatment is often faulted. The person is considered unmotivated. In some cases, that may be true. But I think there's a bigger reason.

The field of addiction is one of the few that has relied on only one method of treatment and expected people with all kinds of addictions to benefit from it. This attitude has resulted in many failed recoveries.

Quite early in my research, I realized that one type of therapy simply won't work for everyone. Even though people may seek treatment for their addictions through an individualized program, they too often discover (if they investigate) that their "special" treatment program is different only in title from the garden-variety program. Nearly all of the addictive treatment programs have come down to a twelve-step program.

You can't change your addictions until you know what to do. No one really wants to be addicted. Yet it's less painful to be controlled by an addiction than to live without the relief the addiction offers—even if it's only temporary.

— 2 —

Misunderstandings About Addictions

Much of the information available today about addictions is not true. Many myths have developed because of fear and misunderstandings about addictions.

"Everybody knows that..."

"The facts have proven..."

"Through our years of experience, we know without doubt that..."

There's a problem with all the known facts about addiction:

They are just not true.

Or they are true in some cases but not in others.

Or they are partially correct.

In the treatment of addiction, a number of statements have been around a long time. They have been repeated so often, they have taken on the meaning of TRUTH.

That doesn't make them true, even if 100 percent of the world's population believe them. Think about all the outlandish notions successfully promulgated by con artists or misguided reformers or careless researchers.

When I started to work in the field of addiction, I confronted these "facts" about addiction. Experts hurled so-called irrefutable evidence at me, repeating what they had been taught. When I questioned such statements, I saw arched eyebrows and frowns and heard skeptical replies.

If a treatment method is true or correct, it produces results. What I saw as recovery from addiction often didn't work. Or the addicted traded one addictive behavior for another kind. Or the addicted stopped doing a

11

particular action such as drinking or overeating but wasn't victorious over the problem. Daily, that person continued to think about doing it.

So I began to treat addictions from the perspective of a simple, basic concept: *If people want to recover effectively from addiction, they need to rely on something that works.*

That concept led me to question the assumptions made by men and women I respected. I could not accept something as true because "Everyone knows that..."

With years of successful treatment of addiction behind me, I've uncovered many commonly known facts—the so-called truths that everyone knows and repeats—that aren't necessarily true. Here are six mistruths that many people believe.

Mistruth 1: A twelve-step program is essential for recovery

A client named Ronald was a physician who voluntarily sought treatment for his alcohol problem. On his first visit to me he said, "I think I'm an alcoholic." He had made his diagnosis after he had seen his routine laboratory blood screen. Ronald described his blood profile as one that "looked like an alcoholic profile."

After a lengthy discussion, I said, "Yes, you're an alcoholic. You need to attend AA (Alcoholics Anonymous) meetings."

Because I wanted to be certain that Ronald was comfortable with such meetings, I suggested he attend one session before he committed himself to AA. Following his first AA meeting, Ronald returned to my office and stated he "would never go to another meeting like that again."

Ronald and I talked about such problems as denial and pride. "I don't care," he insisted. "I'm not going back to an AA meeting."

We finally agreed that he should try a different AA group. When he returned for counseling after his second AA meeting, he again said he didn't want to attend any more such meetings.

I wasn't sure what to do, but I suggested that he have breakfast with a friend of mine who was recovering through the AA fellowship. A week later, after he had eaten breakfast three mornings in a row with my friend, Ronald came to see me. "Joel," he said, "the principles of AA are really great!"

What does this story about Ronald tell us? Simply that he responded better to one person than to a group. For him, group fellowship was ineffective and produced a negative experience.

Many people don't like group gatherings, and consequently, they don't respond positively. Their dislike has nothing to do with denial, pride, or self-confidence. Such individuals get no "reward" from working with groups.

The twelve-step programs are essential for some to recover, but they don't work for everyone.

Mistruth 2: Inpatient treatment is necessary to "break the cycle"

John was arrested for driving under the influence of alcohol. Previously he had never had trouble with the law. The situation caused him to realize that he had a drinking problem. His attorney advised him to go to a thirty-day inpatient program to treat his alcoholism.

"But why an inpatient program?" John asked his attorney.

"That's the most effective form of treatment," he answered. "The judge and the prosecuting attorney agree."

"But why can't I do this on an outpatient basis?"

"Because," said the attorney, speaking as if John didn't quite understand the seriousness of the situation, "it also proves to them how serious you are. If you just checked in each day and went to a few groups, they wouldn't be nearly so convinced of your seriousness."

"Okay," John shrugged.

This way of thinking, as stated by the attorney, has permeated our society. Practically everyone assumes that the only successful way to recover from addictions (or at least the most effective means) is through the most extensive and expensive methods.

The truth is, the best inpatient program doesn't work for some individuals. Many individuals respond well to outpatient programs. My concern and my treatment involve matching patient to treatment.

But why are these inpatient programs so popular and so well received? Simple: Dollars talk. Inpatient programs have money behind them. They have the marketing personnel and resources that yell to society, "We have the answer at Cozydale Hospital!" However, many people have recovered from alternative outpatient programs. My home recovery system is effective *and* convenient.

What works is what's effective.

Inpatient programs work for certain people but not for everybody.

One issue used to get inpatient admission is that it can help some individuals overcome the personal stigma. By signing the admission papers, they are subconsciously saying, "I am so out of control, I have to be locked up and pay a lot of money to highly trained individuals to show me how to get control of my life. They keep me for at least thirty days."

Those same patients may not realize that after they use all their insurance benefits, they may have to become part of an aftercare program for at least two years. The rest of their lives, they will be expected to stand up in groups and say, "My name is Sam, and I am an addict."

Society implies that the more expensive something is, the better the results. Two generations ago, when women were given options to deliver babies through less-medical-oriented means, they were resistant. Hospitals marketed their intensive obstetrical services as safe and state of the art. They proclaimed their highly trained physicians and sterile operating rooms. Fathers had comfortable waiting rooms, and the babies had immaculate and sterile nurseries. The expectant mothers needed all the up-to-date services for their week-long stay for an uncomplicated delivery.

Today, birthing rooms and other alternatives are known to be safe, more natural, and more comfortable for the mother, the father, and the newborn. Consequently, hospitals changed their marketing techniques. Now they promote natural childbirth and shorter hospital stays.

The treatment of addictions is going through a similar stage. Soon treatment considered the only safe alternative and the state of the art will be viewed as archaic and impersonal.

Assuming that all people have lost control of their lives to the point that they need to be protected from themselves is untrue. Compare, for example, people who are mildly depressed with people who are obviously psychotic. Psychotic individuals need protection from themselves, but the mildly depressed don't. In the same way, some people seeking treatment from addiction need a protected environment, while others don't.

Another consideration in seeking protected and professional treatment in the mental health field is the ability of professionals to help you overcome a problem. Most grief counseling has been done by untrained, caring family members or friends. No degrees or professional training was necessary, only care and understanding.

Treatments that meet persons' needs and personalities allow them to break their cycle of addiction.

Mistruth 3: Recovering people are better at treating addictions

When Sally was diagnosed as being a compulsive gambler, she thought it was important to seek treatment with "someone who can identify with my problem." She went to Gamblers Anonymous meetings.

"I figured only another gambler could understand the compulsion," she said.

In the group every woman introduced herself as a "recovering gambling addict." They shared stories that Sally identified with, and she understood the pain and the drivenness. Some of the stories left Sally laughing hilariously, and others brought tears to Sally's eyes.

Then one recovering woman became Sally's friend and sponsor. According to the program, Sally made herself accountable to the sponsor. At first that worked fine. She obediently did everything the woman asked.

But one day Sally asked *why* several times. "I mean, it doesn't make a lot of sense to me," she said after her sponsor gave her a heavy dose of advice. Most of the advice (that sounded like commands) involved attending more and more GA meetings.

"But why? Why so many meetings? Why do I have to keep going through the same thing again and again? Why three times a week?" The more Sally asked, the more clichéd answers she received.

"I don't need more meetings."

"That's denial," the woman said. (*Denial* is one of the biggest pitfalls for recovering individuals.)

"I'm not denying anything," insisted Sally. "I'm tired of meetings. The same thing happens over and over in every single meeting."

"Reinforcement," stated the woman. "You need a lot of reinforcement."

Despite Sally's insistence that she didn't "need" more meetings, her sponsor argued that Sally shouldn't give in to that thinking because "it will only lead you back to gambling again."

For the next few weeks, Sally continued going to meetings three or four times a week. Then she had enough. She limited her attendance to once a week. She was concerned when she came to see me. Would she slide backward? If she didn't go to all those GA meetings, would she still progress?

"Sally," I said, "I think you're doing what's best for you. Recovering people understand you. Having had the same problems, perhaps they do understand better than anyone else can. They've been there. But they have their limitations."

Sally sighed in relief. Inwardly she had known she was doing the right thing for herself, but her sponsor persisted in warning her of the dangers she was setting herself up for.

When persons decide to seek treatment for their addictions, they

FIGURE 2-1
Popular Beliefs About Addiction

Mistruth	Truth
1. A twelve-step program is essential for recovery.	1. The twelve-step programs are essential for some to recover, but they don't work for everyone.
2. Inpatient treatment is necessary to "break the cycle."	2. Treatments that meet persons' needs and personalities allow them to break their cycle of addiction.
3. Recovering people are better at treating addictions.	3. The ability to identify with the addicted is one important characteristic. Helping persons recover takes other skills.
4. Psychotherapy is necessary to treat addictions.	4. Psychotherapy itself isn't the answer. The answer is recovery from the addiction. Psychotherapy is *one recovery method*.
5. The answer to addiction lies in "gene theory" or brain chemistry research.	5. Addictions don't happen just from brain chemistry or gene theories. Recovery involves body, spirit, and mind.
6. Multiple addictions must be treated one at a time.	6. Neurochemical (brain chemistry) treatment can be tailored specifically to include all related addictions at the same time.

have to decide where to get help. Often they will be told to seek a person recovering from the same addictions.

But not everybody needs such people to identify with. Knowing how to fight emotional or physical problems is helpful, but not all recovering people or groups are effective.

If addiction is a disease—and the American Medical Association has declared it to be so—why not treat it like a disease? Individuals who insist that only recovering people can provide adequate treatment are decreasing the validity of the argument of addiction's being a disease.

Identifying with someone who has been through a similar experience is valid. Equally valid, however, is the fact that sponsors may be prejudiced about their own method of recovery.

Addicted persons who don't respond to the care and understanding of family and friends may respond to professionals. Because they're all different, many addicted people respond to knowledge, support, and caring, while others need professional involvement.

The ability to identify with the addicted is one important characteristic. Helping persons recover takes other skills.

Mistruth 4: Psychotherapy is necessary to treat addictions

George was an alcoholic who became violent and uncontrollable when he drank. He showed symptoms of schizophrenia such as sleeplessness, grandiosity, and delusions. His family doctor referred him for psychiatric care.

The psychiatrist was well trained in addictions and observed the alcohol as contributing to the behavior. He was able to show George that the alcohol caused a change in brain chemistry similar to schizophrenia. George stopped drinking, and his bizarre behavior cleared up.

The psychiatrist felt George needed no counseling after he gave up alcohol.

Psychotherapy *is* an option for people recovering from addictions but not the only one. While actively participating in the addiction cycle, most people seem to need psychotherapy. After they have stopped the addiction cycle, such help may no longer be necessary.

Psychotherapy itself isn't the answer. The answer is recovery from the addiction. Psychotherapy is *one* recovery method.

Mistruth 5: The answer to addiction lies in "gene theory" or brain chemistry research

In 1991, a report linked alcoholism to metabolism and genetics. One client named Alice was initially excited about the news. (Unfortunately, this information proved inconclusive.) Then she thought more about what she read and said, "Okay, but so what? The report describes, but it doesn't cure."

Alice grasped an important concept. New theories about old problems don't help the addict. Theories cure nothing. People like Alice learn what caused their problem, but that bit of knowledge doesn't provide a cure by itself. Unless addicted persons receive practical information and solutions that embody the spiritual, emotional, and physical aspects of their lives, the information won't be very effective.

Brain chemistry plays an integral part in the recovery from addictions. Many answers and clues to recovery are known now and more will yet become available through continuing neurochemical research. A person can learn to think differently, respond differently, and achieve freedom from addiction through application of certain principles.

Intimacy, faith, and love are affected by, and affect, brain chemistry.

Resolving what causes chemical imbalances is not the answer to achieving freedom from addictions. Life will still be as miserable and empty as it was before. The answer to addiction lies in treating the whole person—body, spirit, and mind. A gene theory may explain more about addictions and where addictions developed, but it won't cure the lack of peace.

Addictions don't happen just from brain chemistry or gene theories. Recovery involves body, spirit, and mind.

Mistruth 6: Multiple addictions must be treated one at a time

When Randy entered a center for treatment of his alcoholism, he was still allowed to smoke. Later he attended AA meetings. People there talked of how long they had been free from alcohol. But Randy wondered. Of the thirty-three people present, all but one of them relied heavily on the drug called nicotine. He noticed two large coffee urns. Without exception, every member went for refill after refill of caffeine.

Randy did right to wonder. That's when he came to see me. If drugs are affecting the mind and personality—and both nicotine and caffeine *are* drugs that alter moods—there is an addiction. To be free from addiction, the brain needs to become healthy, not partially healthy or only 60 percent better.

Yet professionals in the field of addictions believe they must treat one addiction at a time to prevent the person from getting overwhelmed and discouraged. When addictions are separate and unrelated, that makes sense. This treatment lets one type of addiction remain active while persons are working on others. (This method actually teaches people to switch addictions back and forth.) However, if addictions are interrelated, treating one at a time might postpone recovery.

As I explain elsewhere, the study of brain chemistry reveals that multiple addictions, *when they are neurochemically similar,* should be treated concurrently. Related addictions vary from one person to another and shouldn't be routinely determined for all. With the knowledge of brain chemistry, treating all related addictions simultaneously is not only an option but a preference.

Multiple addictions can be treated simultaneously using neurochemical (brain chemistry) treatment.

— 3 —

The Best Recovery Option

*The recovery option that is best for you is
the one that works.*

In the addictions field, the assumption is that the counselors are always right. They determine what persons must do to recover. If persons don't get better, that same therapist or another will label them as being in denial and not ready for treatment.

Mistruth 1: Denial is the major problem in
treating addiction

Helen is twenty-eight years old and has a relationship addiction. Twice divorced, she is now going with a man she plans to marry soon. Her friends confronted her: "Helen, he is exactly like the other two you married and divorced."

Helen justified her relationship with the new boyfriend. Her friends accused her of being in denial and were frustrated with her.

Helen then came to see me. Working together, we discovered that she had read about relationship addictions and went to codependency meetings two years earlier. Both the meetings and the books accurately described her symptoms. Although she accepted the symptoms, she disliked the conclusions. As she put it, "Their management of my problem does not fit with my personality."

No one suggests that anybody has received the wrong treatment, and yet that's what happened. Their support system is now gone, and no one believes in them. They are without hope for Recovery, and they return to the addiction cycle.

Truth 1 **A sense of hopelessness is a greater problem than denial.**

Mistruth 2: Pride must be broken to attain recovery

Zeke was a professional athlete who developed a sex addiction. His coach said, "You need to get help," when the athlete's problem began to affect his career. Zeke contacted the team counselor who referred him to a twelve-step program for sex addictions. Zeke was provided a list of programs in each of the major cities he would be playing.

Zeke never attended any meetings. When he returned, the counselor told him the major problem was his pride: "You won't ever recover without admitting to the problem."

Zeke sought a second opinion from me because I understood addictions and athletes. Zeke had not attended any public meetings because of the hero complex that triggered his addiction. He knew he would be recognized by women and idolized, and then he would fall prey to his addiction. He had stayed in his hotel room when he wasn't practicing or playing.

When Zeke came to me, I said, "You need to work on your addiction your way, not the way that works for someone else." We set up a program for him. For the past two seasons, he has had no serious problem with his former addiction.

People resist change unless it provides some kind of reward. Someone who appears to be too proud to admit to the addiction is actually trying to maintain the rewards the addiction provides. Often such persons are labeled as having too much pride to change. The real issue isn't their pride; they just don't believe recovery will give them the same level of rewards they got from their addictions. Most individuals know what they will or won't like. They choose what they like instead of what is best for them.

Change may be uncomfortable, but it can be rewarding. When change becomes rewarding, persons follow the healthy choice.

Pride can help in the recovery process. Being too proud to stand up in public and declare, "I am an addict," doesn't mean anything. Although some therapists and recovering people argue that these people won't share in private, either, it isn't a problem of pride, only a statement of different needs. They are stating that they don't share private issues in public.

If someone stood up in public and continued to declare he broke his leg on a motorcycle three years ago and is proud he doesn't ride one anymore, we might question his sanity. Private people may be willing to discuss their problems with individuals they trust. If such individuals know that admitting to a problem requires them to attend a large group meeting, they will resist admitting to the problem.

Truth 2   Pride is not the real issue. Some people don't believe that recovery will give them the same rewards they received from their addictions.

Mistruth 3: Family members can't help in the beginning of the recovery process

Family therapy is accepted and encouraged by all treatment programs, and they usually invite the family to participate around the third week of recovery. The family is basically educated about the disease and support concepts. The family still doesn't know what to do and how to do it. Left out as the primary support system, the family is replaced by twelve-step programs. The family members feel as if they can't offer much support to the addicted person. In reality, if they know what's wrong in the addicted person's brain and what can be done to fix it, they can provide tremendous support and intimacy.

Most people in recovery don't want the family involved because

- They feel guilty.
- They feel they have failed the family.
- They are angry with the family for not being supportive.
- They feel the family created their problems.

Most family members are angry or frustrated or feel a sense of hopelessness about the addicted person. The communication has probably become negative and accusatory, with listening being replaced by demands. The safest option is to avoid communicating with one another, which results in unhealthy and unsupportive relationships.

When people struggle through trials together, a bond develops. The strongest bonds are family bonds. So, families can be effective if they have direction and understand what they are fighting.

Most individuals in treatment develop social or therapy bonds. Or they bond with a twelve-step group. That's where they get their acceptance and love. Yet whether they turn to groups or therapists, a lack of intimacy still exists. People need acceptance and approval from families and spouses.

Including a family in the recovery process requires giving them help in communication, attitude, and techniques that are supportive. Most families can develop these techniques when they understand their own emotions as well as those of the addicted persons.

Truth 3   If they know how, families can be of immense help
throughout the recovery process.

Mistruth 4: A high level of self-esteem is necessary before recovery can happen

Mike, a workaholic, has guided his business to outstanding success. He likes to be in charge of things, and he knows everything that goes on. This means he often works fifteen hours a day. His family is falling apart around him. Two sons are using drugs; two daughters avoid him; two other daughters married workaholic husbands.

Mike is unhappy, fearful, and angry. Everyone is "out to get him," and his children don't respect what he has done for them. He knows his work is causing the problems; however, he receives businessman of the year awards, much praise, and frequent social accolades.

When he turned fifty, Mike decided to seek a new life-style. He started to spend time with his family and to work less. The family members were cautious and held back. Frankly, they didn't know this new person. Mike's business praise and awards decreased. Unfortunately, he didn't continue with his new life-style; within two months he started putting business before family commitments again.

His insecurity, low self-esteem, and constant need for approval couldn't give him what he needed to develop a new form of reward.

If he continues this way, Mike will die successful in the world's eyes; in his family's eyes, he'll be a failure. They didn't need or want more money; they have always needed a father and husband.

Mike has a low sense of self-esteem. When society measures self-esteem by power and money, few achieve it. Those who do achieve money and power status realize it has nothing to do with how we feel about ourselves. Many people, confident in their work, are mistakenly assumed to have a good self-esteem. Yet they may be confused about themselves because they have mixed what they do with who they are.

Many people appear to know everything and brag excessively. Their loud voices may be covering up for their insecurities.

A good self-esteem is the product of recovery from an addiction. Far too many individuals maintain their addictions along with their low self-esteem because they don't know any other way.

Recovery can take place when they can grasp that they have alternatives—the kind that provide rewards. When they get rewarded, they will change to achieve the reward. Developing a healthy sense of self-esteem requires forgiveness and acceptance, which will come after the addiction is no longer controlling a person.

Truth 4   A healthy level of self-esteem is the product of recovery from an addiction.

Mistruth 5: If they have enough faith, God will deliver them

When one part of a person is affected, all parts are affected. A conflict in any area causes a change not only in the level of self-esteem but in the belief in God. Just because persons appear to be spiritually healthy or think they are healthy doesn't mean they are.

Many times I've met people who have been in programs that speak of God or a Higher Power. They sometimes hear, "If you believe in God, and if you have enough faith, that's all you need." It's a subtle way of pushing them to believe more.

This just isn't true. Faith in God helps immensely. In fact, I believe

FIGURE 3-1
Requirements for Recovery

Mistruth	Truth
1. Denial is the major problem in treating addiction.	1. A sense of hopelessness is a greater problem than denial.
2. Pride must be broken to attain recovery.	2. Pride is not the real issue. Some people don't believe that recovery will give them the same rewards they received from their addictions.
3. Family members can't help in the beginning of the recovery process.	3. If they know how, families can be of immense help throughout the recovery process.
4. A high level of self-esteem is necessary before recovery can happen.	4. A healthy level of self-esteem is the product of recovery from an addiction.
5. If they have enough faith, God will deliver them.	5. God can deliver anyone from addiction. God does not always do so—even when people have faith.
6. People have to "hit bottom" before they change.	6. When addicted persons have alternatives, they may not need to hit bottom.
7. Defenses must be broken before a person recovers.	7. Defenses are the mind's natural attempt to avoid pain.

it's a necessary ingredient for a total recovery. But God may also use any number of people, options, and resources for recovery.

Too often I've met persons who were delivered from addictions through a spiritual experience. They did nothing else. "God has delivered me," they said in defiance. Unfortunately, I've also seen those same individuals later suffering from emotional difficulty.

All persons have their focal point, the place where they are most vulnerable or need the most help. People will often allow change to occur at their entry point of their area of confidence because it takes less effort and makes them less uncomfortable. Some individuals begin to change by using the spiritual realm as their entry point, while others begin at the physical or emotional realm. The most important consideration is that all realms *must be treated eventually,* regardless of the entry point.

Some would destroy persons' spiritual recovery by trying to force spiritual insight when the entry point is elsewhere. Forcing faith or spiritual growth when persons aren't ready causes hardening of the heart.

Truth 5   God can deliver anyone from addiction. God does not always do so—even when people have faith.

Mistruth 6: People have to "hit bottom" before they change

Carol came to therapy because her husband had not sought treatment for his alcoholism. She was familiar with twelve-step programs through Overeaters Anonymous. She wanted help on dealing with her husband "until he hits bottom," she said. She stated he resented her twelve-step program and claimed he would never seek any type of program for his problem.

I suggested another approach: "Carol, why are you waiting for him to hit bottom? Get involved now."

Despite the well-meant advice from her OA friends, Carol listened and followed my suggestion. She decided that attending church would be the best entry point for both of them. It wasn't easy to get her husband to go with her, but he did. Soon they both became active. Within weeks they were attending a weekly Bible study in homes. Shortly after that, Carol's husband sought counseling from their minister.

Had Carol waited for him to hit bottom, it may never have happened.

The "hit bottom" idea is one of the most frustrating to deal with because it's been around for so long and most people accept it as truth without question. But think about it this way. Those with addictions know they are hooked. They also know they don't want their addictions. But few people know what to do to recover from their addictions. Why, then, do they have to wait until they are at the point of despair (which is the definition of hitting bottom)?

When people hear about only one program for recovery—one that may not work for them—they have no alternative but to keep on going until they hit bottom. If alternatives were available, they might not have to go through so much pain.

Truth 6   When addicted persons have alternatives, they may not need to hit bottom.

Mistruth 7: Defenses must be broken before a person recovers

Ralph knew he was addicted to videos and television. His family complained constantly. His young daughter was beginning to become distant from him. For a few weeks, he defended his viewing compulsion: "I'm under a lot of stress at work. This is my one chance to relax."

To stop the nagging, Ralph decided to spend more time with the family and less time in front of the television set.

The first night he tried to avoid the TV set, he felt nervous and anxious, and no one had a good time. He kept trying, but he was under stress. Television had become his medication for stress. Consequently, if Ralph didn't watch TV, he stayed under stress. If he did watch it, he felt guilty. If his stress had dropped, he wouldn't need the television to relax. He was trapped in a cycle.

As in Ralph's case, defenses protect people from pain they can't handle. If an alternate solution to pain can be provided, there is no need to justify whatever medicates. Persons can't drop their defenses until they feel confident and adequate to make changes.

Often they're asked to drop defenses before they're equipped to handle the pain. That causes the addictive cycle to resurface—in another form. When the addictive cycle resurfaces, it normally comes in a form that gains them approval.

In Ralph's case, he could have become overly religious or addicted to attending a recovery group. His defenses would still be present, but they would have become socially acceptable. Defenses are seen as an I-am-right attitude in the recovery program and remain as strong as they were when persons were actively practicing their addictions.

Change is a process that involves the right timing. Determining the time to seek the entry point and what to change first is important in the recovery process. If persons try to change in an area before they're ready, they stop. They'll feel frustrated and have feelings of failure. Then they become defensive in their thinking because of their fear. They appear defensive, but they are protecting their pain.

Many people are like Ralph in that they want to change but the brain won't let them. No matter what they do, they are in conflict. If the brain won't cooperate, persons won't change. They become defensive because they feel better with the addiction.

Truth 7   Defenses are the mind's natural attempt to avoid pain.

— 4 —
Where Recovery Can Take Place

Recovery doesn't have to be painful or involve group therapy, self-help groups, hospitals, rehabilitation centers, or individual counseling. Recovery can take place in the home environment.

"**Y**ou can expect two years of misery," a member of AA told Agnes. "After that," he said with a smile, "you got it made."

After two years? *Is that recovery?*

If Agnes had stayed with AA, she would never have made the two years. "It's just too long," she told me. "I've been living with my drinking problem for ten years. I can't go through even another six months of this!"

"It's going to be a tough period," one sponsor insisted. "It ain't going to be no fun for a long time, but just remember, that's how we all licked our problem." The man saying it had been in the program for thirteen months. He admitted he was still depressed.

Is that recovery?

"I haven't done drugs for months," thirty-year-old Carl said with a beam. Then sadness filled his face as he added, "But sometimes ... well, sometimes I still get a little confused about what's real and what isn't."

Is that recovery?

I've heard those stories—and thousands of others. I still hear them regularly. This so-called truth of two years of depression already sets people up to be miserable, they don't know how to enjoy their new way of life, and it cuts them off from the people closest to them.

"Why?" I finally asked a social worker who repeated all the words of gloom. "Why does it have to be that way?"

"Well," he said defensively as if I were attacking him personally, "you know as well as anyone, Joel, that it takes time to get back to normal. You know, to break the old habits, to change attitudes, to—"

"Maybe," I said. That was sixteen years ago. Even then I was doubtful. For some individuals, this might be true, but is this the way it has to be for everyone? I didn't believe it. My research and work later proved that my instincts were right.

Since then I've concluded that many individuals in recovery programs are depressed, filled with negative attitudes, and have a low level of self-esteem. Many struggle with knowing if they are correctly perceiving reality. They may be *in recovery programs,* but they aren't *in recovery.*

These symptoms they talk about after going through their programs are symptoms of chemical imbalances in the brain. That is, they are still symptoms of addictive behavior.

Sometimes people stop doing a type of behavior, such as quit drinking alcohol or smoking. The act of not doing the behavior is not recovery.

Why?

Just stopping doesn't change the chemical imbalances in the brain. Persons are still addicted, even if they don't drink or smoke or give in to the compulsive action.

In the following chapters, I have written a lot about these chemical imbalances because they're so important for recovery. For now, trust me as you read this fact:

True recovery includes physical or brain recovery as well as emotional and spiritual recovery.

Recovery is like a religious conversion. It changes people. Afterward they're different. That's how we know they're cured. They think differently. They don't behave the way they used to. Their brains are different! And if the chemical makeup inside their heads is different, they enjoy their recovery.

Unfortunately, most compulsive people are controlled by the recovery process. They are not in charge of their lives.

Think about control this way: They are controlled in the number of meetings they must attend. Or they'll hear, "You must avoid . . . ," or "You must never. . . ." They are controlled by rules. Laws. Regulations. Do's and don'ts. They're not recovering! They're living defensive lives because they have never treated their brain chemistry.

Because the so-called truths I've been talking about keep many people from seeking recovery from their addictions, I'm going to take time to debunk them. In this chapter, I want you to read about five of these so-called well-known truths that often hinder people from moving into recovery.

Mistruth 1: Focus on the problem daily. Admit the problem daily. This concentration is essential for recovery

Jackie developed alcohol problems over a five- to six-year period. She is shy and rather quiet and enjoys a one-to-one conversation. After she decided alcohol was a problem, she attended her first AA meeting. She became extremely uncomfortable with the offensive language, the blue cloud of tobacco smoke that filled the room, and some of the recovery stories.

"I didn't hear much about my problem," she later told me. "I didn't hear much of anything except little slogans. You know, that I had to take it one day at a time. 'Easy does it.' That, and a lot of other clichés that might mean a lot to some of them."

Jackie couldn't identify with those she met. She wanted to be with people who were like her. Even though she hadn't been to church in years, she contacted her minister who directed her to a women's group Bible study.

Now, two years later, Jackie is free from addictions. Not once did she ever feel anyone pushing her to stand up in her Bible study and announce her problem. (She wouldn't have been able to do that anyway.) Yet she recovered.

Jackie also discovered what worked for her. She began to focus on making the most of her life, on being a better person, on serving others and learning more about God.

Even so, this mistruth about constantly focusing on addiction gets passed on because some have stated that successful recovery requires people to be willing to openly discuss their problems. The popularity of programs such as AA, Al-Anon, Al-Ateen, and other fellowships stems from their ability to attract personalities that do best when they focus on their problems. But it's wrong to expect all persons to respond in the same way.

Some persons are uncomfortable admitting they have a problem because they want to focus on solutions—and move on.

If some persons are told their recovery is based upon admitting their problem in a group, they would avoid therapy. They feel that recognizing a problem, changing it, and then forgetting it are more compatible with their style. Many persons with this philosophy are drug- and alcohol-free today.

Mistruth 2: Attendance in group fellowships (such as AA) is essential to maintain sobriety

Harold went to AA meetings for several weeks. He learned the principles of the group and then said, "Now I'm ready to live this on my own." Despite the protests of persons who predicted his downfall, he hasn't been back in four years. He has also remained free of his addiction to alcohol. Like the popular song of a decade ago, Harold can say, "I did it my way."

Providing only one option for recovery rules out most people who want to recover.

People like Harold aren't wrong for responding to or preferring a different type of treatment; they are just different. They won't even try to recover under a system that is foreign to their nature and needs.

Mistruth 3: Recovery occurs when the addiction is eliminated

Betty

Betty was a compulsive overeater and weighed 120 pounds more than her ideal weight. She was usually depressed, disliked sex, and argued with her husband constantly. She hated herself, God, and everyone around her. Friends finally dropped her because she was negative and complaining.

In desperation, Betty decided to attend a weight loss program at a local hospital. In four months, she lost 120 pounds. But she remained depressed, still disliked sex, continued to argue with her husband, and had no friends.

Betty slowly realized that dieting consumed her life. Her definition of success had been to lose at least 100 pounds. "I've done that," she said. "So why am I so miserable?"

Within two years she was overweight again, this time by regaining the 120 pounds plus an additional 30. For Betty, defining success by eliminating negative behavior didn't treat her addiction.

This third so-called truth grows from inappropriately applying twelve-step principles. In twelve-step programs it often appears as though success is measured by how long persons have stopped a negative behavior such as overeating or using alcohol.

When persons base their recovery on the fact they haven't had alcohol for fifteen years, the success of their recovery raises questions. Calling treatment successful because persons aren't doing negative things is like saying I'm a nice person because I didn't kick my cat this morning. All people who didn't kick their cats this morning aren't necessarily nice people. Nice people also do positive things, and we don't measure their niceness by focusing on what they don't do.

Many individuals who stop drinking become miserable. Their relationships suffer as much as they did when they were using the substance. They actually trade one negative behavior (drinking) for another (poor relationships).

This is not successful recovery.

Recovery includes eliminating negative behavior and developing positive attitudes and behavior.

Mistruth 4: Once addicted always addicted

Tom became addicted to gambling by trying to cure his depression and loneliness. He was single and insecure and felt unlovable. Gambling gave him temporary relief. Eventually, Tom's gambling intensified until he couldn't afford to buy a decent car. He moved into a cheaper, undesirable apartment complex.

One evening a friend introduced Tom to an attractive woman. She found Tom interesting. They started to date. After a few months, they were married. After eighteen months, Tom bought a new car, and the following year, they signed a mortgage for a house.

Years later, while reading an article about gambling addictions, Tom realized he had been a gambling addict. Yet he no longer had a desire to gamble. He hadn't even thought about the habit since he had become engaged. He has never been tempted to return to gambling. Why? Because he developed alternatives to handle loneliness and depression that caused his addiction to gambling.

I don't want to say that "once addicted always addicted" isn't true. It's safer to assume that it's universally true. Those with a genetic addiction (such as alcohol) usually find it's true. If they acquired the disease, it is generally false.

Realistically, healthy persons won't want to try the behavior they were addicted to before recovery, especially if that behavior caused them pain. Healthy people learn from their mistakes and change.

On the other hand, unhealthy people tend to think in terms of absolutes. For them, everything is yes or no, right or wrong. They focus on what they shouldn't do or can't do. They could decide not to do certain actions or to substitute positive actions.

Think it through. If "once addicted always addicted" holds true, recovering addicts should never participate in their addictive behavior again. That would then mean people once addicted to food should never eat again; the sexually addicted must give up all sexual activity.

Individuals like Tom never got labeled addicts because they never went to a professional for labeling. If they had, they might be expected to focus on avoiding their addiction the rest of their lives.

"Once addicted always addicted" is sometimes true. For others, addictions may be acquired. The addictions go away when their life situations change.

Mistruth 5: Your recovery won't last long

Wayne was a cocaine addict whose business partner told him to get treatment. Wayne had promised to quit so many times that his partner finally handed him a check: "This amounts to a fair share of the company. Either get treatment or cash the check." He told Wayne that he would no longer tolerate the problems caused by his cocaine usage.

Wayne completed a specialty cocaine rehabilitation program. He discontinued the cocaine usage and started to attend twelve-step meetings. He got into a moderate exercise program. Over the next three months, his exercise needs increased, and they soon reached bizarre levels. He would exercise before he went to work; he would often not eat at noon so that he could exercise. He spent most of his evening exercising at a spa. No one questioned or confronted Wayne because everyone was so thrilled he wasn't using cocaine. Near the end of his sixth month in recovery, he became ill. He couldn't exercise and became depressed. Within three days he was using cocaine again.

"Wayne relapsed," a friend said. "I knew it wouldn't last."

The fact is, Wayne had never treated his addiction. He transferred it from drugs to exercise.

Most people who discontinue an addiction don't experience recovery. They haven't really stopped the addiction; they have transferred the *form*. When persons discontinue an addiction and transfer all the chemical changes in the brain to another behavior, they have not accomplished recovery. The addiction resurfaces.

These individuals learned how to recover from the *symptoms* of the addictions. They focused on discontinuing "negative rewards," and nothing changed in their thinking.

FIGURE 4-1
Popular Beliefs About Recovery

Mistruth	Truth
1. Focus on the problem daily. Admit the problem daily. This concentration is essential for recovery.	1. Some persons are uncomfortable admitting they have a problem because they want to focus on solutions—and move on.
2. Attendance in group fellowships (such as AA) is essential to maintain sobriety.	2. Providing only one option for recovery rules out most people who want to recover.
3. Recovery occurs when the addiction is eliminated.	3. Recovery includes eliminating negative behavior and developing positive attitudes and behavior.
4. Once addicted always addicted.	4. "Once addicted always addicted" is sometimes true. For others, addictions may be acquired. The addictions go away when their life situations change.
5. Your recovery won't last long.	5. When people treat their addictions, recovery is highly successful and long lasting.

When people treat their addictions, recovery is highly successful and long lasting.

———— ◆ ————

The growth in heart disease research and treatment has exploded in the past twenty years while the treatment of addictive disorders has changed little. If physicians practiced medicine as they did twenty years ago, they would be liable for malpractice suits. Yet the addiction field considers twenty-year-old treatment methods to be the standards by which to judge other methods.

Most professionals who avoided treating addiction didn't know how to treat it and were afraid to try. Consequently, individuals who got involved as therapists in addictive clinics and programs were usually people who were themselves recovering from alcoholism and other drugs. It was a natural response since the medical community turned their backs on these needs. Only after health insurance companies agreed to pay for treatment did professionals get involved.

Once involved, the medical professionals started a PR campaign that claimed they were better equipped because of their education. The recovering community claimed they were better because they understood.

A battle began within the mental health field that resulted in separating treatment of the psychologically ill from the addicted. Today dual diagnosis is treating the psychological issues in an addictive disease unit, which allows the addiction field to treat psychological issues. Different standards and rules have been set up for each type of program. Thus began competition for addicted persons. Each type of program was trying to prove it was better. Marketing ploys became treatment standards.

Alcohol addiction was forced to expand. Soon it became common to use terms such as *substance abuse*, which included drugs, and then certain types of compulsive behavior were added.

Originators of programs suddenly became specialists for a specific addiction. To make their role even more impressive, they claimed that each addiction had to be treated differently. They have continued to do this even though some of us shout back, "Nonsense! Addiction is addiction."

When addiction expanded to include eating disorders, gambling, sexual disorders, and other dysfunctions, new "truths" developed. The only model they had, the twelve-step approach, was stretched to fit all the people all the time and for all addictions. No studies showed if twelve-step programs would be effective for overeating or gambling or other addictions. People were simply told, "Use this or fail."

Because addiction has been a political diagnosis as much as a medical diagnosis, people in the field have developed a defensiveness about the way they do therapy. A field that justifies its actions, instead of learning new information, will develop a great number of strongly held beliefs, whether they are facts or not.

The purpose in revealing these mistruths and how they began is not to be critical but to open eyes and hearts to other approaches. Alternatives must be sought if we want to affect the people who need help.

— 5 —

Getting Free

Freedom from addictions has no set formula. It is an individual process that only you can determine—if you have the right information.

"**I**'m free," Rhonda told her family after she had completed an inpatient program for addiction to prescription drugs. "I'll never, never take another pill again."

"I won't be controlled again," said Gene, a compulsive eater. "I've got it all sorted out now."

"My life is changed forever," said Tim, "and I'll never touch another drop of liquor."

We like hearing those enthusiastic statements. And the people mean every word.

UNFORTUNATELY, all too often their enthusiasm shatters. They have a bad day, and things don't go right.

"Just once," they whisper to themselves.

The addictions sneak up and take over again. Soon they are smoking, drinking, overeating, or gambling. Not only do they struggle with guilt over failing themselves, but they admit, "I let down everybody." Their supportive and caring friends often became angry and disappointed and begin to distance themselves.

The regressed addicts feel overwhelmed by failure, or they take the reverse strategy and deny that they feel anything. Often they hide the problem, denying that they have returned to the addiction.

At that point, their lives become a replay. The cover-up begins. The denial, sneaking, lying, and guilt are all there—and much stronger. They are now more deeply involved in the addictive cycle.

"Oh, that's part of how it goes," one longtime member of an AA

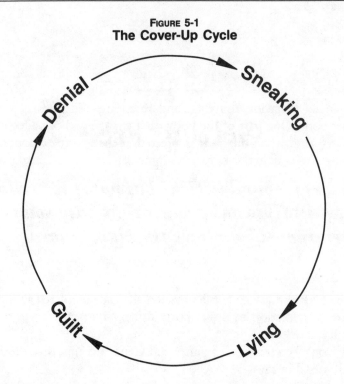

FIGURE 5-1
The Cover-Up Cycle

group told me. "But eventually they get sober and stay sober if they're serious."

"But why do they have to keep repeating the same cycle?" I asked. The person gave me a lot of words in response but no real answer. I insisted that if the initial recovery had been effective, the addictive cycle would have stopped. Supporting friends and goal fulfillment would have remained intact.

Principle 1   To break the cycle, recovery must be effective the *first* time

If you have failed in several attempts at recovery, I want this to be the *last* time you'll be enmeshed in the cycle.

As I say throughout this book, recovery is more than discontinuing drinking, drugs, overeating, or smoking. Recovery changes how persons think, react, and deal with life. To overcome addictions, persons must know how to make those changes.

I have developed a method that doesn't try to treat all addictions or addicts the same way. No single treatment works for everybody. Each individual needs a personalized program to be effective.

The Help Yourself Recovery System has its foundation in helping hurting people understand human behavior, brain chemistry, hormones, emotions, and even God. They also learn the value and place of activity, diet, changed behavior, thinking, and reactions, and how all of these affect the body. One part of the body can't change without affecting the other parts. And when the body is affected, it changes the emotions. My program stresses that the body, the mind, and the spirit are interconnected. When one part hurts, all parts hurt in some way.

Principle 2   An effective recovery program is personal and individualized. One size doesn't fit all

People who seek a lasting recovery need more than help on stopping their addictive symptoms. They need to understand what causes their behavior and how to successfully change so that they eliminate their addictions *forever.* In this process, they come to understand their feelings and frustrations.

I like to tell people who come to our clinics, "Having answers will make the fear of change less frightening to you. If you know what to expect, you can face it a lot easier."

Through the research and practical experience at clinics, I have shown in several thousand instances in the past ten years that this method works. I rely on current research, but I've also realized that some of the truths go back thousands of years. The Bible, for instance, is a storehouse of practical as well as spiritual information. Too often old information gets thrown out to accommodate new information. The Help Yourself Recovery System makes use of both.

Principle 3   Recovery begins with knowledge— the knowledge of where to start, what to do, and how to get there

Many claims and marketing techniques about recovery are confusing to those seeking to recover from addiction. They find it difficult to know what will be effective for them and where to get the help they need. To recover, they need to know what they are fighting and what to do.

Effective recovery decreases denial, destroys false hopes, and eliminates the support problems. When individuals decide to stop their addictions, share their expectations and dreams of life without addiction, they find abundance of support from the church, friends, and family. Suddenly, the whole environment seems supportive and caring. Everyone is proud of the persons recovering from addiction. Even distant relationships begin to develop closeness. Those formerly addicted develop consistent life-styles. They move on with their lives.

This process starts with self-knowledge. To understand themselves, persons need to assess their physical, psychological, and spiritual strengths and weaknesses, which isn't an easy task. People today tend to compartmentalize themselves.

A good example is Ben. He thinks and behaves one way at work but another way at home, still another way at a party with close friends, and yet still another way at church. While all people have various facets to their personalities, the tendency in our Western world is to acknowledge only small parts of ourselves in each situation.

This is much like the approach in medicine for at least the past fifty years. Instead of treating the whole person, doctors have specialized. Today we have a seemingly infinite number of physicians with medical degrees and their own limited fields. We have psychiatrists, psychologists, family therapists, hypnotherapists, massage therapists, cognitive therapists, and a dozen other varieties.

Although persons get the benefit of superbly honed skills in these limited areas, the loss comes because doctors don't view their clients as whole beings. Or they are limited in understanding the way each part of the body, mind, emotions, and spirit affects other parts.

Much of the frustration of not being able to change comes from the lack of understanding of the brain and how it controls behavior. Knowing the brain better offers insight into behavior.

A Key to Addictions

The search for a key—the one special key—to cure addictions is on. Millions of dollars in research grants get spent each year to determine what causes addictions and other compulsive disorders. Researchers ask questions such as:

- "What is the gene or key to the cause of addiction?"
- "What is the most effective treatment?"
- "Do twelve-step programs work?"

Specific answers to those questions may not be important. Understanding all the answers to the questions of addictions is impossible. Those who wait for every answer before they change won't change.

Principle 4   There is no single best way for all people to recover from addiction

Each addicted person fights an individual battle. Don't be discouraged!

This information actually offers more hope than all the programs presented today. My Help Yourself Recovery System begins by stating the obvious: The only ones who can understand their addictions are the addicted. No one else's recovery program or problems are theirs.

Here's the better question to ask: "What will free me from my addiction?"

We have to stop the addictive cycle. Only the addicted persons themselves can do that. And only when they stop the cycle will they have the peace for which they have searched so long.

FIGURE 5-2
Basic Principles

Principle 1	To break the cycle, recovery is most effective the *first* time.
Principle 2	An effective recovery program is personal and individualized. One size doesn't fit all.
Principle 3	Recovery begins with knowledge—the knowledge of where to start, what to do, and how to get there.
Principle 4	There is no single best way for all people to recover from addiction. Each addicted person fights an individual battle.

I recall an experience with adolescents (ages twelve to eighteen) who were in outpatient treatment. It had been decided the most effective way to bring about change in adolescents was through activities that offered some life-changing experience.

Our own experience told us that psychotherapy with adolescents was difficult and often unsuccessful. Their changing thought patterns, a result of hormonal imbalances, were part of the reason psychotherapy was replaced with experiential conditions. Life experiences, we thought, wouldn't require the same amount of self-reflection as psychotherapy demanded.

This particular activity was a backpacking trip to northern Michigan. The adolescents were to be ready to leave the clinic at 8:00 P.M. They had endured the speeches about having to carry all their food, clothing, shelter, and anything else they felt they needed. We reminded them that the items on their backs would get heavier as they walked. They would grow tired. We urged them to take only absolutely essential gear. Even when we said that, we knew they would consider "boom boxes" (powerful tape recorder-radio combinations) and butane-powered curling irons essential gear.

From the clinic, we had a six-hour drive north. We set the time so that they would feel exhausted when we arrived. Although they didn't know it, all of us adults had taken long naps during the day.

The backpacking experience we designed included physical and emotional stress. As adults, we knew our own stress would be automatic. After all, we were spending a weekend with adolescents.

After arriving about 2:00 A.M., we had a four-hour hike to the campsite. The adolescents, still wound up and excited about the experience, hadn't slept. The van trip had been a party to them.

Their first experience was to help one another as we trekked through the dark night on a narrow trail. The first person through announced any places where those following might stumble. Trust began to develop within the group.

By 6:00 A.M. they started to pitch their tents. We let them go to sleep—until 8:00 A.M. It was time to begin the experience. Since the adolescents were exhausted, some started complaining about life. We assumed most of them wanted to sleep in, but we didn't give them a choice. Others tried to prove their toughness by their readiness for the hike.

Ignoring the grumbling, we made them put everything in their backpacks. After they hiked six hours without a rest of more than fifteen minutes at any spot, the complaints intensified. In the beginning they called us their fearless leaders and "insightful friends," but we became jerks or worse. They focused their pain on blaming someone else. "Our leaders got us into this," they grumbled. Several asked aloud, "Why did we come anyway?"

Despite their growing dissatisfaction, the hike continued for another two hours. They were a determined group, and their blind faith and pride kept them going. Yet more and more we heard their complaints about "this dumb group," and "I'm about ready to check out of this hike" became a refrain. No longer did anyone express concern for those behind or those who walked slower. It had become a matter of each looking out for himself or herself. In that period of time, they had turned into a rather selfish group.

The pain of walking with heavy weights on their backs became unbearable. Soon they were discarding weight. Not one of them discarded a boom box or curling iron. They did drop food.

Just before 4:00 P.M., a mass rebellion broke out. They were exhausted and angry, and they wanted to quit. Silent, internalized anger had been brewing for at least the past hour. Then they attacked us, their leaders.

When I asked, "What's wrong?" they let me know.

"We're tired."

"I just want to quit."

"My back's killing me."

"My legs are giving out."

"You're killing us by making us go on like this."

Then a small group announced, "Hey, we're quitting the hike."

I said, "All right. But where are we going?"

Silence filled the area as they shifted their glances from face to face. They didn't know. They had no idea how far they'd gone or how far they still had to travel before they got there. In fact, they didn't even know where "there" was.

We talked quietly. I told them their present location, how far we still had to go, and how long it would take us. Immediately, their attitude changed. They were determined to go on. Teamwork resurfaced.

"Hey, we can do it," someone said.

"Yeah! It's not far!"

"Come on! Let's speed it up!"

From then on, the experience took on an air of exciting anticipation. They were still tired, but that didn't seem to matter. They were on their way to where they were going. We adults became their friends again; once again we became insightful and special people.

We leaders hadn't changed. The adolescents weren't any less tired. *But* their attitudes and thoughts had changed.

So often I've thought about those kids in the matter of addiction. The hike to recovery can be exhausting. When people don't know where they are going or if they'll even get there, they become angry. Often they direct their anger against those who have been most trustworthy and helpful. They feel they are being forced into changing by everyone around them. Those who want them to change don't understand that the pain to change is too great.

Also, when persons don't know where they were when they started, how can they measure their progress? Recovery involves knowing where to start, where to go, and how to get there. When they have an end in sight, the pain becomes a challenge. Knowing what they can achieve keeps them motivated.

The hike in the woods taught those adolescents about addiction. As we discussed the hike in connection with their addictions, they were able to make the connections. Their knowledge and understanding of what lay ahead enabled them to endure the pain of change.

— 6 —

Learning from the Twelve-Step Programs

The twelve-step programs have taught us some very important things about recovery. These things can be used at home with support from the church, family, friends, or others.

Persons who have benefited from the twelve-step programs have often said, "I couldn't have made it without them."

The various twelve-step programs do work. Many people recover from addictions because the members in such groups are accepting, understanding, honest, and helpful.

The twelve-step programs and other support groups work because of a simple principle: Before recovery begins, persons need to have supportive people in place. Mutual-help groups are already in place, waiting to lend a hand to those who begin their recovery.

For more than fifty years, the twelve-step programs—based on the foundation of Alcoholics Anonymous (AA)—have helped millions of people in recovery. When persons want to recover, it's natural that they assess the strengths that twelve-step fellowship groups offer—and there are many.

Although I don't think twelve-step programs are the answer for everyone, I want to point out eight things I especially admire about their principles.

1. Twelve-Step Programs Teach Accountability

An effective part of twelve-step fellowships is their focus on accountability through sponsorship and group attendance. Accountability is not control but a loving questioning of actions and motives. People just won't keep promises they make to themselves. They have an uncanny ability to lie to or deceive themselves, explain their own inconsistencies, and justify their actions. Accountability keeps members honest and positive.

Accountability takes place when persons in recovery are able to say, "I need help. I need someone to be accountable to." Unless those in recovery ask for *and want* such help, it has proven ineffective.

To be effective, accountability must be voluntary. It must be requested by those in recovery.

2. Twelve-Step Programs Provide Reality Checks

Twelve-step programs refer to group consciousness or, as we call it sometimes, a form of reality checks. What persons think or feel may not be true. When they are in pain or feel confused, unloved, euphoric, or excited, they may set themselves up for unrealistic expectations. In moments of joy, they may feel total confidence in their ability to "go it alone" and never be tempted to return to their addictions. Or they may be going through a time of depression and believe they'll never change. In both instances, the truth isn't based on how they "feel" at the moment, and their perceptions aren't necessarily reality. Through one-on-one discussions—a vital part of the twelve-step recovery process—persons learn to define what is real.

Reality isn't based on feelings. Reality is based on facts. People starting in recovery often get their feelings confused with the facts.

3. Twelve-Step Programs Supply Identification

People like to be understood by others who know their situation. Although nobody truly knows exactly what another feels, those who have been addicted have a strong sense of identification with those who are coming out of addiction.

In our culture, people spend their lives hiding their true selves and covering up their faults and weaknesses. In twelve-step programs, members share their struggles, failures, faults, successes, and newfound strengths, which allows newcomers to identify with the group. "These people understand me" is a common response.

Knowing what others are going through can be helpful. But their experiences or problems don't have to be exactly the same. The individuals don't have to be from the same social, racial, or ethnic background to identify with a person's problems.

Nowhere does this matter of identification with those in pain seem more apparent than in the Bible. One instance comes to mind. Paul, a leader of the early church, wrote to the people in the city of Philippi who were being persecuted for their faith. At the time he wrote to them, he was in prison because of his preaching. Quite obviously they realized that he did understand them when he wrote,

> For it has been granted to you on behalf of Christ not only to believe on him, but also to suffer for him, since you are going through the same struggle you saw I had, and now hear that I still have. If you have any encouragement from being united with Christ, if any comfort from his love, if any fellowship with the Spirit, if any tenderness and compassion, then make my joy complete by being like-minded, having the same love, being one in spirit and purpose (Phil. 1:29—2:2 NIV).

People need to feel they are understood. They identify with those who have had similar experiences.

The confidence persons feel at being accepted just as they are—which is part of what happens when others identify with them—is essential to fight the battle of addictions.

4. Twelve-Step Programs Allow People to Feel They Belong

"I used to feel that I was the only alien alive on planet earth," said Doug. "When I joined Overeaters Anonymous, I knew I wasn't alone. These were aliens like me. I belonged."

Twelve-step programs bring the feeling of belonging to the recovery process. The addictive cycle destroys or diminishes self-esteem so badly that those in recovery need to be convinced that they belong and that they have a supportive group who feels what they feel. Once they feel part of a group or fellowship, they can venture into the world of change.

I like to think of twelve-step programs as those that require members to have problems; most other organizations require people to conceal their problems.

"It was the first time I could take off my mask," a woman in AA said. "It was more than just feeling I belonged there. They made me feel as if they cared more about me than I cared about myself." She laughed

Figure 6-1
Characteristics of Twelve-Step Programs

Characteristic	Lesson
1. Twelve-step programs teach accountability.	1. To be effective, accountability must be voluntary. It must be requested by those in recovery.
2. Twelve-step programs provide reality checks.	2. Reality isn't based on feelings. Reality is based on facts. People starting in recovery often get their feelings confused with the facts.
3. Twelve-step programs supply identification.	3. People need to feel they are understood. They identify with those who have had similar experiences.
4. Twelve-step programs allow people to feel they belong.	4. Everyone needs to belong someplace. When individuals know they fit, they are able to receive help.
5. Twelve-step programs offer validation.	5. To keep changing, people need to feel validated.
6. Twelve-step programs educate.	6. Part of recovery involves self-education. People need to learn who they are.
7. Twelve-step programs offer direction.	7. Those in recovery need to have voices that say, "This is the way."
8. Twelve-step programs point to reliance on God.	8. Spiritual recovery is the cornerstone of recovery.

and added, "Maybe that's what I needed. For the first time in my life, I had found a place where I fitted in."

Everyone needs to belong someplace. When individuals know they fit, they are able to receive help.

5. Twelve-Step Programs Offer Validation

When persons change, they need others to recognize the change. They need to hear comments such as:

- "You're different."
- "You've changed."
- "I like the new you."
- "I'm proud of you for what you're doing for yourself."

They need appreciation. Respect. Recognition for their hard work and their self-honesty. When they receive all this from others, that's validation.

Validation boosts their self-esteem. They begin to think better of themselves because others encourage them and point out that they are not failures and misfits.

To keep changing, people need to feel validated.

In meetings, the group provides coins, tokens, or certificates to reward recovery time and to mark recovery anniversaries. These are also forms of validation that encourage members to keep changing.

6. Twelve-Step Programs Educate

"I'm forty-seven," said a one-year member of Gamblers Anonymous. "This year I've learned who I am. I've lived with myself all these years, but I didn't understand who I really was. It's now an exciting journey for me as I learn more."

At their best, such groups educate their members and help them see the behavior pitfalls and attitudes that lead them into addiction. Those in recovery begin to learn about themselves—who they really are.

The education goes outward, too. AA and the twelve-step programs have made society more aware of addiction. Their educational efforts have affected law enforcement as well as judicial, medical, social, and religious organizations. They have worked to overcome misinformation, fears, and prejudices of addiction.

Part of recovery involves self-education. People need to learn who they are.

7. Twelve-Step Programs Offer Direction

AA and other twelve-step programs provide a sense of direction to persons who need it most. Those in recovery, especially in the beginning stages, are often confused, or they misinterpret reality. They need others to point them in the right direction. Such people are like road markers that cry out, "This is the right direction."

Twelve-step people guide by sharing their experiences and resources. Slogans such as "Easy does it" and "One day at a time" offer encouragement and direction.

Those in recovery need to have voices that say, "This is the way."

8. Twelve-Step Programs Point to Reliance on God

Even though I've left this for the last point, I believe it's the most important. Some recovery programs try to ignore or deny the place of God (or a Higher Power). I think that's a serious mistake.

For recovery to take place, people need to know that God cares about them personally and about their problems. Some people don't like my statement. They tell me, "Joel, you sound like a fanatic."

I respond by telling them, "Then you don't know or haven't grasped what has taken place through the fifty years of AA. My years of neurochemical research and its results say essentially the same thing."

I've said to clients, "The Bible has every answer you need." Even so, some try to avoid it. Maybe they don't know how to read the Bible. Maybe they have misconceptions about how to read it. Maybe they've seen too much religious manipulation and will cite the failure of religious leaders. Yet this much I do know: No other book is as awesome or as helpful.

Spirituality isn't limited to faith in God but refers to a way of living. A healthy spiritual outlook produces healthy thoughts, positive attitudes, and a more optimistic view of the world and the self.

Spirituality includes giving up (surrendering) power over addiction and replacing it with the power (strength) of God. I like to think of spiritual recovery as giving up self-centeredness for Christ-centeredness.

I've included the famous twelve steps here. Notice that the first three include the need for God as the center of life.

Spiritual recovery is the cornerstone of recovery.

The Twelve Steps of Alcoholics Anonymous*

1. We admitted we were powerless over alcohol—that our lives had become unmanageable.

2. Came to believe that a Power greater than ourselves could restore us to sanity.

3. Made a decision to turn our will and our lives over to the care of God as we understood Him.

4. Made a searching and fearless moral inventory of ourselves.

5. Admitted to God, to ourselves, and to another human being the exact nature of our wrongs.

6. Were entirely ready to have God remove all these defects of character.

7. Humbly asked Him to remove our shortcomings.

8. Made a list of all persons we had harmed, and became willing to make amends to them all.

---

*The Twelve Steps are reprinted with permission of Alcoholics Anonymous World Services, Inc. Permission to reprint the Twelve Steps does not mean that AA has reviewed or approved the content of this publication, nor that AA agrees with the views expressed herein. AA is a program of recovery from alcoholism. Use of the Twelve Steps in connection with programs and activities which are patterned after AA but which address other problems does not imply otherwise.

9. Made direct amends to such people wherever possible, except when to do so would injure them or others.

10. Continued to take personal inventory and when we were wrong promptly admitted it.

11. Sought through prayer and meditation to improve our conscious contact with God as we understood Him, praying only for knowledge of His will for us and the power to carry that out.

12. Having had a spiritual awakening as the result of these steps, we tried to carry this message to alcoholics, and to practice these principles in all our affairs.

Here are similar twelve-step programs and fellowships:
Bulimics/Anorexics Anonymous
Child Abusers Anonymous
Cocaine Anonymous
Debtors Anonymous
Emotions Anonymous
Gamblers Anonymous
Incest Survivors Anonymous
Narcotics Anonymous
Overcomers Outreach (Christian-based twelve-step programs for
    alcoholics and adult children)
Overeaters Anonymous
Parents Anonymous
Pills Anonymous
Sex Addicts Anonymous
Sex and Love Addicts Anonymous
Shoplifters Anonymous
Smokers Anonymous
Workaholics Anonymous

NOTE: All the answers aren't in twelve-step programs. The answer to recovery includes the twelve-step principles, biblical principles, and brain chemistry issues.

Most important, recovery is individual. What works for one may not work for the other.

— 7 —
Staying Free

Support, accountability, and understanding your brain chemicals are essential to recover from addictions.

Years ago someone asked, "What do I need to do to get free of this thing forever?" His question really got to the heart of the issue. Theory about addiction can help, but hurting people want more—they want relief from their pain. They cry for something to change them permanently.

"I can stop smoking," she said with a pained expression. "I've done it twenty times." She was asking for a recovery that would last and would change her way of life.

That's what I want to present in this chapter—what people need to *permanently* break the addictive cycle and to recover *for life*.

As I related in an earlier chapter about backpacking with adolescents, when persons know what they need to do to recover, the journey becomes less painful and stressful.

The exciting journey of recovery, once begun, can continue for the rest of life. I believe that when people know what they need and where they're going, they do better. Those who want to keep moving ahead need to know nine specific things.

1. They Need Ongoing Support

Vic was recovering from sex addiction. He spent his days trying to mellow out and alleviate his excitement. Someone took him to a meeting of Sexual Addicts Anonymous (SAA). He left after half an hour.

When Vic came to me, he said, "I'm not a prude or anything, but the language appalled me—all the swearing. Besides, I've never smoked, and I felt I needed a gas mask to sit through the gray haze of smoke. I'd be wired out if I got into any of that."

Vic got no reward from the SAA meeting or from any other similar group fellowship system. He did find help when he joined a Bible study of six men that met every Saturday morning. They knew of his addictive history and were supportive. "They are just what I need," he remarked.

Just before they broke up the first time, each of them said to Vic something like, "Here's my telephone number. Call me anytime." Those men were there when he needed them—and not just on Saturday morning.

Individuals need other people to make them feel acceptance and approval for their actions and even for their existence. Looking in the mirror isn't enough—it takes real people to affirm and respond.

Persons need ongoing support. They enter into recovery in a state of low self-esteem. That is, they don't feel good about themselves; they are aware of their failures, lies, deceptions, and weaknesses. Because their self-esteem has been badgered so much, gaining approval for who they are and what they're doing is a top priority.

Everyone in recovery needs somebody's support and approval.

Individual needs and personalities determine where they get support. Group fellowships and Bible studies aren't for everyone. Some don't get a reward or feel good from group activity. In fact, belonging to a group could actually be negative for them.

Persons who avoid twelve-step programs or mutual-help groups need to make sure this is a personality value issue and not just another act of denial. They may try to use denial to hide their anger or other emotions. Unless they are clearly hampered by being in a group, those who want to recover need to give themselves the opportunity to try such fellowships.

2. They Need to Be Accountable

Ryan had a hard time with accountability. "I'm not going to be a prisoner going up to the warden every week," he said.

"Let's look at it another way," I told him. "Think of accountability as a process. Before you make a decision to act, you describe what you're going to do. This shows your intention. If necessary, you then explain your reasons for choosing this behavior."

As we talked, I explained to Ryan that he might be thinking idealistically or wrongly. Just having another person—someone who cares—to listen and respond can make a lot of difference.

"This person can lovingly question your perceptions. Or challenge you if you deviate from your planned approach. All of this means you'll have someone outside yourself, someone who can help you rethink your behavior," I said.

Ryan did change his viewpoint when he realized that this wasn't a legalistic imposition but a chance for him to think out loud and to get feedback.

That's freely accepted accountability. But when accountability is imposed, it usually fails. Often families impose this burden on addicted persons by keeping track of their attendance at meetings and the length of time they aren't "doing" their addictions. Those in recovery didn't ask them to do this. The concerned families defend their actions by saying, "We thought we had a right," or "We're doing this for their own good."

Such family setups require the addicted persons to change *before* family members offer their support. This approach makes me think of some religious people who want only the good people to come to church. By contrast, the Bible illustrates that Jesus always reached out to sinners. Read about an incident where religious leaders criticized Jesus for doing this:

> While Jesus was having dinner at Matthew's house, many tax collectors and "sinners" came and ate with him and his disciples. When the Pharisees saw this, they asked his disciples, "Why does your teacher eat with tax collectors and 'sinners'?" On hearing this, Jesus said, "It is not the healthy who need a doctor, but the sick. But go and learn what this means: 'I desire mercy, not sacrifice.' For I have not come to call the righteous, but sinners" (Matt. 9:10–13 NIV).

Today, Jesus might very well chastise leaders and congregations and say the same thing He said two thousand years ago. Too many church people have refused to reach out in loving support. In their place, twelve-step programs, cults, and occult groups have come along. They have replaced the church in allowing "sinners" to belong.

Accountability works right when it's linked with love that imposes no conditions. If families can offer this kind of accountability, they can greatly improve the recovery process.

Accountability also works on a mutual level. The Bible describes the perfect accountability system in Ecclesiastes 4:9–10:

> Two are better than one,
> Because they have a good reward for their labor.
> For if they fall, one will lift up his companion.

But woe to him who is alone when he falls,
For he has no one to help him up!

That is true accountability—helping the other not to fall. If the other does fall, the friend holds out a hand and says, "Here, let me help." **Accountability helps persons move in the right direction at their own pace, and there's no keeping score.**

3. They Need to Define the Battle

Fighting the symptoms of addiction doesn't work. That is, *not* smoking or *not* overeating by sticking to a strict diet isn't a cure.

For success, persons have to define their battles, which may be spiritual, emotional, or physical. Regardless of the primary battle, the war affects them in all three areas.

Emotional battles come in the form of depression, anxiety, and just about every known emotional upheaval. Often these struggles focus on unresolved conflict, or they are created by the addiction cycle. These emotional battles weaken persons spiritually and physically.

When persons fight a spiritual battle—and addiction is a spiritual battle—their emotions and bodies are also affected. They can't feel peace and comfort and often are controlled by anger, fear, and insecurity. They develop physical symptoms such as headaches and ulcers.

Spiritual battles center on issues such as acceptance, unconditional love, and self-discipline. They affect addictions, relationships, and everything persons do.

Over the years I've noticed that spiritual battles are often the most difficult. Such fighters are struggling in foreign territory or with intangible items or issues that involve more than logic. For most, it is a battle of faith—believing in the goodness of God and also in God's love for them.

Trust doesn't come easily to those who have felt betrayed, isolated, unwanted, and rejected. While they may know they want to believe, they can't "reason" themselves into faith, and they don't learn about God purely through the intellect.

The apostle Paul addressed this issue:

And my speech and my preaching were not with persuasive words of human wisdom, but in demonstration of the Spirit and of power, that your faith should not be in the wisdom of men but in the power of God (1 Cor. 2:4–5).

The addiction is an obvious symptom; the cause is more diffi-cult to determine.

4. They Need to Identify Chemical Imbalances

Hormonal and chemical imbalances may create addictions and emo-tional, spiritual, and physical problems. Physical illnesses may result in pain or depression or chemical imbalances in the brain. When the body is out of balance, persons often misperceive their own emotions or God. The cycle of physical affecting emotional affecting spiritual begins.

Neurochemistry can provide valuable insight into the spiritual, emotional, and physical realms. I think of Reese and others like him who have been through traditional recovery programs but still find themselves depressed and uncomfortable. For several months, Reese had been a model of behavior in overcoming his compulsive overeating. He did everything that was supposed to make him feel better, but nothing positive happened.

"I just don't know what to do next," he said in a dejected voice. "I've tried everything, but it doesn't really work for me."

When we started to work with Reese, we quickly realized that a chemical imbalance in his brain caused his depression. He actually had achieved success, but because of the chemical imbalance, he would per-ceive everything negatively.

Whatever persons think, eat, drink, feel, and do affects the body on all three levels: physical, emotional, and spiritual. Balancing the brain is part of the recovery process.

Chemicals become unbalanced because of genetics (inherited genes or tendencies). If a genetic predisposition caused the alcoholism, overeating, or other compulsive disorder, the way to eliminate the disor-der is to correctly balance the brain chemistry. Trying to stop an addiction in someone with an out-of-balance brain is not effective.

Normal chemicals become unbalanced through the addictive proc-ess. Persons develop feelings of insecurity, fear, dread, depression, and anxiety from the altered brain. When the addiction is discontinued, the brain can return to normal. But it doesn't do this naturally.

Life-styles also cause a chemical imbalance. All factors—especially diet, exercise, thoughts, and behavior—affect neurochemistry. An un-healthy thought or behavior pattern creates chemicals in the brain that cause an imbalance, which leads to negative emotions. These chemical changes show themselves through depression, anxiety, the inability to experience rewards, the need for excitement, or overeating.

Often addictions actually treat these chemical needs. Persons with a depressed neurochemical makeup may participate in activities such as gambling, sexual promiscuity, or cocaine use to alleviate their depression. The opposite occurs with excitatory excesses.

Addictions can provide relief to an imbalance because they are a form of self-medication for the brain.

5. They Need to Make Sure What They Think Is True Really Is True

One of the greatest struggles people with addictions experience is knowing what's true. Conflicts created by addictions sometimes make people feel they're crazy. Their moods change, their concept of reality shifts, they break promises, and they feel guilty. Then they condemn themselves and feel hopeless, knowing they can't stop their behavior. No one around them believes in them any longer. Soon, they question their own sanity.

The mind plays tricks on people in the middle of conflicts. Most of us have observed attitudinal changes in people when they undergo stress. Quiet people get abusive; other people just become silent. Stress produces fears. When fear takes hold, the view of life can't be relied on. These changes come about because of chemical changes in the brain brought on by the stress. The stress releases chemicals into the nervous and cardiovascular systems. As a result the emotions shift.

The same chemical imbalances affect the body and bring on physical ailments, such as ulcers and migraines and even heart attacks. When persons are physically suffering, they view everything in life differently.

Although addicted persons need to discuss love, timing is important. When they're angry isn't the appropriate time. Their anger creates chemical changes that distort (even momentarily) their view of life.

Those who seek recovery from their addictions must know the chemical alterations of the brain. Treatment will be incorrectly perceived if their chemicals remain out of balance.

I want to tell you about Doris, an eighteen-year-old girl referred for treatment by her mother. "Doris is sexually promiscuous," she said.

During the initial interview process, Doris said she knew her real problem: "My father doesn't love me enough." So she was looking for love from other men.

"How do you know your father doesn't love you enough?" I asked.

A startled expression came to her face. For a long time she stared at me as if no one had ever asked that question before. (No one had, as I learned later.)

Finally she said, "Well, he doesn't hug me much. Almost never touches me."

As we talked, I realized that Doris thought of parental love in terms of the amount of displayed affection.

While I worked with Doris, another therapist talked at length with her father. He had grown up in Germany during World War II. He spent most of his early childhood in a concentration camp. At the end of the war, his family immigrated to the United States. Although his father was trained as a medical doctor, his license wasn't recognized in this country. He was also too old and too poor to get the additional training to qualify. He finally got a job as a mason. He worked long, hard hours and saved money to educate Doris's father. The family lived in poverty and worked hard to save money. He got his master's degree in chemical engineering.

This was the man Doris was asking to be demonstrative and emotional. It was impossible for him to be more responsive. As a boy, he had survived the concentration camp by his wits and couldn't afford to express feelings to his captors or to those dying around him every day.

When the other therapist asked the father, "Do you love Doris?" tears filled his eyes.

"Of course," he said, "I love her very much. She's everything in the world to me." He said he wanted to show her how much he loved her by sending her to a top-rated college—and it would be a financial strain. He did say he patted her on the head each time she came home from college.

"Do you think you should be a little more emotional toward her?" the therapist asked.

He gave her a blank stare, then replied, "I am a very emotional and loving person."

A week after the father spoke with the other therapist and I got the report, Doris had her second appointment with me. We began to talk about love. Even though I talked to her about how much her father loved her and what he was trying to do for her, she didn't understand.

Yet her father felt that he showed her physical affection by patting her on the head each time she came home from college. Growing up, the father had received pats on the head as expressions of love. He was simply repeating what he had learned.

Doris's sex addiction was based upon inaccurate conclusions from her father. He did love her, but she didn't accept his way of loving her. Her need for other men was a misperception of her father's love.

Eventually, Doris began to understand that he did love her in his way. His patting her head was then all right. Her addiction dissipated with the acceptance of her father's love.

Many people who feel rejected and unloved don't understand the language spoken by their parents or spouses. They can't feel love because of their own addictions. They focused so much on the others' failure to express love the way they want them to that they haven't grasped the reality of how deeply those very people care. They reached unreal conclusions caused by chemical imbalances, unrealistic expectations, or misperceived truths.

How people feel at the moment determines their perception of reality. Their perception may be faulty.

6. They Need Rewards

Physicians often complain about patients' noncompliance—not doing what they're told to do. The doctors become frustrated and say, "They could do better or get well if they'd just follow instructions."

Immediately I think of Oliver. He was seventy pounds overweight and also had a heart condition aggravated by his high-fat diet and lack of exercise. His physician gave him a diet and exercise plan and insisted, "Oliver, you have to follow this strictly. If you don't, you can have even more serious health problems."

When Oliver returned a month later, he had not followed instructions. The frustrated doctor concluded, "He doesn't care about himself. He's one of those noncompliant patients."

Because of what the doctor called "his self-destructive personality," he referred Oliver to me for counseling.

When I talked with Oliver, it was obvious he did care, but he just couldn't stay on a strict diet. "It offers you no reward, does it?" I asked.

When I explained what I meant, Oliver grinned: "Yeah, now I understand. No wonder every diet failed."

Together, Oliver and I decided to try something else. We wanted to change his brain chemistry through behavior and activities that provided him a reward. Once we had worked out a plan for him, he became one of the most compliant clients I've ever seen. Two years have passed. Oliver is at ideal weight and doing well.

Compliance is actually related to brain chemistry. Persons won't continue to do something if they don't get a reward. When persons do something that provides no reward, they'll find ways to discontinue it.

Rewards create reinforcement for continuing behavior. No matter if

FIGURE 7-1
Requirements for Staying Free

Requirement	Reason
1. Ongoing support.	1. Everyone in recovery needs somebody's support and approval.
2. Accountability.	2. Accountability helps persons move in the right direction at their own pace, and there's no keeping score.
3. Definition of the battle.	3. The addiction is an obvious symptom; the cause is more difficult to determine.
4. Identification of chemical imbalances.	4. Addictions can provide relief to an imbalance because they are a form of self-medication for the brain.
5. Assurance of truth.	5. How people feel at the moment determines their perception of reality. Their perception may be faulty.
6. Rewards.	6. When persons get no reward for their behavior, they will find ways to stop that behavior.
7. Realistic expectations.	7. When persons know what to expect in their recovery, they prepare themselves to handle it.
8. Directive, useful knowledge.	8. People need knowledge that directs them in the recovery process. Following the advice of the last person they talked to is a sure setup for failure.
9. Knowledge of God.	9. True recovery is a spiritual recovery.

addicted persons promised themselves, their parents, children, mates, or God. Their failure creates a cycle of hopelessness and frustration. The addiction cycle continues because they have no alternative.

That's why knowing about brain chemistry is so crucial. This information unlocks the mystery of reward centers. It explains why twelve-step programs won't work for everyone, why some people will exercise or diet but not others. It explains why many set themselves up to fail when failure could be avoided.

When persons get no reward for their behavior, they will find ways to stop that behavior.

7. They Need Realistic Expectations

Maxine had struggled with bulimia for a long time. She would seemingly get better and then relapse. Among other things, she had faulty expectations. Somehow she believed that she would never have to confront the issue of her body again, as if all the issues magically disappeared.

On the other hand, I've encountered persons convinced that they will always battle the addiction; that if they let up, they'll lose. When they realize they're not greatly troubled, they panic, feeling certain that something is wrong. This is another example of unrealistic expectations.

Undergoing the recovery process can be like riding a roller coaster. The ups and downs are created by the changing chemicals in the brain. The shock of being brought down unexpectedly can be lessened through the understanding of brain chemistry. When persons know what is going to happen, they'll be much more prepared to handle it.

If they understand their emotional, spiritual, and physical makeup, they can predict what will most likely occur in each phase of recovery. The persons will be prepared for problems before they begin. Offensive treatment obviously lessens the severity of mood swings and frustration levels.

When brain chemistry is understood, persons can manage unpredicted changes much better. When they understand which chemicals are out of balance and what rewards they can achieve, they can set up a program that prevents them from feeling too badly when their emotions go haywire.

In the Help Yourself Recovery System we actually prescribe the form of behavior. When certain chemicals respond in one way, we prescribe the type of behavior to correct them. Addicted persons then treat their addictions instead of transferring to another form of abuse. They follow new forms of behavior that provide the same chemical rewards.

When persons know what to expect in their recovery, they prepare themselves to handle it.

8. They Need Directive, Useful Knowledge About Themselves

Knowing what to do and how to do it results in successful recovery. Increasing motivation isn't necessary for most people. They want to change; they just don't know how.

Addicts who give up cocaine and turn to excessive exercise are still addicted. The persons may argue that the addiction is now positive. Although exercising is more positive than using cocaine, the addiction still controls them. The new addiction is based on being physically healthy and looking youthful. When they become ill or when they begin to age, the exercise compulsion will no longer meet their needs. They will then be vulnerable to cocaine again.

Exercise isn't always good for everybody because of its effects on brain chemistry. Individual chemical levels will determine what form of exercise persons need and how much is good for them.

Assuming whatever feels good must be appropriate isn't the answer. This attitude can allow the compulsion to continue—and grow. Exercise is appropriate only for those who obtain a reward such as positive emotional and physical health. Although exercise may be healthy for most people's physical needs, it may be negative for their emotional needs. The Help Yourself Recovery System prescribes activity based upon an individual's brain chemistry and the activity's effect on the brain.

Diets also affect brain chemistry and shouldn't be chosen solely by caloric count. An improperly prescribed diet may result in anxiety or depression.

The recovery process allows for individual and group support. But persons have to know what kind of support is best for them. Once again, brain chemistry answers the question. Most people attend groups because they assume such attendance is best for them and for everyone. But for many, group activities are negative and will set them back in recovery. The type of therapy and the setting are individual and should be prescribed, not chosen because of popularity.

People need knowledge that directs them in the recovery process. Following the advice of the last person they talked to is a sure setup for failure.

9. They Need to Know God

Persons with addictions have chemical imbalances in the brain that create misperceptions. They misperceive God, themselves, and others. It is more important to act on faith when one is misperceiving than to try to understand through inaccurate conclusions. Faith means the ability to accept something as true even when it's not fully understood. Defining truth through the understanding of a misperceiving brain is dangerous.

They need faith most when they're afraid or defensive or when they avoid taking care of their spiritual needs. The fears, defensiveness, and avoidance are part of the problem with their thinking. A misperceiving brain draws the wrong conclusions and defines truth inaccurately.

True recovery is spiritual recovery.

— 8 —

The Battle to Recover

Addiction isn't the battle you are fighting.
The battle is with your thoughts and the
psychological needs the addiction meets.

Soldiers dedicate themselves to fighting a war when they know why they're fighting. People just don't fight to the death without a cause. In the same way, we can say that addiction is a war. To have the heart to fight to the end, persons need to understand the cause they're struggling for.

In the matter of addiction, the battle front is the brain. Fighting first takes place among the thoughts that seem to strike randomly. If such thoughts are not overcome and changed, battles inside the self result in fear, guilt, shame, inadequacy, and hopelessness. Addiction—whether eating, drinking, using drugs, gambling, or spending—is a result of unchecked thoughts and conflicts.

Here's the motto of this war:

Win the inner battle, and the addictions stop.

Many times I've seen this happen. People struggle against the symptoms of addiction, but it's not effective. The best result of such action is that they transfer to another addiction. When they focus on the addiction and eliminate it by not doing it anymore, the chemical changes in the brain still haven't changed.

Often these transferred addictions aren't obvious to most people. "He doesn't drink anymore," they say. "She dropped two hundred pounds and has kept them off." They see results of fighting one addictive symptom, but observers don't realize that the mind and the emotions are still addicted.

Battling the symptoms of addiction actually creates special problems. Persons may stop doing the negative behavior, such as drinking or smoking, but they don't have peace. If they're constantly thinking about cigarettes or whiskey or cocaine, they're still addicted.

Here are nine common problems created by fighting the symptoms of addiction and not the cause.

1. The Problem of No Significant Change

Friends gradually diminish their support, not because they don't care, but because they don't recognize any significant change. Often, the changes addicted persons make are self-centered or based on selfish reasons. These new activities make them feel better, but in their new way of thinking, the family exists for them and their needs. They spend three nights a week at AA and have no time to be with the family. As much as friends and family want to be supportive, they won't continue long if nothing much happens.

A popular cliché, "People have to want to change for themselves," goes back to the idea of taking care of number one. Unfortunately, such frequently mouthed sayings have permeated the addictions field. BUT they aren't true. People don't change only for themselves.

All of us are social creatures. All of us need approval and acceptance from the significant others in our lives. This inborn human need can be an invaluable tool in recovery. When we recognize that part of developing a healthy self-esteem comes from knowing that we have been respected, accepted, and valued by others, we can use this in recovery.

Healthy self-esteem is a product or a result of treating the cause of addictions, not the symptoms. When persons change their view of themselves, others notice. They comment positively. They affirm the action, and they are likely to offer their support.

A healthy self-esteem results in validation and respect by those who love us.

Healthy relationships are not selfish. Intimacy comes through giving, not getting. Our society has learned to become so selfish that any concept that includes doing something for others is too often rejected.

2. The Problem of Motivation to Change

Because of my experience and research, I think that people are much more dependent on others than society would like us to believe.

When others encourage and show their support, addicted persons can change. Often they need voices outside themselves that say, "You can do it. I'll take your hand and walk down the road with you."

I've also noticed that those with compulsive habits "name" their addictions fairly early when the addictions negatively affect the important people in their lives. When their "have to" habits interfere with family or social relationships, they hear about it. Sometimes they are directly confronted. If those significant others give them a double message, they can help addicted persons want to change.

The double message is (1) you are addicted and (2) I care about you and want to help. Persons then have powerful motivations to change. Remember: Most people want approval from others.

The motivation to change includes the impact of the change on others.

3. The Problem of the Need for Support

Persons find support from others when they are honest enough to share that they need to change. A sense of humility and forgiveness is essential to get support. The Bible speaks of the need for humility: "When pride comes, then comes shame; but with the humble is wisdom" (Prov. 11:2).

All too often, society has perceived humility to mean being taken advantage of by others. Humility involves recognizing limitations and asking for support from others.

When persons fight only symptoms, they focus on their addictions. They need to strengthen their relationships that provide acceptance and intimacy.

Persons who know it all and want no help stand alone. When persons can admit to a problem and ask for forgiveness and support, they won't have to go it alone. There is strength in numbers. The Bible teaches, "For where two or three are gathered together in My name, I am there in the midst of them" (Matt. 18:20).

Fighting alone is a lonely battle.

4. The Problem of Family Support

Friends, families, and others often have unrealistic expectations about recovery. That's also why treatment of the whole family is necessary. And the family's treatment can occur only when members know they are important and are part of the solution, not simply enmeshed in the problem.

Because families don't know what to expect and how to offer support, they often feel part of the problem. And they exhibit negative attitudes when they feel they are the problem. Ignoring or not including the family in the recovery process tells them they are the problem.

The longer family members are left feeling they are the cause, the more reinforced such feelings become. The greater the feelings, the less support they can give.

Family members can learn acceptance in a short time—if they are included in the recovery process. The family can become the primary source of validation for the person.

The more families feel they are responsible for the addiction, the less supportive they can be.

When family members become part of the solution from the beginning of the recovery process, they are more open to change. Knowing the battle allows them to join the fighting force. When family members understand that the rejection they feel and the blame they receive are part of the symptoms of addiction, they are more supportive.

5. The Problem of Denial

When persons fight symptoms and lose by returning to the addiction or transferring it to something else, they tend to deny they have the problem. They have feelings of hopelessness. Whether they say the words or not, in their hearts they are thinking, *I'll never overcome this problem.* To avoid the overwhelming guilt and depression of hopelessness, they make the natural (and unconscious) response of denial.

When persons with addictions fight the addictive symptoms and nothing happens or they fail, their first tendency is to deny the problem. Or they blame another cause for the problem such as their boring jobs, their demanding supervisors, or their nagging families.

The brain is chemically imbalanced. As long as persons continue their addictions, the brain remains out of balance. If they have no hope of ever being normal, denial of a problem is usually an automatic response. It is too hard to live with a problem day after day after day and feel there is no solution. It's easier to convince the mind that there is no dilemma.

Denial is the option for the defeated, imbalanced brain.

Denial occurs when people don't know any other way. Denial is a result of narrow vision or closed minds. But persons can overcome denial by opening themselves up to new ideas.

Bob and Don are brothers who went into business together. They put a great deal of energy and money into making their business successful. They dedicated their lives to it, to the point they were workaholics. Then the business failed, forcing both brothers to take a look at their options and themselves at the respective ages of forty-five and forty-seven years.

Six months later, Bob was positive and restructuring his life, while Don was getting a divorce, had moved, and was drinking heavily. The difference in the two had to do with their recovery from their addictions.

Bob recognized he was a workaholic, and the failure of the business forced him to face this truth. He and his family began to work on the problem together and fought the battle.

Meanwhile, Don thought everything would be better if he could "just get a job and make some money." He focused on meeting his workaholic needs and denied the real problems. Eventually, he transferred his workaholism to alcoholism, but he still denies he has any problem.

Most of the denial in recovery results from the feeling of having no other options. Life is too painful, and the real world hurts too much. Denial alleviates some of the pain.

6. The Problem of Hopelessness

Although I've already mentioned it, I have observed no other emotion more frequently in addicted persons than hopelessness—the feeling that there's no solution. Anger, fear, and denial are the emotions stemming from hopelessness. Hopelessness comes from focusing on symptoms or trying to eliminate an addictive life and then failing.

Some watch others drink alcohol or overeat and not have the addictions they do. Other individuals direct their anger toward the people who are free from addictions.

Often persons who feel the sense of hopelessness refuse to associate with those who have overcome their addictions. Some alcoholics can't stand AA meetings. They are actually expressing anger at their feelings of hopelessness.

Hopelessness is the emotion of untreated addictions. Hopelessness says, "I tried and I failed."

Another expression of hopelessness centers on blame. Such persons vent their rage and hurl blame on parents and grandparents because of genetic conditions or the way they were raised. They are convinced their parents made them sex addicts, alcoholics, gamblers, or smokers by the way they were raised as children. Their anger is a sense of hopelessness that says, "I can never change." Persons who focus on their addictions develop a subtle form of hopelessness.

Hopelessness is also fear. Addicted people are afraid they will never get out of the prison they are in. They fear the loss of the relationships that are already in trouble because of their addictions.

Depression surfaces, then they feel like giving up. They feel that they must live with their addictions the rest of their lives. They often look at the alternatives and see a life they don't want, either. They can't imagine going to meetings and talking about their problems the rest of their lives. Recovery scares them as much as their addictions.

Hopelessness is a symptom of being in a war against addictions and not knowing what to do.

7. The Problem of Causal Personalities

Addicted people who fight—but don't know what they are fighting—develop causal personalities. Causal personalities feel they must prove something or must make statements. They have a yes-or-no, right-or-wrong attitude. They tend to look for *the* right way to do something,

FIGURE 8-1
Common Problems Created by Fighting Symptoms Instead of Causes

Problem	Explanation
1. No significant change.	1. A healthy self-esteem results in validation and respect by those who love us.
2. Motivation to change.	2. The motivation to change includes the impact of the change on others.
3. The need for support.	3. When persons fight only symptoms, they focus on their addictions. They need to strengthen their relationships that provide acceptance and intimacy. Fighting alone is a lonely battle.
4. Family support.	4. The more families feel they are responsible for the addiction, the less supportive they can be.
5. Denial.	5. Denial is the option for the defeated, imbalanced brain.
6. Hopelessness.	6. Hopelessness is the emotion of untreated addictions. Hopelessness says, "I tried and I failed." Hopelessness is a symptom of being in a war against addictions and not knowing what to do.
7. Causal personalities.	7. No one was raised in a totally healthy environment. Getting help is more important (and healthy) than blaming or controlling.
8. Constant approval seeking.	8. Approval seeking behavior is a direct result of fighting symptoms.
9. Religion and religiosity.	9. True faith in God does not promote selfishness or expect God to respond to selfishness.

forgetting there may be many right ways to do the same thing. Often they will argue about little things, believing their thinking is correct and others are mistaken.

Anger is common among causal personalities. They become enraged over the injustices of the world. If they got sober through AA, they become crusaders for the system. Anyone who dares to speak of alternatives doesn't really know the disease.

Some women are angry with men, have no peace, and are still addicted. Their lack of personal peace has resulted in being angry. Because they were hurt by men, men become the focal point. Narrow vision and compulsion are still their trademarks. They haven't been able to move on. They have a point that must be proven at the expense of personal peace.

Men who are addicted or in recovery may have destroyed their family systems. They have blamed their wives and are filled with inner rage toward women. Some marry, but they still dislike women. Others become sexually promiscuous and in this way show that they have no respect for women. They are controlled by their anger and have no peace.

They aren't able to provide for intimate and fulfilling relationships. Paul writes in Ephesians 5:21–33 on the subject of healthy spousal relationships. Verse 21 sets the tone for the entire section, which tells readers to give themselves mutually to each other. *Submit*, *respect*, and *love* are three different terms that bring out the idea of mutual self-giving:

> Submit to one another out of reverence for Christ. Wives, submit to your husbands as to the Lord. For the husband is the head of the wife as Christ is the head of the church, his body, of which he is the Savior. Now as the church submits to Christ, so also wives should submit to their husbands in everything. Husbands, love your wives, just as Christ loved the church. . . . This is a profound mystery—but I am talking about Christ and the church. However, each one of you also must love his wife as he loves himself, and the wife must respect her husband. (NIV).

In healthy relationships, each party builds up the other's self-esteem. **No one was raised in a totally healthy environment. Getting help is more important (and healthy) than blaming or controlling.**

8. The Problem of Constant Approval Seeking

Fighting a war and not knowing what is being fought can create the need for constant approval. All persons need approval, respect, and a feeling of importance from others. When persons change their values and beliefs for approval, however, they have developed an addiction to approval seeking.

Approval seeking can be seen in people who volunteer or work excessively. Sponsorship in a twelve-step program and membership in volunteer committees are excellent ways to achieve approval and can become addicting rather quickly.

Persons involved in these activities receive much praise for their caring and supportive personalities. Often these praises replace the reality of their lives. They are searching for intimacy in relationships but can't find it. The status of a magnificent volunteer or sponsor can alleviate these needs temporarily.

Voluntary work and sponsorship are to be commended. *But* if persons cease to look at their own problems or sacrifice existing relationships for this approval or don't feel approved except through serving, they have an approval seeking addiction.

Workaholism can be a form of approval seeking. Society teaches that hard workers are good. Managers and bosses praise their most productive workers. Persons addicted to approval may become addicted to their jobs.

Those suffering from eating disorders may become so involved in helping others they have no time or energy to change. Many individuals suffering from compulsive overeating develop approval seeking addictions. They have given up on their disease and look for their self-esteem by getting others' approval, which may be in the form of church activities or other areas to achieve praise.

Approval seeking behavior is a direct result of fighting symptoms and not the cause of addictions.

9. The Problem of Religion and Religiosity

People who don't fight the real issues can become religious fanatics. The Bible describes the Pharisees as religious leaders who had high standards but no real faith in Jesus Christ. They were so scrupulous about everything that they sometimes made the laws of God a mockery. For example, they were to give one-tenth of their goods to God. According to Jesus, they even counted out one-tenth of the herbs from their gardens. Unfortunately, they ignored the more important matters of law. Many people are like the Pharisees, and their legalistic religions have the same symptoms as addiction. They are addicted to their perceptions and way of thinking. They believe they are right and use the Bible to prove it. The Pharisees relied on the same methods. But Jesus Christ challenged the legalistic law-oriented Pharisees and Sadducees: "Hypocrites! Well did

Isaiah prophesy about you, saying: 'These people . . . honor Me with their lips, but their heart is far from Me' " (Matt. 15:7–8).

Jesus spoke at length about the superpious teachings of the Pharisees. And they have their spiritual counterparts in churches today. Jesus declared,

> Woe to you, teachers of the law and Pharisees, you hypocrites! You give a tenth of your spices—mint, dill and cummin. But you have neglected the more important matters of the law—justice, mercy and faithfulness. You should have practiced the latter, without neglecting the former. You blind guides! You strain out a gnat but swallow a camel (Matt. 23:23–24 NIV).

A new religious movement, the opposite of the Pharisees and legalism of many churches, has emerged in recent years. It is the religion of a compulsive and controlling society, including few standards and a faith that says, "God will fix everything if we only ask."

Such persons try to control God. They pray with their "wish list" in one hand and Bible in the other, extracting the verses that say God will provide if they have enough faith. They have been taught, and they themselves teach, that God always wants to make Christians wealthy and give them the best of this world. Wealth, inner peace, and freedom from pain and disease are parts of their routine prayers. This teaching claims faith will provide for anything but silently teaches selfishness is everything. Such attitudes offer no help to persons trapped in addictive behavior.

True faith in God does not promote selfishness or expect God to respond to selfishness.

Addictive personalities want internal change without action. This type of faith is all-receiving and self-centered; it requires no action. Compulsive and selfish people can so easily become caught up in the attractiveness of this religious movement.

———————— ◆ ————————

Now you know the common battles of those trapped by addictive behavior.

Problems? Yes. But there is help.

— 9 —

A Healthy Brain

A healthy brain sees things accurately. A brain that is imbalanced causes addictions or behavior that leads to addictions. Diet, activity, and thoughts affect brain chemistry.

The brain controls everything—all the muscles, the heart, and every other part of the body. This wonderful, unique brain enables us to make a variety of muscle movements. The brain tells the muscles to run or to relax if we want to sit.

Sometimes certain parts of the brain get injured or diseased. When someone has a stroke, the portion of the brain that controls the muscles is injured. This means loss of control over the muscles. They are still functional, but the brain can't tell them what to do.

The brain also controls thinking—what we think and how. Every day the brain must effectively filter out unnecessary information. If the brain wasn't so efficient, our thoughts and conclusions would get confused. We might start thinking about snow when we're planning to swim.

Again, injury and disease cause trouble. Certain illnesses, such as schizophrenia, don't allow the brain to think clearly. Consequently, thoughts get confused; we could be feeling afraid when we're in a peaceful and safe situation.

The brain does all of this, but we also control the brain. Here are a few examples:

• We decide what to eat.
• We choose to exercise.
• We decide when to sleep.
• We reason and make decisions.

73

Thoughts also generate emotions. For example, Rodney begins to think about an unpleasant situation he is involved in with his boss. As he dwells on his feelings (consciously or not), his anger causes his brain chemicals to change, which creates anxiety. Now that he is anxious, Rodney has to do something to lessen his anxiety, so he drinks alcohol. This is the beginning of his addiction cycle.

Thoughts—*all* thoughts—affect brain chemistry. As simple as this may sound, it is the foundation of this chapter.

All thinking affects brain chemistry

Our thoughts, attitudes, spiritual perceptions, and views of life affect the balance of brain chemicals. That means our emotions affect the brain in some way. This effect can be negative or positive.

A positive effect causes us to think more clearly and remember more accurately. The brain then stores positive information. The next time we need to recall a similar experience, the memory sends us positive information.

When we react negatively to situations, pessimistic thoughts get stored in the brain. In the future, when we call for stored information, the brain will pull out gloomy information.

We base most of our decisions and choices on information we have stored in the brain. When we come upon situations similar to those we have faced before, we pull memories out of storage. Most of have learned, for example, that when we see a red eight-sided sign with the word *STOP*, we apply the brakes of the car. This is called a learned response.

Every action in the brain brings about a reaction

Negative thoughts can't store positive responses. Obvious? Of course, but we seldom think about it this way. A negative cycle develops from the effect of negative thoughts on our brain chemicals.

Persistent, ongoing negative thoughts cause a dark outlook on life. *Negative thoughts also cause chemical imbalances in the brain*. When chemicals are out of balance, life is out of balance. We see everything differently, that is, unrealistically. This unrealistic view affects every part of life: relationships, work habits, appetite, and self-esteem.

If negative thoughts persist so that the brain becomes increasingly imbalanced, we can lose control of our thoughts. That's when emotions such as anger, rage, and depression emerge. These compulsive negative emotions can become our controlling forces. No matter what we see or hear, or who we talk to, we remain controlled by the forces that we helped shape.

The worst part is that we don't easily break this pattern because our brain chemistry has affected our interpretation of the information. Let's see how this works with Brett.

Brett joined a therapy group. Other members reached out to him, trying to make him feel wanted. They called him likable. Someone even used the word *lovable*. Brett didn't "hear" those words because his stored knowledge said, "Brett, you are worthless and unlovable."

No matter how often Brett heard the positive statements, the messages didn't get through to him. The explanation is simple. His negative thoughts changed the chemicals in his brain. This condition then created a negative conclusion about himself. No matter how much positive affirmation the group showered on him, his mind still insisted, "I'm worthless."

Brett doesn't have to remain with negative thoughts. He can change—but he'll need help. The fact is that only when he changes his conclusions about himself will he be able to accept himself positively.

Our brain chemistry affects our interpretation of information and our emotions.

A healthy, positive brain can win the war against addiction

The key to understanding the brain lies within the central nervous system, which is made up of the brain and the individual nerves. This part of the nervous system controls emotions and rewards. It is also the part of the nervous system that we can control.

Think of the nerves as electrical wires. The electrical impulse in nerves, although small, is the same type of impulse that an electrical wire carries. Where the nerve ends in the brain determines the response the impulse creates.

For instance, the optic nerve affects vision. This nerve goes from the eye to the part of the brain that interprets sight. The brain controls whether seeing is important at that moment. When we're asleep, the optic nerve rests or is turned off. This is an off-on type of nerve.

The heart muscle, however, is controlled by a different type of nerve. When we run or walk, the heart pumps harder. The nerves that connect the brain to the heart increase their electrical impulses. The greater the electrical impulses, the faster and harder the heart will pump. That same heart needs to slow down when we sleep. In this case, the nerve can't just turn off or the heart will stop.

Think of a man who plays golf. The walk to the tee requires certain muscular activities. As he walks along, he can talk to his companions about the weather or the stock market with little concentration. As soon as he gets ready to hit the ball, he changes his concentration. This action requires highly individualized muscle coordination, with the eye on the ball, left arm straight, and feet set apart. As a result, if everything is coordinated, his club hits the ball.

This illustration reminds us that we can control some nerves. When a light switch is turned on, the electricity moves through the wire and turns on the light. The light switch controls the electricity from the main power source and directs it to that particular light. However, switching on the living room light won't turn on the hallway light. In the example of the golfer, he selectively switched on different lights. The five senses of touch, taste, smell, hearing, and sight bring information into the brain. The brain responds back to swing, run, jump, or whatever needs to be done.

When one or more of the five senses switch on a nerve that leads to the brain, the brain then interprets the information and determines the action. The nerves carry the action from the brain by using electrical impulses to the organ, muscle, or emotional part of the brain.

Let's say the golfer paused to think about what he had learned from previous mistakes. Sometimes he missed hitting the ball. Or he had to chase it when it got lost in the dense brush. So now he knows the necessity of concentration to hit the ball. He has learned that his thoughts will straighten his left arm, position his feet, and cause a follow-through with the swing.

When the brain interprets information and has options to respond, it is called a voluntary response. Voluntary responses—those responses that we can control—are affected by what we have previously learned. Running a race, watching birds, and feeling a piece of fabric are voluntary responses. These voluntary responses require stored information to be recalled from the brain so we can make a conclusion. Past experience has taught the golfer to keep a straight left arm, follow through, and keep his eye on the ball.

Some nerves aren't controlled directly by thoughts or decisions. When a response doesn't require the brain to interpret information, when it occurs regardless of our own thoughts, we call that an involuntary response. Reflexes, breathing, and the heart beating are examples of involuntary responses. Someone who touches a hot stove and immediately jumps back doesn't even need to think about moving a hand from that hot stove.

———————— ◆ ————————

Let's see how this information works on an emotional level. Phil's father and grandfather bought only Fords. While he was growing up, Phil was taught that Fords are superior. No car is as well made or has the styling and control of a Ford. Phil won't buy a Chevrolet, even if the salesman offers a better price than the Ford dealer. No matter what anyone tells him, Phil "knows" the superiority of a Ford.

If we transfer that to what we believe about ourselves, it's obvious that many of us believe certain things are true about ourselves, regardless of the evidence. Often these things we "know" about ourselves are wrong. That they are untrue doesn't change anything. In childhood, we heard certain statements from our parents or others close to us, so we believed them without question, especially if we heard them often.

Here are typical statements that many of us accepted as true and never questioned:

- "You're a bad girl."
- "You can't do anything right."
- "Why are you so stupid?"
- "You'll never amount to anything."
- "Your sister is the pretty one in the family."
- "You're just plain lazy!"
- "You're exactly like your father."

If we accept such statements as true, we believe them. We may be the brightest people around, but if we accept the statement that we're stupid, we're convinced we're mentally slow. Or unlovable. Or unwanted. Or ugly. The brain stores such information as truth.

Suppose we've heard directly or we've concluded from statements made by our parents that we're worthless. We stored that information as true. When we seek a job, think of marriage, discuss a news event, or whatever we do, inside the brain, we still believe we're worthless. This self-appraisal occurs automatically and almost involuntarily every time the brain has to make a determination about our worth.

Few people understood this concept until early in this century. At that time, a Russian physiologist named Ivan Petrovich Pavlov, already famous for his studies on digestion, proved the principle often called conditioning or conditioned learning or Pavlovian response. He conducted an experiment using a dog, food, and a bell.

Each day just before feeding the dog, Pavlov rang a bell. That set the sequence. First came the ringing of the bell, then the dog saw the food.

Once this ringing-followed-by-food became a habitual experience, Pavlov rang the bell, and the dog began to salivate in anticipation. Whether food followed or not, the dog salivated when he heard the bell. He had learned a response to a specific situation or condition.

We could say it another way. The dog developed a connection with one sense—hearing. A diagram would look like this:

bell → food

Once this conclusion was imprinted in the brain, the animal prepared to eat. How? By salivating. So the diagram then becomes:

bell → food → salivation

After that, hearing a bell caused a physical response of salivation (even when no food was present) because the bell became associated with the presence of food. We call this *conditioning*:

bell → salivation

The same effect occurs in human behavior.

When we talk about recovery from addiction, we go back to the Pavlovian response. The way to change our response is to *interrupt* the sequence of a ringing bell that results in salivation when no food is present.

Here is how this works with Brett: If Brett wants to be free from his addiction, he needs to understand what he can control. If he had total control over his brain, he could stop his addiction by choosing to stop. If the addiction is involuntary and automatic, he must remain addicted for life. Brett *does* have control, although he may not realize it or he may not choose to use it.

Suppose Evelyn's parents expressed their love for her, but they used such expressions of affection to get her to do exactly what they wanted. A kiss, a hug, a pat on the cheek—all these signs of affection developed a Pavlovian response in her. As Evelyn grew older, a hug, a kiss, or any overt show of affection from either mother or father became interpreted as "They're trying to manipulate me to do what they want. They want something from me. They want to control me. They want to force me to do what they want."

If Evelyn takes this conditioning and applies it to every relationship (which often happens), she almost automatically responds with a feeling of anger over being manipulated whenever anyone expresses affection. She might grow up to believe that every relationship is one of manipulation and pain. That situation conditioned her as a child. If every relationship Evelyn develops causes her pain, she soon believes that all relationships are painful. No matter how much she wishes to believe differently, she has no choice. The logic of childhood response still controls her thinking.

Changing the thoughts changes the behavior

Dick came to see me because of conflicts in his marriage. He was the child of an alcoholic father and a controlling mother. His mother expressed love openly, although she seemed never to approve of anything he did. He felt that he couldn't do anything good enough for his mother.

Thirteen years into his marriage, Dick realized he was becoming a romance addict. He sought approval from women around him, which created conflict with his wife. In therapy, he described his wife as controlling and nonapproving.

Later, Dick discovered he had developed a Pavlovian response to his wife's actions. When she expressed love and care for him, he interpreted her actions as control—a response he had learned from his relationship with his mother. His wife's controlling attitude wasn't as real as Dick's brain had interpreted. When he finally broke the Pavlovian response, the relationship improved, and the romance addiction soon disappeared.

Or take the case of Barbara, who felt lonely. One night she ate compulsively. Afterward she felt a little better. Because she found relief from her loneliness, she repeated the behavior when she felt the same way again.

If Barbara repeats this compulsive eating frequently, the response will become automatic. She "cures" her loneliness by eating more. She then develops an addiction to food. If this happens, despite the logic and all the diets she'll ever try, Barbara won't change the addiction.

Any repeated cause-and-effect type of circumstance can develop a Pavlovian response

Breaking the addictive cycle means learning that our thoughts and acts can control certain nerves. If we can reprogram the brain, we then reprogram the conclusions the brain will reach. When this happened to Dick, he no longer had to interpret relationships to mean control. If it happens to Barbara, she won't have to eat to relieve her loneliness.

Let's look at the brain again. The nerves we control are like dimmer switches. The electricity in a regular switch is either on or off. A dimmer switch controls the amount of electricity allowed to pass through the switch. This provides the option of a dim light or a bright one, depending on the amount of electricity that passes through the switch.

Certain nerves control the intensity of the response. The mind slows down so we can sleep, and muscles in the legs and arms relax when we sit. When we sleep, the television may still be on, but our response to it has changed. Our responses to stimulation are governed by nerves and are almost automatic.

We can change the input of information received or the external factors in life. To change the conclusion to the input or the response, we reprogram the brain. Let's see how this works.

Barbara, the compulsive overeater, changed jobs, and she broke off troublesome relationships. Did she solve her problem? No, because she remains depressed and compulsive.

Resolving the inner problems requires changing *conclusions* to outside responses. She needs to learn that her problem isn't just that "I eat too much." It's still not enough for her to realize, "I eat when I'm lonely." She needs to think of the interpretation of emotions as a neurochemical issue. In every emotional, physical, and spiritual response, Barbara will have to see the involvement of brain chemistry.

Take the emotion of anger, which is the feeling that triggers Alex to overeat. He has two ways to approach his anger. The first is to change what makes him angry. He has to gain a true perspective of reality, and the level of reality depends on the chemical balances in his brain.

Alex's second approach is to change his response to anger because anger leads him to overeat. This is the Pavlovian response. Anger is the ringing bell that prepares him to overeat. Changing Pavlovian responses requires neurochemical manipulation.

Alex has to understand the elements involved in the complex nervous system. Several types of neurochemicals affect nerves. When these neurochemicals are affected, so are thoughts, actions, and anything else the brain controls through the central nervous system. Alex *can* change his brain chemistry when he understands his neurochemistry and how it responds to different emotions or stresses.

In the following chapters I'll explain how to make these changes.

Part II

---◆---

THE SYSTEM

— 10 —

Reward Centers

In order for a behavior to become addicting, a reward must be received from it. The circumstances of our upbringing and our brain chemicals will determine the reward.

Ever wonder why people don't follow through with their promises to do things that will make them more healthy?

Doctors sometimes plead with patients to follow exercise programs and diet plans. Yet professionals also know that most of them won't. Even when physicians make clear the importance of change, patients still resist change.

Why don't they follow through?

People joke about New Year's resolutions. They might as well be called fantasies because they're not the reality of what will be done.

Why don't they follow through?

If it will do people good, why won't they change?

Why do they continue on a road of self-destruction when the solution to change seems so simple and defined?

Just knowing what they need to improve their health or lengthen their lives won't bring about the desired change.

Why won't people change to do things that are good for them?

I've figured out the answer: People don't change because they don't get rewarded for the change.

For people to make changes, they must be rewarded.

Can anything be more simple? Maybe that's the trouble. It's too obvious. To prove my theory, I have to indicate how addiction begins. I start by pointing out six factors that contribute to the choice and creation of addictive behavior: (1) Pavlovian (or conditioned) response, (2) the social environment, (3) baseline neuro-transmission levels, (4) neuro-chemical personality, (5) internal factors, and (6) external factors.

All six factors revolve around the following principle:

If a behavior results in a good feeling, it has the potential to become addictive.

Here is another principle involved:

Once persons understand the relationship between neuro-chemistry and rewards, they can learn what they need to change and how to make the change.

The brain wants rewards. Individuals will stop doing something for a while without a reward but not for long. *People change because they get rewards from the change.* They don't change because it's good for them or because someone tells them to. Or put another way, the primary motivation for change is that it feels good. The change relieves pain, reduces stress, or lifts the emotions—all are rewards.

The brain has what I call a reward center. This part of the brain gets stimulated (rewarded) and causes the individual to feel good or lessens a bad feeling. The reward center and its role in addictions are complex issues.

The six major factors enable individuals to understand which behavior has become/can become addictive, what triggers the addiction, and even what caused the addiction. They then use this information to begin their own recovery program.

The Pavlovian Response

Johnny was taught to avoid conflict by his father, although his father didn't realize that he was actually teaching this behavior. Johnny learned by watching his father walk away when an argument started. Sometimes his dad turned on the television set when a conflict arose. At any early age, Johnny learned how to respond to conflicts—run away from them.

As he got older, Johnny started walking away from conflicts. He avoided the pain of confrontation, just as his father had taught him.

When he got married, Johnny continued the learned behavior of avoidance without even knowing what he was doing. In fact, he didn't even recognize there was conflict. His marriage ended in divorce, leaving him confused. He complained that he couldn't figure out "his wife's problem." His brain never seemed to pick up the message, and Johnny walked away.

Rebecca's story illustrates another Pavlovian response. Rebecca was taught that being overweight would make her undesirable to men. Society planted the seeds with advertising of diets, fashion trends, and societal attitudes. Her friends made fun of fat people.

After she grew up, Rebecca developed a relationship with a young man. He abused her emotionally and occasionally beat her. She eventually left the relationship, but she was scarred for life. Men asked her out, but she refused them because she could remember only the hurt. Unconsciously, she concluded that close relationships cause pain, and she decided to become unattractive. She began to eat compulsively. Before long she was overweight, and she neglected her physical appearance.

A few years later when Rebecca met a man who liked her for who she was, she wanted to be attractive. She tried dieting—frequently. All of the diets worked for a few weeks; none worked for long. Rebecca said, "I felt constantly hungry. I just had to eat."

She didn't know that feeling hungry wasn't true hunger because she had become addicted to overeating. Diets didn't work because diets *restrict* food intake. They deprive. Rebecca needed reward, not punishment.

Johnny and Rebecca are two examples that show how the brain develops rewards from behavior. In both cases, they received their rewards by escaping emotional pain. These weren't healthy forms of behavior, even though they produced the positive reward of feeling good (or better).

Johnny had learned a Pavlovian response to avoid conflict or pain. He learned that avoidance kept him from experiencing the discomfort of conflict.

Rebecca showed three learned, uncontrolled forms of behavior. The brain received rewards by avoiding pain: being overweight meant she was unattractive; close relationships with men caused pain; and overeating relieved the pain of relationships. (She combined the first two responses.)

The brain gets rewarded by receiving pleasure from something. Once the brain learns this, persons seek the form of behavior that brings a pleasant response so they will feel better about themselves and about their situations.

Rewards are good feelings. They come from decreasing pain or increasing pleasure.

Persons obtain pleasure by a wide variety of methods. For example, Bill is insecure and doesn't really like himself. He feels he is ugly and unintelligent and has no personality. Since childhood, Bill's parents had told him these things in many different ways. His father never let him do anything difficult because he might mess it up. So he "learned" that he wasn't good at doing anything. He was stupid.

Bill's sister was popular with girlfriends and with boys. Loner Bill never had more than one or two friends, all male. He felt he couldn't talk to girls because they thought he was ugly.

By the time Bill was in high school, his parents kept trying to get him to change the way he looked and behaved. They urged, "Go out and mix more. Dress better. Let people get to know you." That's how his sister behaved. But he didn't learn to mix.

When he was sixteen, Bill met a girl who was friendly. After a few dates, they had sex. At that particular moment, Bill felt great. For the first time in his life, he felt adequate, desirable, and normal. He repeated the sexual experience a few times. Every time he had sex, he had the same response—a wonderful feeling about himself. The feelings didn't last long, but they were the best feelings in his otherwise drab life.

Soon Bill developed a sexual compulsion (addiction). Whenever he felt bad about himself, he needed sex to get the good feeling. Because the feelings were so short-lived, he began to think about sex, plan sexual activities, and focus much of his energy on ways to get more sex. By the time he was seventeen, he had become a sex addict.

The examples of Johnny, Rebecca, and Bill show that people repeat behavior that rewards them by decreasing pain or increasing pleasure. These pain-and-pleasure issues may be emotional, physical, or spiritual in nature. When persons are addicted, they need only *think* of the reward, and the Pavlovian bell rings in their heads. The involuntary response that began as a reward becomes the addiction.

Brain chemical rewards are stronger than value systems.

Obviously children born in a family in which alcohol is used to reduce stress and to celebrate tend to turn to alcohol to relieve pain or to feel good. They base their choice on patterns within the family system. If the same family had used exercise for these needs, the children would probably try exercise to reduce pain or feel good.

The Social Environment

Samantha comes from a family that believes the stomach is the way to the heart. For generations, the family has expressed love by preparing large and delicious meals. The result? Most family members have been overweight.

As Samantha grew toward adulthood, she felt a need for acceptance.

She began to eat but found no reward from the generations-taught method. Since eating provided no reward, she turned to perfectionism. Perfectionists tend to try to make everything about themselves and their environment perfect. If things are perfect around them, no one will criticize them—and therefore they must be okay. Perfectionism provided the reward and became her addiction.

People naturally imitate what they know. They opt for the behavior style taught by their environment. If they receive a reward, they may develop Pavlovian responses to maintain the behavior; that is, it becomes an addiction.

Samantha's first choice was eating because her family (the environment in which she was raised) taught her that. It failed, so she tried another behavior.

The choice of addictions relates to social and peer pressure. This principle means that if persons come from backgrounds that reinforce their behavior, they are more likely to repeat it. If their behavior receives disapproval from their peers or family, they may never do it again. In the beginning, social pressures influence the internal reward system.

Whatever gets rewarded gets reinforced.

Fifteen-year-old Colleen was from a religious background. She struggled with being accepted at school. She had run for class secretary and lost. Several friends said, "You're just too religious for most people to like you."

That information shattered Colleen. Acceptance was important to her. After weeks of brooding confusion, one Friday evening she attended a party with some of the kids she wanted to like her. They offered her cocaine, which she accepted. Using the drug was a rebellious attempt to break the religious image that Colleen believed was preventing her from having friends and finding acceptance. She was not being rewarded for being religious.

Cocaine gave Colleen no internal reward. But the group responded, "Now you're being cool," and "Colleen, you're a real human being after all!"

Colleen went to more parties. Each time she used cocaine because it rewarded her with peer acceptance. In time, the cocaine itself became a reward.

The social environment largely determines the behavior chosen to relieve pain or increase pleasure.

Being rewarded for taking cocaine was the beginning of addiction for Colleen. Each time she took the drug, she received acceptance by that particular peer group. And she felt good about herself because social acceptance was important. However, if the group had not rewarded her behavior the first time, she might not have become addicted to the substance.

As I think of Colleen, I think of many religious parents I've met who have addicted children. They feel guilty when their children become addicted. "We've failed" is what I hear most often from them. "We've failed to instill in our children the right value system."

They often fail to realize this vital principle:

The choice of addiction isn't an issue of values. The power of the rewarded behavior determines the addiction.

Baseline Neurotransmission Levels

An individual can be depressed or anxious by nature. The neuro-chemical baseline, or basic brain chemistry, of a depressed person may be caused by too few chemicals that excite or too many chemicals that inhibit. The neurochemical baseline of an anxious person may be caused by too many chemicals that excite or too few chemicals that inhibit.

The behavior of that individual will be determined in one of two ways. First, behavior is caused by alterations to the baseline. For example, the neurochemical baseline of an anxious person is altered when he or she does exciting activities like running or mountain climbing, or the neurochemical baseline of a depressed person does inhibiting activities like eating or controlling.

The second way an individual's behavior can affect the neurochem-ical baseline is through compensation. In this case, the behavior is an attempt to medicate or change the abnormal neurochemical baseline. The depressed person, for instance, may run or climb mountains to overcome depression.

Let's see how this works. Howard doesn't know how to relax, and he hates lengthy conversations. He is actually depressed, but he doesn't know it. Because he is always busy, his natural neurochemical level has little opportunity to settle and affect his outlook. When it does, he will be depressed. Howard's behavior is addicting because he is trying to treat his depression.

Neurotransmission baseline refers to the normal rate or speed of transmission of chemicals within an individual. *Neurochemical personality* determines the level of behavior that provides a reward for each indi-vidual. Some may receive a reward from exciting behavior while others from mellow or quieting behavior. This is different from the neurochem-ical baseline. In the baseline, the chemicals affect the choice of the behavior. Behavior is a reward. Some people enjoy fast-paced activities; others enjoy slow ones. The preference for a fast pace is caused by enjoying excitatory chemical release; slow-paced individuals enjoy decreased excitatory release. Baseline neurochemical levels can take years to change and are often associated with the use of medication. However, by following prescribed diet, activity, and behavior that will change the baseline and provide a reward, persons can achieve immediate relief.

Understanding neurochemical baselines is important to determine why a behavior becomes an addiction. Yet baselines may be difficult to determine for some people. The determination is helpful in recovery but not essential.

The baseline is a fine balance of excitatory and inhibitory levels that the brain tries to maintain. This level may not make a person feel good. Genetics and other factors affect the level the body believes to be normal. For example, the brain may consider a certain level of neurotransmission to be normal, and it will try to maintain this level. However, this level may cause feelings of depression or anxiety. In these situations, persons will naturally increase or decrease the level through behavior or addiction.

Jessie, who struggled with alcohol abuse, was an anxious person by nature. Her baseline neurochemicals were elevated. During her menstrual cycle, she drank alcohol to overcome the anxiety. The drinking resulted in feelings of depression. Her cycle, combined with genetic anxiety, pushed her too high to feel comfortable. The alcohol depressed her levels, making her feel better, but it also helped to cause an addiction.

Neurochemical Personality

A behavior that feels good to Bill may have no effect on Colleen. Or it could make Samantha feel worse. Reading and watching television relax my wife. For me, such quiet activities create stress.

Some people find their comfort in high-energy activities while others are more comfortable with low-energy behavior. The level a person enjoys is the neurochemical personality. A satiation personality might enjoy low-level activities because of neurochemical baselines or use them to treat neurochemical baselines.

Neurochemicals change rapidly, making the person feel better temporarily. When the temporary effect is gone, the brain returns to the baseline neurochemical level, which is either depressed or anxious. The neurochemical personality is based on the level of activity the person wants—either in response to or caused by the neurochemical baseline. The behavior performed is the temporary change in neurotransmitter.

A neurochemical personality is related to, but different from, baseline neurochemical levels. Neurochemicals can be altered quickly, and behavior can be performed quickly to change them back temporarily. A neurochemical personality has to do with the behavioral choice that causes the immediate response or creates instant good feelings for a person. Neurochemical baselines are the result of long-term neurochemical changes that may be inherited or created from an addiction. Psychiatrists and psychologists used to refer to one of these changes as endogenous depression. That is, the brain caused the depression because of a deficiency of chemicals in the brain. Anxiety could also be caused by an excess of chemicals. These situations may be inherited or may occur as a person develops. A baseline is actually the level that is "normal" or natural for you. It isn't necessarily good or bad, high or low, just the level at which you naturally will function. These altered baselines will be seen as persons' overall emotional level, such as depression or anxiety.

Phil had a high-vitality workaholic personality that thrived on energy and stress. His personality functioned well, actually making him feel good. His neurochemical personality was one of high excitement and excitatory neurochemical release.

He also had a compulsive overeating disorder. His overeating was more of a low-energy (inhibitory release neurochemistry) addiction, and he received no emotional rewards from it. He overate to treat a chemical imbalance.

For Phil, a recovery program that would correct the neurochemical imbalance would then change his behavior. It would not work for him to attempt to change his behavior (such as go on a strict diet) to correct a neurochemical imbalance.

Many persons are like Phil. Their chemical imbalances cause their addictions. Participating in a traditional recovery program won't work for Phil. He won't stay with it very long. Although he couldn't explain it, the recovery program wouldn't provide him with a neurochemical reward. Until he gets the chemical imbalance treated, he won't come out of his addiction.

Internal Factors

Internal conflicts develop at different stages in life. They are powerful factors in shaping addiction.

For instance, Melinda was popular and active throughout her life. She married Ted, her childhood sweetheart, when she was twenty-three. Over the next five years, she bore two healthy children. Ted and Melinda attended church regularly, had many friends, and pursued various hobbies and recreational activities. From all appearances, they were the ideal family.

After ten years of marriage, Ted left Melinda. "I just need a change," he said lamely. "I can't explain it, but I can't stand this anymore."

Ted's sudden action shattered Melinda. She was sure she had let him down, but she didn't know how. The experience destroyed her self-confidence, and she began to feel guilty for not being a better wife. Soon she felt insecure about everything. Instead of having a calm faith, she sometimes doubted God's existence; at other times she worried about being punished by God.

Almost in desperation, Melinda got more active with her church. Within a period of fifteen months, her life became centered on her church. All her friends and the children's friends were of the same faith. She cut off contact with everyone else. If the church needed someone to volunteer for an activity, she rushed to the front of the line. She attended three weekly Bible studies and jumped into almost every church function. At home, she kept the television tuned only to a religious network.

Although Melinda wasn't aware of it, she actually wove a net around herself to soothe her feelings of guilt over the divorce. In the process, she became addicted to her religion. She wasn't active because of a love for her faith; it was a means to show other people she was a good person and not at fault in the divorce.

Internal conflict can cause people to seek a behavior to soothe pain, just as it did with Melinda. The choice depends on behavior that offers relief, meets the internal needs, and provides rewards.

If the same behavior gets repeated often enough, the Pavlovian response can make it a compulsion.

External Factors

The death of a loved one, marriage, the birth of a child, a job change, or a move to a new city is a stressful time that creates temporary neurochemical alterations. Other alterations may occur because of an exciting situation, such as traveling, fighting in a war, winning a race, or getting a job promotion. Any of these temporary alterations may so reward a behavior that it will eventually become an addiction.

I think of Phyllis who was raised in a thrifty middle-class farm family in Iowa. In college, she met and fell in love with a brilliant investor. Early in their marriage, because of her thrift and his wise investments, they had more money than she had ever thought possible.

One day Phyllis bought a few extravagant things for her husband: three hand-painted ties, a Rolex watch, and two pairs of Gucci loafers. "I feel you deserve all this," she told him. He was pleased, and she was delighted by his reaction.

More than that, Phyllis had gotten an emotional "high" when she walked through the exclusive store, spending money lavishly. Shortly afterward, she bought expensive gifts for her now elderly parents. Again, she experienced the emotional uplift.

Soon Phyllis regularly bought things she didn't need. Often she left the newly purchased items in the original boxes, never using them or thinking about them again. Whenever she began to feel depressed or anxious, she instinctively went shopping. Phyllis had become a compulsive spender.

———————— ♦ ————————

When the people mentioned in this chapter thought or did something that relieved pain or gave them pleasure, their brains released chemicals that caused a good feeling. This good feeling is a reward, and it is actually a physical response within the body. The interweaving of emotional, spiritual, and physical systems works through the "neurochemical reward center." The phrase means that the thought or behavior that feels good is determined by any of the six factors previously discussed (Pavlovian response, social environment, baseline neurochemical levels, neurochemical personality, internal factors, and external factors).

Another way we can look at this is to say people seek reward for behavior in two general instances: (1) when they feel down or depressed and (2) when they feel up or excited. In either instance, all persons have a "comfort zone" that lies somewhere between anxiety (high) and depression (low). The comfort zone varies from person to person.

Louis is employed by a financially unstable company. He is aware that the plant may close down any day. Whenever he thinks about the future, particularly supporting his family, he becomes anxious. From the time he gets home from work until he goes to bed, he works in the garden. He rarely interacts with the family. At work, his thoughts center on what he can do when he gets home. He appears distracted and not as efficient as he had been. At home, Louis and his wife have argued repeatedly over his behavior.

Louis has tried to relax and interact with the family. However, when he's anxious (which is most of the time) and he can't or doesn't work, he feels terrible and gets more anxious.

Actually, Louis has chosen to work and tinker around the house rather than maintain a good relationship with his wife. His reward center demands work, and his body has made neurochemical changes.

In recent years, scientists have classified chemicals related to the reward center. They are the endorphin/methionine/dopamine class. These chemicals are released when individuals enjoy a particular thought or engage in a certain activity. When the chemicals are released, the neurochemical effect is an increase or a decrease in neurotransmission.

It works like this:

Increased neurotransmission decreases depression. Decreased neurotransmission decreases anxiety.

The release or retention of neurochemicals results in a pleasurable feeling by the neurochemical reward center. Persons who feel better from being mellowed out or who seek antianxiety effects receive rewards by decreasing excitatory neurochemicals. They could achieve the same effect if they increased the inhibitory neurochemicals. The net result is decreasing nerve transmission or slowing them down. The choice of approach will vary with how persons were taught to respond and whether they have an addiction. If they are addicted, the choice will be automatic—they will seek to balance their needs.

Individuals who enjoy or feel good about being hyped up or seek antidepression activity obtain a reward from the release of excitatory chemicals. A decrease in the amount of inhibitory chemicals would have the same effect.

Often the same behavior can increase or decrease neurotransmission. At one time shopping may lift persons out of depression. At another time shopping may bring them down from an anxious day. The behavior creates a release of the reward center chemicals. When the same behavior can relieve anxiety and also relieve stress, it becomes a powerful compulsion. Most addicted people use their addictions in both situations.

— 11 —

Psychological Needs

Addictions treat psychological needs. We must determine what our psychological needs are to be able to treat addictions. It is important to replace an addiction that treats a psychological need with something else that still provides a reward.

Basic to an understanding of the Help Yourself Recovery System is this law:

A theme refers to a psychological need. An addiction is the method used to meet that need. Persons won't repeat what doesn't feel good to them.

Themes develop from lack of fulfillment. We all have themes, but many of us find healthy ways to meet those needs. Others, not finding healthy ways to satisfy those needs, develop the themes through years of thoughts and feelings about themselves and their interactions with others. Since people are what they think about themselves, these themes influence the way they behave. And individuals may have more than one theme operating at one time.

Neurochemistry affects themes in two ways.

First, an out-of-balance brain triggers themes. I sometimes say, "The best you can feel is equal to your worst theme." That is, if brain chemicals are depressed, persons begin to feel the major theme surface. Once it comes to the level of consciousness, they respond to it by behaving in a certain way. The more out of balance the brain, the more often the theme resurfaces and the more frequent the behavior.

Second, by focusing on their themes (such as worrying about the

95

need), persons cause changes in their thoughts. Then chemicals become imbalanced.

The cycle begins with the out-of-balance brain.

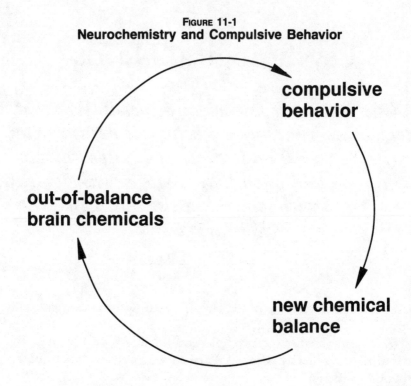

FIGURE 11-1
Neurochemistry and Compulsive Behavior

Compulsive themes are the result of behaving certain ways, according to individual personality. Compulsive behavior is an attempt to treat the chemical imbalance.

If the addiction has a genetic (inherited) base, the addiction changes the thoughts and creates the compulsive theme.

If it is an acquired (or learned) addiction, the thoughts create the theme that changes the neurochemicals and thereby creates the addiction.

Compulsive themes are the sickness. Addictions are the symptoms. Persons with *acquired* addictions start their recovery by changing their behavior. Persons with *inherited* addictions start their recovery by changing their neurochemistry through diet and exercise.

Here are the steps needed to work with compulsive themes.

1. Addicted persons need to identify their behavioral themes to recover

FIGURE 11-2
The Compulsive Theme Cycle

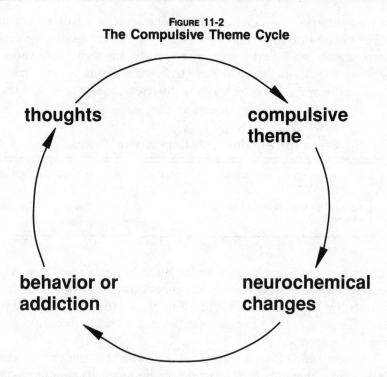

thoughts   compulsive
                            theme

behavior or   neurochemical
addiction   changes

Genetic addictions will probably begin in most cases with neurochemical changes. Acquired addictions will begin in most cases with alterations of thoughts.

completely from an addiction. Knowledge of their themes allows them to fight a specific war and not to engage in a variety of confused battles.

2. *Addicted persons need to change their thoughts, which will change their Pavlovian responses.* Individuals vary. Some may show two or three compulsive themes and half a dozen types of compulsive behavior. Obviously, it is wiser to fight the themes (or causes) than the reaction (behavior).

To recover, persons need to concentrate on the cause of the addiction and not on the addiction itself.

Compulsive themes develop. It's a process. When emotions, needs, and behavior come together, they form the theme. The example of Ray may make this clear.

Ray believes he has outstanding leadership ability. He also feels that his coworkers and employers don't respect this talent. Over a period of time, his frustration has developed into a theme of (a need for) recognition. He will now do something because of this theme. His need becomes so great that he *must* find some way to satisfy this theme. He chooses some form of behavior, and it is likely to become a compulsive behavior. For instance, Ray could become a compulsive exerciser or a cocaine user.

FIGURE 11-3
Steps for Working with Compulsive Themes

Step 1	Addicted persons need to identify their behavioral themes to recover completely from an addiction.
Step 2	Addicted persons need to change their thoughts, which will change their Pavlovian responses.

Billy was depressed because he felt his father didn't like him. After all, Dad was never around. Then a neighbor named Mike invited Billy to play baseball with a few other friends. Billy agreed to play because he felt wanted. He hit a home run that won the game, and he became a hero accepted by everyone.

The next time Billy got depressed, he thought about that baseball game. He remembered how he loved the attention and recognition. So he called his friends to see if they could play baseball. Although not conscious of the theme that was developing, Billy knew that if he played baseball well, he could overcome his depression. Unknowingly, he was developing a theme of recognition through sports.

Later in life, Billy's recognition theme may come from work or some other area where he can do well enough to receive a reward. Unless he deals with the need (theme) for recognition, he has already determined his theme for the remainder of his life.

Compulsive themes usually cause several addictions:

- The workaholic may become both an alcoholic and a sex addict, with a theme of power.
- The overeater may seek to overcome a theme of adequacy through perfectionism and control of others.
- The cocaine addict who is also addicted to risk taking and excitement may be following a theme of pleasure.

Understanding the themes that cause addictions is important to understanding the Help Yourself Recovery System. These themes cause changes in brain chemistry.

Harry was dominated by women. His parents divorced when he was two years old, and he was the baby of the family with three older sisters. He felt manipulated and overpowered by them. Consequently, he developed a need (theme) for power.

By the time Harry was fifteen, he had his first sexual experience. During those moments of being with a woman, he felt powerful. By the time he was nineteen, he was having sexual experiences daily. Before he was twenty-one, he had a fully developed addiction to sexual orgasm because only then could he feel he had power in his life and power over women.

Harry could join Sexual Addicts Anonymous (SAA) to treat his addictions. However, if he does not cope with the theme of power, he has done nothing but stop the *form* or outlet. He will return to some other form of sexual release such as pornography. Or another addiction will surface, possibly gambling or drugs.

But if Harry gets help at SAA related to the theme of power, the outcome will be different. Let's say his sponsor talks with him about his problem with women and Harry finally admits his need for power over them. If he can satisfy his need, he will then have to correct his chemical imbalance for no new addictions to surface. Habits and inclinations persist, but Harry can eliminate compulsive behavior by taking care of his theme.

Once persons know their themes, they need to identify the addictions they use to treat them. Some "treatments" are obvious, but not all. Workaholism, compulsive cleanliness, and romance addiction are frequently applauded.

Addicted persons often don't recognize their inner needs. If they are willing to examine their behavior, they can determine their themes. Unfortunately, most individuals develop an excellent defense system that makes it difficult to recognize their themes directly.

We're going to look more closely at these six general themes. If you want to know your themes keep two things in mind. First, you need to be open to what you discover. (It's part of the healing process.) Second, you need to remind yourself that everyone has themes. No theme is worse (or better) than any other.

1. The Adequacy Theme

From my perspective, the most devastating disorder in society today is the feeling of inadequacy. Attempts to acquire possessions, money, prestige, and control often come from feelings of inadequacy, especially when other areas of one's life suffer because of these attempts. When persons feel insecure (inadequate), they attempt to make the outside look successful to compensate for the lack of peace inside. No matter how outwardly successful or how talented they are, all their accomplishments don't matter if they don't like themselves.

Others who develop a theme of adequacy show signs of giving up, or they behave as if nothing really matters. They no longer set goals. They settle for a life of apathy. Joy becomes elusive, and peaceful existence is their highest standard.

One such person was Roger, who worked in a factory as an assembler. He was consistently on time and valued as a loyal employee. One day the management team at his plant announced a contest because they were seeking creative ways to cut costs and yet increase productivity. Roger submitted an idea.

The contest judges gave him the award. The executives sensed they had discovered a hidden talent within Roger. They offered him a promotion to a management position. He would be in charge of monitoring the efficiency of several plants.

"I don't think so," Roger said. "I like what I'm doing just fine." The dumbfounded executives tried to reason with him, but he insisted he was happy where he was.

Roger didn't (and maybe couldn't) speak of his overpowering sense of inadequacy. The other managers had college degrees—or so he thought—and he had quit high school in his senior year. He was convinced that his grammar was bad (it was adequate) and that no one would listen to him (he was quite articulate). Despite what they said and the inducements they offered, he was certain that he would fail if he took the position.

Because of his feelings of inadequacy, Roger remained an assembler.

2. The Approval Seeking Theme

Healthy approval seeking is a natural human characteristic. Who doesn't want to be liked and appreciated? Approval seeking becomes a theme when individuals sacrifice beliefs, values, and opinions to get the approval of others.

Approval seeking shows up in many ways:

• Few people feel comfortable expressing opinions without knowing how others will accept them.
• As soon as a clothing fad changes, they have to buy the new item.

• If the group they're with decides to act contrary to what they believe, they go along anyway.

I've especially noticed individuals who seem confident and speak up boldly so that few would accuse them of seeking approval. However, by listening closely, I've observed that they don't state opinions as such— they present their opinions as facts. That is where their insecurity shows. Since no one can reasonably argue against facts, they push away rejection. Their insecurity and fear of rejection sometimes cause them to be labeled know-it-alls.

3. The Pleasure Theme

As society becomes more pleasure oriented, individuals' reward centers need more and more to stimulate them. The demand to be constantly entertained shows a need to overcome feelings of isolation and loneliness. This sickness prevents communication, growth of relationships, and intimacy. Many persons feel more comfortable spending time in groups or being entertained than engaging in one-on-one conversation with a spouse or child.

Pleasure themes are evident when people seek recreation, emotional highs, and sexual activities. Recreation as a form of relaxing is popular today and usually healthy. The pleasure theme can become an issue when bowling, golf, or video and computer games take the place of interaction with the family. Drugs, alcohol, sex, and other high-energy addictions directly relate to the search for good feelings or a theme of pleasure.

Seth worked hard and provided more than adequately for his family. He wasn't a workaholic, but he spent evenings and weekends away from the family. He had a pleasure theme.

Here's how it worked. He golfed two evenings a week and every Saturday. Two evenings a week he worked on the lawn. On Sunday, he watched television almost continuously from the time he got up in the morning. Since he spent most evenings and weekends at home, he appeared to be a caring, giving husband and father.

Yet his golf, yard work, and television were so pleasurable to him that he allowed nothing to interrupt his schedule. He spent his free time doing things for himself. That's how his pleasure theme worked.

His wife and kids assumed his activities would be beneficial to help Seth relieve the stress from work. While they understood, they also wanted to share in his life. But Seth was so wrapped up in a pleasure theme, he took little notice of them. His perceptions and conclusions were all self-oriented.

4. The Power Theme

The power theme often directs itself toward obtaining money, getting a better position, controlling others, enhancing beauty, and/or emphasizing intelligence or education. And society tends to use these very things to measure individuals. Most people unquestioningly accept these standards and rely on them as the basis for their self-esteem. Those with a power theme frequently have a low self-image but are generally unaware of it.

Outsiders usually observe that persons' need to be in control takes precedence over family, friends, or job. Of course, those with the power theme usually deny its existence. That's their defense system at work.

Power theme becomes a problem when individuals seek to meet their needs at the expense of others. When climbing the company ladder takes precedence, here are frequent ways it shows up:

- They neglect spending time with their children.
- They have no time to be with their spouses.
- They don't relax with friends.
- They complain about how much they have to do.

Such behavior strongly indicates the power theme is at work.

After Jackie worked five years in a company, her supervisor offered her a prominent position. Unfortunately, it would take her away from her family because of frequent out-of-state travel.

The pay increase was more than offset by the increase in expenses. In reality, Jackie made less take-home pay. However, she refused to consider that aspect. "I'm the vice president of marketing," she said. "It's a responsible position, and who knows where it will lead?"

Just having the position, Jackie thought, would show others her importance. She was important because she had risen to the top. She felt good golfing with friends and talking casually about her travels and her powerful position.

All the while, her husband and children were missing her and needing her. Jackie had fallen prey to the need for power so that she could feel good about herself.

5. The Recognition Theme

Everyone needs to be recognized, appreciated, and respected. The difficulty comes to those whose lives are controlled by their need for recognition. They calculate their actions so that others will applaud what

FIGURE 11-4
Six Most Common Compulsive Themes

Theme 1	Adequacy.
Theme 2	Approval-Seeking.
Theme 3	Pleasure.
Theme 4	Power.
Theme 5	Recognition.
Theme 6	Responsibility Avoidance.

they do. Internal recognition isn't good enough. For them, approval and recognition of their good deeds must come from other people.

If they serve others, they want the world to know. They serve from a desire not to help but to look good and be recognized as caring.

Often they brag and exaggerate their accomplishments. Or they tell others what they have accomplished. I once knew a wealthy man who gave virtually nothing to charity. A friend who was in charge of a local charity drive was aware of the man's need to be recognized, and he began asking him to contribute to the charity so that everyone "will know how concerned you are." They soon got enough from him that they helped spread the word that he was "the most generous man in the community." For the next dozen years the man lived, he gave enough to keep that recognition.

Unfortunately, I think community leaders preyed on his weakness, which I don't condone. But they did understand the man's theme.

6. The Responsibility Avoidance Theme

Many times I've heard people speaking of feeling responsible, and somebody quickly pipes up, "You're only responsible for yourself," or "Just do your own thing."

Some pop therapists have chided people for feeling responsible, sometimes implying it's a weakness or even a sickness to feel a sense of commitment to others. Few people see it as character strength.

Persons who avoid responsibility show this quality frequently by refusing to get involved in anything. They back off from

- making job commitments.
- obligating themselves to help others.
- volunteering in churches and civic organizations.
- giving themselves in relationships.

Sadly, in many homes, the commitment to families has shifted to a search for selfish fulfillment of individual needs. No longer are parents asking, "What's best for the family?" Now they're declaring, "I have to live my own life. I have to take care of *my* needs." I don't want to imply a neglect of self-care, but it's often an excuse for selfish living.

I saw a painful example of this in the film *Clara's Heart*. The upper-class husband and wife had a son, and they hired a Jamaican maid named Clara (played by Whoopi Goldberg). Both parents were so self-absorbed they ignored their son's needs. Clara soon took over the responsibility for the boy's upbringing. The parents, so addicted to the principle of avoiding responsibility, seemed quite unaware that their son had needs. After all, their attitude implied, we hired a live-in, full-time cook and housekeeper. What more did the boy need?

--------------- ◆ ---------------

These six themes are the major ones that cause neurochemical changes and compulsive behavior and addictions. Naturally, it's easier to fight a single theme.

When you recognize that you have more than one theme, I encourage you to focus immediately on the most powerful one.

--------------- ◆ ---------------

"I don't know who I am," Nick moaned. "I've never known who I am."

Originally Nick had come to see me because of his weight problem. "I've tried every diet I know, and nothing works permanently," he said. He was nearly a hundred pounds over what the weight charts called normal. "And I guess I gamble a little too much," he added.

As I learned later, Nick's father had dreamed of being a professional pitcher in the major leagues. He made it all the way to the minor leagues for two years and was then let go.

Nick told me that his dad would come home from work around four o'clock every afternoon. "Grab your mitt," the father called as he walked inside the house. Until dark, the boy pitched to his dad. During the summer, the playing went on for as long as five hours.

As the practice sessions continued, Dad yelled, "You're going to do it, son. You're going to be the best pitcher in the National League!"

Nick did reach the major league and played one season with a professional team. But his constant weight problem, unproven allegations of illegal betting, and hints of sexual harassment of women meant his contract didn't get renewed.

"You know," Nick said, "that was nine years ago. My dad has never spoken to me since I told him I had been dropped."

Nick didn't know who he was. How could he? As a boy, he never had a chance to find out. In reality, he was an extension of his father. His failure as a player was his father's failure.

Nick and his eventual recovery make me think of the work of Abraham Maslow. He developed what he called a hierarchy of needs of all human beings. Maslow said that only when the lowest need is met are people ready to move upward.

> self-actualization
> self-esteem
> to be loved or to belong
> protection and safety
> basic need, food and water

When persons' basic needs are met for food and water, they search for protection and safety. Once these needs are satisfied, they seek to be loved by others and to belong. Only after they feel loved are they able to develop a healthy self-esteem. When they have developed a healthy self-esteem, they move toward self-actualization. When they reach that point, they can help others, enrich their own lives, and move toward maturity.

Most children live in an environment where these basic needs for food, water, protection, and safety are provided. Some of them, but not all, know that they are loved and that they belong. Whenever children feel threatened or their needs aren't met in any area, the rest of their lives are affected. I think of needs unmet by parents as abuse—and there are many forms.

Unmet needs are reflected in abuse.

I will describe six forms of abuse listed alphabetically.

1. Emotional Abuse

Emotional abuse is often unrecognized in parents and children alike. Children are young when the abuse begins, and they have no way to know it is wrong behavior. Whatever life-styles prevail in the home, they accept as the norm. Unfortunately, parents are usually ignorant of the long-term effects of their actions.

Emotional abuse occurs when parents minimize their children's feelings or imply that the children are wrong or immoral for feeling a particular way. Often cultural, racial, and ethnic issues come into play in emotional abuse. For example, children's anger may be minimized or rejected by families who believe anger is a weakness or even a sin. Their culture may have taught them that crying because of happiness or pain is a sign of weakness. Unknowingly, they teach their children they should not have these emotions. Consequently, the children learn to deny having such feelings.

Emotional abuse takes place when parents say,

- "You know you can't sing."
- "You're so awkward, you'll never be any good in gym."
- "You can't spell. Nobody in our family can spell."
- "You look just like your dad's side of the family. They are all too fat."

Sometimes children receive the message without actually hearing the words. Yet they know (or assume) how their parents feel.

Another form of abuse comes from comparison with a brother or sister. Parents declare,

- "Well, everyone says that Lena is the pretty one."
- "Billy always was the smartest kid in the family."
- "Her sister has the voice of an angel, but Judy sounds like a bullfrog."

When children hear comparisons, no matter how the parent means the words, they tend to interpret them as if the parent points a finger at them and says, "You aren't good enough."

Power, pleasure, and recognition themes are often the result of trying to alleviate the emotionally abused children's fears through their accomplishments. These fears often lead to alcohol, drug, work, gambling, sex, exercise, physical appearance, intelligence, material, spending, risk taking, violence, stealing, and activity addictions.

Adequacy, responsibility avoidance, and approval seeking themes develop to cover up conflicts of emotional abuse. From such situations, addictions also develop. These addictions include control, overeating, eating disorders, relationship dysfunction, hypochondria, religious fanaticism, perfectionism, cleaning, and media fascination.

Does This Information About Emotional Abuse Describe You?
□ Yes   □ No

2. Identity Abuse

Some parents live their dreams and desires through their children. They fail in reaching their goals so they push or force children into becoming successful and do what they themselves didn't or couldn't do. The children may become athletes or intellectually focused children because their parents are acting out of their own desires. Many grow up feeling as if they never had a childhood. Or they know who they are because their parents kept them focused on what they wanted them to be. Others don't match their parents' expectations and get criticized for who they are. Perhaps they look different, prefer different music, or have different occupations from their parents.

Parents often measure their own sense of self-worth by what their children do or how their children appear to others. Children may feel pressured to pursue their parents' dreams or to rebel. Parents may fail to consider who the children really are; they only criticize children for what they aren't. In such cases the children's identities are abused.

Identity abuse causes the development of power, pleasure, adequacy, responsibility avoidance, approval seeking, and recognition themes. Power, pleasure, and responsibility themes are developed because parents have taught them they are better than others. They become addicted as adults. Work, alcohol, drug, gambling, sex, and material addictions are frequently evident with adult children. (Adult children refers to persons who are adults because of the years they have lived but are still emotionally children because of their unhealed hurts of childhood.)

Does This Information About Identity Abuse Describe You?
□ Yes   □ No

3. Intellectual Abuse

Often, families are intellectually abusive to their children through their communication techniques. Parents call children stupid, won't listen to them, and ignore their ideas. Each time, they intellectually abuse their children.

The ramifications of such behavior are devastating. Few children of these families are naturally self-confident, believe in their abilities, and like themselves when they become adults.

They grew up insecure, and they never felt their ideas were worth mentioning. As adults, they won't share an opinion without first knowing the opinions of the people around them. Many follow the example of their parents and sneer at or won't listen to others' opinions. Like their parents, they insist that they know what they're doing. Both types typify victims of intellectual abuse.

Children affected by intellectual abuse develop themes of adequacy, responsibility avoidance, and approval seeking. They seek approval through alcohol, drug, work, gambling, sex, food, exercise, physical appearance, religion, material, spending, and activity addictions.

Does This Information About Intellectual Abuse Describe You?
☐ Yes   ☐ No

4. Physical Abuse

Physical abuse threatens children's feelings of protection and safety, love and self-esteem. When children's thoughts include fear of being hurt, they can develop neurochemical imbalances. They're afraid to make mistakes or to say the wrong thing. Because physical beating is always a threat, they live in a fear that creates conflicts and inconsistency. The nervous system, still underdeveloped, is vulnerable to such stresses.

These fears release excitatory neurochemicals in the brain and put stress on the nervous system. Long-term and consistent stress, such as that seen with physical abuse, can contribute to altered baseline neurochemical levels.

Physically abused children frequently develop themes of power, adequacy, and approval seeking in adulthood. Those who operate with the power theme often continue the generational physical abuse by abusing their own children. Drug addiction, workaholism, gambling and sex addictions, exercise and physical appearance addictions, materialism, spending and risk taking, and violence appear in adults who were physically abused as children and developed a power theme.

Most of the time, these children, unable to reason that they were victims, actually believe they deserved the beatings and mistreatment they received. That belief also can lead them into a full range of addictions.

Does This Information About Physical Abuse Describe You?
☐ Yes   ☐ No

5. Sexual Abuse

Sexual abuse threatens children's security as well as their need for love, self-esteem, and identity. Sexual abuse is a combination of physical, emotional, intellectual, and identity abuse. The effect of sexual abuse on neurochemicals is powerful because it releases chemicals and causes the development of themes that lead to compulsions.

Sexual abuse affects children's ability to mature into emotional adults. Every step in their lives brings conflicts that are difficult to resolve. They often develop themes of power, pleasure, adequacy, responsibility avoidance, approval seeking, and recognition.

Power, pleasure, and recognition themes also come from trying to prove they weren't at fault for the abuse, although they may feel that they really were. Sometimes they develop compulsions because they want to feel whole and worthy. For these individuals, alcohol, drug, work, sex, exercise, physical appearance, religion, material, spending, and activity addictions often surface in adulthood.

Many sexually abused victims develop control, food, relationship, rescuing, hypochondria, intelligence, religion, perfection, cleaning, and media fascination addictions.

Does This Information About Sexual Abuse Describe You?
□ Yes   □ No

6. Spiritual Abuse

Spiritual abuse is fairly common within religious communities, often without the abusers being aware of what they're doing. When parents use God or religion to justify their unhealthy or unloving actions, spiritual abuse can develop.

Adhering to essential beliefs and presenting them in a sensible, loving way don't cause spiritual abuse and seldom bring out resentment in children. Moving beyond the clear doctrines and teaching minor issues as if they are matters of life and death can (and often do) result in spiritual abuse.

Parental inconsistency in living by professed values can be just as problematic. However, if parents live and act according to their professed beliefs, their children see and learn consistency.

Inconsistent behavior can generate neurochemical changes in the brain and create compulsive themes. Power, adequacy, responsibility avoidance, approval seeking, and recognition are all themes taught through spiritual abuse.

Power and recognition are often associated with adult children of parents who were guilty of spiritual abuse. Even if the adult children embrace their parents' religious convictions, they become vulnerable to drug, sex, material, work, physical appearance, spending, and other addictions.

Does This Information About Spiritual Abuse Describe You?
□ Yes   □ No

———————— ♦ ————————

If persons stay in conflict long enough, their baseline (normal) neurochemical levels change or adapt. Children are vulnerable because they naturally seek approval, protection, and love from their parents. Regardless of the response, they accept their parents' actions as legitimate and true.

This situation can set up constant turmoil and cause themes to develop. Later, the adoption of addictions is an attempt to treat the imbalanced brain.

Baseline alterations caused by genetic or generational influences cause themes and addictions to develop. The children become adults without having their essential needs met. Because the essential needs of safety, protection, love, belonging, and self-esteem aren't met, compulsive behavior is used to try to fill those needs.

— 12 —

Chemical Imbalances

Chemical imbalances in the brain can be caused by genetics, by our upbringing, or by our present lifestyle. These imbalances can cause us to see life differently and cause addictions.

In college, both Jeff and Rich attended a wild party where everyone drank heavily, and as Jeff said later, "We had a million laughs." Jeff grew up in a home where he heard nothing but criticism and disapproval. At college, he wanted the approval from peers that he never got at home. Approval seeking became a theme for him. Even though he grew up in a home where his mother opposed drinking, Jeff had a need. To get the approval of his college friends, he was willing to sacrifice the beliefs and values his mother taught him. So he drank.

Jeff's heavy drinking at the party was the beginning of his addiction. Within three years, he was an alcoholic.

A theme refers to a psychological need. An addiction is the method used to meet that need.

Although Rich attended the same party, he didn't find the fun and excitement that others talked about. He had two drinks, got upset at his stomach, and vomited. Three years later, Rich still has not touched alcohol again.

The difference was not so much that Rich got sick (a negative response) but that Jeff had a fun time (a positive experience). From then on, *Jeff kept trying to repeat the high he had felt by drinking at the party,* and sometimes he did get that feeling of lightness and excitement when he drank.

Here's Jeff's story: At the college party, he received a reward for

111

drinking. Although he didn't know it, he would soon repeat the behavior to get the same feeling again. Later on in the addiction cycle, withdrawal symptoms (especially in alcohol and drug addiction) may cause reinforcement of behavior. However, the initial reinforcement will be determined by whether it provides a reward or not.

Here's the reason: Reward centers determine whether individuals repeat a particular behavior. If the behavior gets rewarded, and if they continue to repeat the behavior, they move in a compulsive form of behavior or what we call an addiction.

Rich, however, received no reward for drinking. Therefore, he had no reason to continue the behavior or to develop an addiction.

Many things affect the reward center, and each person's reward center works differently. Genetics, environment, and personality are three powerful influences.

As individuals mature, they develop compulsive themes and begin to interact in the world. These themes are affected by and affect neurochemical levels.

Chemical changes in the brain fall into two categories.

1. *Baseline neurochemical alterations.* The brain "believes" a level is normal and will fight to maintain this level—even if this "physiological normal" doesn't feel good.

Let's go back to Jeff and see what happened. Several factors came into play:

a) Jeff had a psychological need for approval (theme).
b) When he drank alcohol, he got rewarded (a good feeling AND approval from friends).
c) Jeff repeated his action (drinking alcohol).
d) He drank consistently over a period of time (three years).
e) During that period of time, his brain chemicals altered.
f) Once altered, his brain adapted to the new norm (altered neurotransmission baseline).
g) RESULT: Jeff's brain now constantly craves the behavior (drinking alcohol) so he can experience the good feeling *because* his brain is convinced that the good feeling is normal.

Jeff is addicted to alcohol. It is a compulsion. He has never resolved his initial conflict (his need for approval), so now he is addicted to alcohol. He MUST drink to get the buzz, the euphoria, the kick, and the lift that alter his brain chemicals.

Jeff's brain is convinced that the buzz is normal. When he is sober or hung over, he is not normal. The brain craves and demands that Jeff get "fixed" so he can be normal again.

2. *Situational alterations*. These temporary changes result from thoughts, activities, diet, behavior, and exercise. They cause immediate changes in the neurochemistry, but the brain returns to baseline levels rather quickly. *Only when a situational behavior is repeated long enough or frequently enough does it alter the baseline.*

Rich's brain chemicals were temporarily altered when he drank. But he had no desire to drink alcohol again. Once the experience was over, his brain chemicals returned to normal (their former level), and the brain continued to seek that level.

Here's another way to illustrate this. Years ago I was sitting in a movie theater where I watched the film *Jaws* about a killer shark. The first time the shark dramatically and suddenly appeared on the screen, people near me flinched, squealed, or screamed. One woman jumped to her feet and let out a horrifying shriek. Two or three more times during the film, members of the audience had their neurochemicals altered; they felt fear. But the effect was temporary. When the film was over, they felt as safe as when the came inside.

Baseline neurochemical level **refers to the level of chemicals that the brain thinks is normal (it may not be). The brain works to maintain that level. A** *situational alteration* **of the baseline neurochemical level is temporary. The brain doesn't try to maintain that level.**

Baseline Neurotransmission Alterations

Baseline neurotransmission imbalances come about in two ways.

1. Genetic

Some individuals are predisposed or have a tendency toward a chemical imbalance. For instance, mothers addicted to cocaine or heroin tend to bear children who are already addicted because the infants are born with a craving for the drug and often suffer withdrawal symptoms.

Regardless of the cause of the genetic alterations, the result is the same. The neurotransmission recognizes this level as its normal level. All other body systems interact to keep the brain chemicals at this level. This may create uncomfortable feelings and thoughts that cause compulsive themes.

If persons turn to forms of behavior (gambling, workaholism, etc.) that maintain the baseline neurotransmitters at this level, they will feel good (or not depressed), *and* they will seek to keep the baseline neurotransmitters working at this same level.

For example, Miles came from a family with a long history of depression and suicidal tendencies. He had inherited a baseline level of neurotransmission that resulted in depression. This depression was evident with his negative attitude, anger, and fear. He developed a theme of adequacy; any accomplishment meant nothing to him.

At the age of eighteen, Miles tried cocaine, and for the first time in his life, he felt normal. That is, his depression, fear, and negativity lessened. The cocaine caused a release of excitatory chemicals that temporarily increased neurotransmission. The drug provided physiological relief from his depression.

Miles's addiction to cocaine was a result of genetic alterations of his neurotransmitters. He chose cocaine, but it was a form of medication—to fix something in himself.

In time, he went into therapy and worked with a mutual-help group. He stopped his cocaine addiction, but he did not change his neurotransmitter levels. What happened?

Miles was so miserable that after two months in therapy, he transferred his addiction to sexual activity. The sexual behavior also increased his neurotransmitters. He had "treated" the cocaine addiction by quitting. But because he had not changed his neurochemical addiction, he would inevitably return to cocaine or transfer to something else.

Recovery from addictions caused by genetic alterations may require a direct change in neurotransmitters through the proper prescribing of psychotropic medication. Others adapt to the baseline alterations and cope with other methods of behavioral changes. If methods other than medication are effective, they are generally preferred.

2. Acquired

Acquired imbalances are just what the term says; they are the imbalances "picked up" or chosen. There are two types: childhood-acquired and adult-acquired.

If persons acquire imbalances in childhood, we call them generational alterations. The way families interact shapes children and their attitudes. Associating with others also affects them to some degree.

Here are the reasons for the term *generational alterations*:

- They usually "picked up" these imbalances in or around the home.
- Other family members probably have the same imbalances.
- These acquired imbalances can usually be traced back one or more generations.

Going back to Jeff and Rich, suppose Jeff had acquired certain behavior in his childhood that predisposed him to alcoholism. In his case, this isn't genetic because alcoholism doesn't run in his family. However, his father and his uncle Mitch handle conflict in the same way. When they get anxious or frustrated, they go out to a bar and have a few drinks. They aren't alcoholics, but their response to stress is to numb the pain with alcohol. They don't do this often, so alcoholism hasn't developed. However, Jeff observed them and unconsciously learned to avoid pain and conflict by using alcohol. He developed alcoholism not genetically but generationally.

There is an increasing focus on the family dynamics that contribute to generational alterations. Several specialty treatments have developed because of this problem, including treatment for now adult children of alcoholics and dysfunctional family systems.

Whenever children have a relationship with those they love or idealize—especially their family members—they are vulnerable to those persons and their problems. They tend to imitate what they observe.

Adult-acquired imbalances are the result of long-term conflicts that produce certain behavior. Rich gets no reward for drinking. In fact, drinking alcohol works against his personality. Drinking means giving up control or being out of control.

Rich has an adult-acquired imbalance that he acts out in violence. (His theme is that of adequacy.) He gets the same kind of fix from violence that Jeff gets from alcohol. Rich needs to overpower others, and he enjoys himself most when he is forcing someone to do something he or she didn't want to do. He has committed rape four times and has never been prosecuted. If temporary or situational behavior is performed often enough—such as Rich's violence—the repeated action causes his baseline neurochemicals to change.

Regardless of the cause (genetic or acquired), repeated behavior can change baseline neurochemical levels, which affect the way persons feel about themselves and others and how they perceive their world. Depending on the personality, some feel anxious, and others exhibit depression.

Even though persons have these feelings, they may not be detected easily. Often those with such feelings deny that they exist even if confronted. Sometimes they mask their feelings or hide them in some way so that others don't recognize what's going on with their emotions.

Remember this: Whether genetic or acquired imbalances, they have the same effect. Imbalances create changes that affect thoughts, themes, and rewards—and they can cause addictions.

Long-term stress or conflict changes the way persons think. Their insecurity levels, fears, and feelings of inadequacies intensify during these occasions. These thoughts and feelings alter neurochemicals, causing depression and anxiety. When the brain is out of balance in this way, persons are predisposed to addictions and compulsive behavior.

They may use the addictions and behavior to make themselves feel better. In essence, the conflicts caused a change in their baseline neurotransmission levels by altering their neurotransmitters.

This attempt to make the brain "feel" better is called compensatory behavior. Alternatively, the out-of-balance brain can create a noncompensatory behavior. In this situation, such behavior is actually caused by the chemical imbalance. For example, depressed neurochemicals can cause a depressed behavior.

This cycle can occur one or several times before persons choose a corrective behavior. Each time the cycle occurs, the chemical balance in the brain becomes more and more out of balance. These thoughts and emotional conflicts continue to strengthen the addiction as long as the brain is out of balance.

Genetic-caused imbalances and acquired imbalances (as a child or as

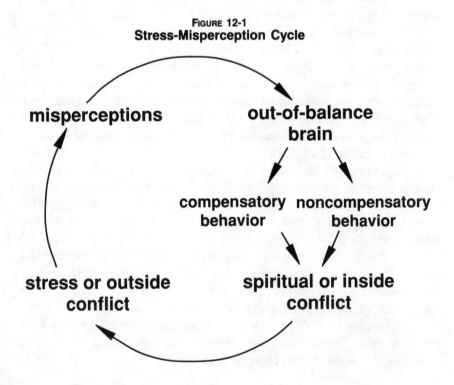

FIGURE 12-1
Stress-Misperception Cycle

misperceptions

out-of-balance brain

compensatory behavior **noncompensatory behavior**

stress or outside conflict

spiritual or inside conflict

an adult) can change baseline neurochemical levels, affect overall emotions, and lead to compulsive behavior.

Let's see how this works with one person. Steve, an executive, is under considerable stress because he is responsible for inventory control of a large corporation. Business is unpredictable, and the nation's economy has taken a turn for the worse. His warehouse is overstocked, and creditors are demanding payment for the stock. Current sales don't come close to meeting the overhead.

Feeling caught in a situation for which he sees no solution, Steve is in a state of helplessness. The only thing that can help is an improved economy—something beyond his control. He feels even more hopeless as he dwells on this fact.

At home, Steve becomes negative and less communicative with his wife. In response, she becomes distant and negative.

He begins the stress-misperception cycle at this point. He feels somewhat inadequate at work. Soon this misperception creates a conflict at home with his wife. Her response to this attitude makes him feel even more inadequate.

Steve's stress level continues to escalate and creates more misperceptions. Soon, his neurochemicals have become so out of balance he feels depressed and worthless. He works excessively and turns to gambling and other forms of risk taking. Soon his behavior becomes a compulsion. Its purpose is to compensate for his depressed feelings.

When Steve is working excessively or gambling, he does feel better. At least, he feels less useless and temporarily loses his sense of hopelessness.

Steve and millions of others develop conflicts that begin small but escalate to tremendous proportions. Addictions, family conflict, avoidance of children, and other forms of behavior begin in such situations.

If the conflict remains long enough, individuals develop a compulsive behavior. Unresolved conflicts change neurochemical baselines.

Any long-term consistently repeated behavior can cause baseline alterations. At first, Steve's brain wasn't out of balance. It functioned without compulsive or addictive behavior. But once he began certain forms of behavior (workaholism and gambling), they altered his neurochemicals. The brain then adapted or adjusted to this condition. Because Steve reinforced this by repeating his action again and again, he created an out-of-balance brain. (See figure 12-2.)

The difference between the *thought-acquired* neurochemical baseline adaptation and the *consistently repeated behavior-acquired* neurochemical baseline is the origin. The thought-acquired adaptation began with an

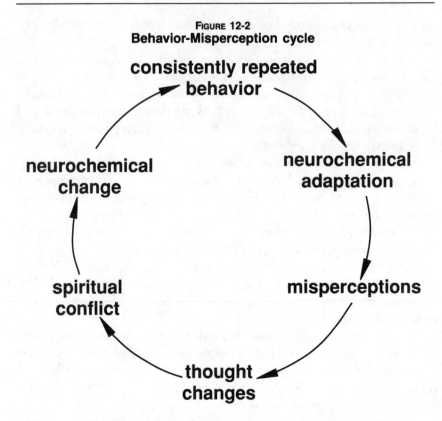

FIGURE 12-2
Behavior-Misperception cycle

emotional or a spiritual thought (Steve's hopelessness and negativity) that eventually brought about the development of types of action (compulsive work and gambling).

The behavior-misperception cycle is caused by the behavior and results in changed thoughts. For instance, Eugene was a Vietnam veteran. He entered the war as a confident, well-balanced individual. For fifteen months, he stayed alert, fearful a sniper would shoot him. This consistent behavior was forced upon him, but even so, it changed his neurochemicals.

By the time Eugene returned to the States, he had changed. He no longer trusted people. He took more risks and began to develop an activity addiction. When Eugene tried to relax, he couldn't. "I just have to be doing something," he said. "I have to be on the go constantly."

Eugene had become compulsive in needing excitatory neurochemical stimulation. These changes created emotional effects of anxiety, fear, and lack of trust. His behavior in Vietnam caused his baseline neurochemicals to adapt or change to a new level.

The understanding of neurochemical adaptations also explains what many call relapse or the common practice of transfer from one form of addiction to another. Whenever baseline neurochemical levels are changed—*regardless of the cause*—they alter behavior and thoughts. If persons eliminate a form of behavior *without changing the brain chemistry,* they create the conditions for a transfer to another behavior or set themselves up to return to the original form of addiction. Their brain chemicals have been altered, but they have not found a new neurochemical reward.

— 13 —

Naming the Addictions

*Addictions that satisfy the neurochemical
personality are often present in more than
one form in the same individual.*

Behavior can become addictive if it satisfies the neurochemical personality.

While satisfying neurochemical reward centers, addictions also bring about changes in neurochemical transmissions. If a behavior relieves depression, it is an excitatory addiction. If a behavior lessens anxiety, it is an inhibitory addiction. The same behavior can provide satisfaction (reward) for the same person for different reasons.

For example, Angie is regularly depressed and receives an antidepressive feeling when she eats. This is an excitatory response. She also eats when she feels anxious, and this causes an inhibitory response.

Here is another significant and perhaps obvious fact about addiction:

Addictions that meet both inhibitory and excitatory needs tend to be stronger than those that meet only one need.

In this chapter I examine twenty-four common addictions listed in alphabetical order. This list isn't exhaustive, but these are the most common ones.

1. Activity

Activity addiction is a compulsion to do things. Persons who must keep busy, always doing something, never relaxing, quite likely are activity addicts. For them, relaxing is uncomfortable and gives no reward. Vacations are fun and relaxing only when they are active oriented (such as scuba diving or mountain climbing).

Activity addiction meets the needs for pleasure, responsibility, avoidance, adequacy, approval seeking, and recognition. Often the pleasure theme causes the constant need for neurochemical stimulation. Persons may actually be depressed or "stressed out" and need action to balance the brain chemicals.

The acceptance by others as fun-loving and active individuals creates recognition and approval seeking and ultimately overcomes the feeling of inadequacy—temporarily. Relationships and intimacy usually suffer because persons rarely set aside times for reflection.

Activity addiction coincides with drug, work, sex, exercise, and risk taking addictions. Activity addiction can meet satiation or arousal rewards.

2. Alcohol or Drug

Alcohol and drug addictions (now often referred to as substance abuse) are the most discussed and written about addictions in society today. They provide direct neurochemical changes through their chemical reactions. They also provide indirect chemical changes by the feelings they create. Eliminating drugs and alcohol won't eliminate the themes or needs that their use will meet.

Often the chemical changes created by alcohol or drugs make persons feel more powerful, sometimes even invincible. Many people who have a power theme seek such emotions. The decrease in inhibitions that comes with consumption of alcohol and drugs provides false courage, making them temporarily feel more confident in their communication and confrontation skills.

Alcohol and drug use meets pleasure needs. The chemicals make persons feel good. The social environment in which alcohol and drugs are used is often a fun place to relax. Many people who struggle with the addiction believe life is no fun without alcohol or drugs.

Chemical dependency can contribute to avoiding responsibility. Excessive alcohol and drug use leads to irresponsible behavior—which persons blame on the alcohol and drug usage the next day. Unless such persons are recognized as addicted, society often accepts this excuse when alcohol and drugs are involved.

Alcohol and drug addictions are always related to feelings of inadequacy. Under the influence of chemicals, people believe they are as good as anyone else. Chemical use improves the self-esteem—temporarily. This constant need to feel adequate requires continued use (and often large amounts) of alcohol or drugs to alter self-perceptions.

Arousal and satiation personalities alike are vulnerable to chemical dependencies. Immediate neurochemical rewards provide instantaneous relief to the out-of-balance brain. All addictions are seen concurrently with chemical dependencies.

3. Approval Seeking

I recently attended a gathering where one of the most subtle compulsions became evident—that of approval seeking. I had breakfast with one man in the group on a previous morning. We had challenged a few values and positions for each other in a rather informal discussion. He then expressed an opinion that he knew I held.

At the gathering, I overheard a conversation he was having with another person on the same subject. This time he took the other person's position. As I listened, I realized that the man operated this way. His opinion was never his own but was always linked to the person he was with at the time. I wondered if he had any opinions about issues. He was an approval seeker.

Approval seeking behavior can become addicting in and of itself. Such individuals change their plans, beliefs, and values to get approval by others. Often they have no plans or values of their own but rely on those with whom they associate to make the choices.

Approval seeking addictions are caused by feelings of inadequacy. To feel adequate and acceptable, individuals must be liked.

Often the approval seeking addiction is associated with alcohol or drug abuse, compulsive overeating, hypochondria, and relationship addictions. Satiation and arousal personalities are equally vulnerable to the addiction.

4. Caffeine

Caffeine addiction isn't usually directed to meet a theme, but it is a neurochemical reward. The feelings provided by coffee or caffeine-containing products can be rewarding and reinforcing. Caffeine can cause a stimulation or a relaxing effect, depending on the beginning level of neurotransmission.

5. Cleaning

A close friend of our family is the least spontaneous person I know. Everything has to be just right at the house, or she won't allow anyone to visit. This woman spends days cleaning and sanitizing. No matter what anyone says to convince her not to work so hard, she answers, "If my house doesn't look spotless, people will think I'm lazy or disorganized."

She hasn't asked me what I think, but I believe she is searching for satiation by not allowing people to see any mistakes so they can criticize her.

After a dinner party, she feels euphoric if she detects no criticism and everyone raves about how beautiful everything is. Or she can end the evening depressed if she detects anything slightly amiss. One time she found a small particle of lint on the floor and burst into tears.

Compulsive cleaning is similar to perfectionism in its attempt to meet compulsive themes. Compulsive cleaning is seen in people who clean far beyond normal levels.

The compulsive cleaners attempt to avoid criticism, and they seek approval in culturally reinforced ways. Many believe their identity is based upon having a spotless home, car, or workspace. They believe they will be better, more ambitious, and more respected if the home or car is clean. The basic truth of that belief is exaggerated, and the rest of their lives suffer because of the addiction.

Many compulsive cleaners are addicted to alcohol, food, relationships, worship, perfectionism, or the media. The satiation personality is most vulnerable to this addiction because of the neurochemical changes that result from compulsive cleaning.

6. Control

At a dinner party I sat next to Deanna. Across the table and down two places sat her mother. Deanna and I were talking about addictions, and she kept saying she wanted to read books on the topic. I suggested several books, jotted down the titles, and gave her the list. As Deanna looked it over, Ellen got out of her chair, came around to the other side of the table, stood behind her daughter, and read the list.

"That one," Ellen said and quoted a title. "I think you ought to start with that one."

Deanna kept her head down as if trying to memorize the list. Finally she said, "I think I'd like this one better." She named the title.

Ellen's feeling of rejection was obvious. Tears filled her eyes. When the daughter turned and saw her mother's face, she said meekly, "Yes, maybe you're right, Mother."

Control addictions are extremely common and destructive to marriages and families. When people attempt to dominate others, they are vulnerable to developing control addictions. They are usually unaware of the addiction until they have destroyed their relationships.

Controlling others is an attempt to feel power or to overcome feelings of helplessness. The power of getting people to do what they ask is unmatched by any other power issue. Soon such dominating individuals expect others to give in to their every request. If others don't comply, the "managers" feel pain, frustration, or personally insulted. "She must not love me enough," a man may say, "or she would respect me enough to do what I ask." They don't consider that their requests may be unreasonable.

Control is a result of feeling inadequate. Control attempts to shape others' feelings and actions to meet their own selfish needs. Their need to feel adequate is so strong persons manipulate and coerce to get what they want. Control is often accomplished by doing things for others so they feel obligated in return.

Control is seen in arousal and satiation personalities, often coupled with workaholism, alcoholism, drug addiction, and perfectionism.

7. Exercise

A fairly new and socially acceptable addiction appeared in the 1970s—exercise addiction. Exercise is generally healthy for people. However, exercise-addicted people keep working out long after they have had sufficient exercise. These are the ones who chant, "No pain, no gain."

Dr. Kenneth Cooper, who gave new meaning to the word *aerobics*, has said that if people run more than twelve miles a week, they are running for reasons other than physical fitness. No matter what the exercise, compulsive types just can't stop at a moderate level.

Exercise addictions involve the themes of power, adequacy, approval seeking, and recognition. Persons may have a sense of power when they feel and look physically fit. They can develop a belief that they are able to do anything they choose because of their physical strength and stamina. Exercise addicts can feel a sense of power over others. Being admired by others for their prowess reinforces that feeling.

Individuals who need to exercise but don't have the self-discipline are often in awe of the exercise addict's self-discipline and achievements. They participate in the addiction by giving approval to the exercise addict. Too frequently the news and entertainment media recognize compulsive exercising as a virtue, thereby reinforcing exercise to become an addiction.

Most exercise addiction is seen in arousal personalities. They enjoy the "high" attained through exercise. Often perfectionism, workaholism, and sex and physical appearance addictions are seen along with the exercise addiction.

8. Food

Elizabeth was always extremely busy. She served on committees and task forces and community panels. She turned down no commitments. She was rarely home and ate compulsively.

Whenever anyone made comments about weight or diets, she'd say, "I need to start on a diet. I'm going to just as soon as I get past all the stuff I'm involved in. Right now I'm just too busy."

When Elizabeth finally entered therapy, she realized within a few weeks that she was quite depressed and felt rejected by her alcoholic husband. These were the issues that made her an overeater.

Food addictions are extremely common today, with compulsive overeating being the most common. This addiction is also the one most bombarded with advertising and enticement to increase its hold.

Diet programs, exercise techniques, self-help books, twelve-step fellowships, and specialty programs are available for persons suffering from eating disorders. The problem is of such magnitude that many options are widely available—but rarely effective.

To begin with, people don't overeat simply because they like food. (They may say that, but it's only an excuse.) Compulsive overeating is an addiction. "Feeding" that addiction may meet the needs of power, pleasure, responsibility avoidance, approval, and adequacy themes.

When overeaters control and manipulate others, they are expressing the power theme. Other people often arrange activities around the over-weight person, often giving them the center of control. Activities that require energy such as walking or volleyball are avoided. Choice of where to dine is affected by overweight persons. Overeaters thus gain social and relationship power as well as control with their food addiction.

Through the sheer enjoyment of eating, they meet their pleasure needs. Just the feel of a chocolate bar in their mouths reinforces their sense of pleasure.

Most frequently I've seen persons with food addictions use them to avoid responsibility and cover up for their inadequacy. They learn to avoid relationship changes, although this is often denied. Because the pain of change is too great, overeating provides a socially acceptable option for resisting it.

Overeating can also meet the theme of adequacy. Individuals often eat excessively when they feel rejected or unworthy. Carbohydrates have a soothing effect on an excited or nervous system.

Overeating can involve an approval theme because a "good" wife or mother stuffs her family. A large meal with meat, potatoes, and vegetables is the minimum requirement.

Most individuals who suffer from compulsive overeating are satiation personalities. Many become compulsive overeaters in an attempt to treat the chemical imbalances of their brains. This type of chemical imbalance is probably treated with the ingestion of excessive quantities of carbohydrates.

Persons with food addictions show this in such behavior as control, perfectionism, and compulsive cleaning.

9. Gambling

People are now more readily recognizing a gambling addiction with the recent involvement of figures such as baseball player Pete Rose admitting to the disease. The addiction varies in intensity from betting on horses, sporting events, or cards to the more common buying of lottery tickets. When money is used to try to increase income or provide excitement at the expense of relationships and financial situations, it is an addiction.

The excitement produced by gambling attracts the arousal personality. The physical rush of winning big stimulates the reward center of the people who enjoy the feeling from "flooring the gas pedal." Just the excitement of gambling lifts depression. This feeling may be temporary, but gambling addicts don't care. Depression is too uncomfortable to bear, even for a minute.

Gambling provides a sense of power, pleasure, and recognition. Gambling says, "I'm having a good time." Just watch the TV ads. The ads for Las Vegas, Reno, and Atlantic City aren't designed to feed gambling addictions directly, but they emphasize that by going to such places, people can find unlimited fun and meet their pleasure needs.

As a secondary theme, gambling can help overcome feelings of inadequacy. If persons win, they'll receive recognition. Society has taught us that having a large amount of money makes persons feel adequate and important.

Gambling addictions sometimes mix freely with cocaine, risk taking, and sex addictions. All these can add to the neurochemical release persons addicted to gambling find pleasurable.

10. Hypochondria

A close friend suffers from feelings of worthlessness, and she's frequently depressed. She experiences constant mood swings, but more distressing, she keeps developing new forms of sickness. This friend spends large amounts of money having tests run because she's convinced that she has some rare disease causing her problems. She and many others have learned that it's easier to excuse behavior when persons are physically ill. We call that hypochondria.

Hypochondria (developing imaginary illnesses) is a sophisticated form of addiction. Doctors find it difficult to disprove pain of certain injuries, which allows the addiction to remain unconfronted. Hypochondriacs have themes of power, responsibility avoidance, and adequacy.

When individuals can do what they want when they want, they are in control. They have power over others. This power excludes or ignores others' needs and allows them to meet their selfish needs. Others won't question their motives because they feel guilty or can't confront sick people. Hypochondriacs avoid taking responsibility for themselves and make others take over.

When persons feel inadequate, physical sickness gets them attention and reduces the expectations of others. When nothing is expected of them, they cannot fail. Feelings of inadequacy are lessened by decreasing standards by which they will be judged.

Hypochondria is seen in satiation and arousal personalities and often with chemical dependencies. Religion, media fascination, and control addictions frequently accompany hypochondria.

11. Intelligence (Education)

Intelligence or education addictions can be present. If persons attend college for several years, we call them professional students. After graduation, some continue to obtain degrees for the sake of their addiction, not as an opportunity for vocational or professional growth.

In Chicago, a friend once rode with a cabdriver who had thirteen earned degrees. When my friend asked why he drove taxis, he said, "With all my education, I'm overqualified for almost every job. This is the only work I can get."

Individuals search for power through education, which causes them to feel intellectually superior. They also know that most people will respect and listen to their remarks because of their advanced educational level or their high intelligence.

Education addiction shows fairly obvious symptoms of not feeling adequate. People may be searching for meaning through their educational and intellectual skills. Often people addicted to intellectualization don't look at emotional or spiritual issues from the heart. They try to intellectualize their purpose or the meaning of life. They end up with a void that can be filled only through relationships. Yet trying to establish relationships would make them feel inadequate.

Education addiction is common in the satiation personality. Workaholism, perfectionism, approval seeking, and materialism are often associated with this form of addiction.

12. Material

It's both interesting and sad to watch the keeping-up-with-the Joneses process in suburban America. A friend told me of an incident in his neighborhood. Three men bought sports cars. Although different brands, they all cost approximately the same amount. Within a short time, one of them decided to trade his in for a newer model that cost slightly more. Not a month later, the second one upgraded. The third man, who my friend said probably couldn't afford higher payments, bought a conservative family car. The other two began to tease him, especially because he had been the first to buy a sporty car.

"I'm buying a car that my family can use," he said. "I've wasted enough money on myself."

My guess is that he was dropping out of that race by appearing to be a self-sacrificing individual. The reality is probably that he wanted a sports car, but he was unwilling to buy one that didn't match up to those of his neighbors.

Materialism, the constant search to acquire more things, is a subtle, but common addiction. Often the degree of the addiction is limited by income or by the credit limit persons can handle. The purpose is to seek power, approval, and recognition by attaining and accumulating things.

Materialism as an addiction often occurs with workaholism; control, sex, and spending addictions; and alcohol and drug abuse. Arousal and satiation personalities are affected equally.

13. Media Fascination

A man in our neighborhood laughs at me because I don't subscribe to cable television. "Hey, Joel, what can you do without having a choice on the tube?" The fact that I still have several channels to choose from doesn't impress him.

This man seems to spend his time switching channels between old movies and sports. Although he calls it his way of relaxing, he allows no interruptions and no significant conversation between the hours of six and midnight. His family see him in the rec room, but they don't know who he is.

Satiation needs of individuals can be met through various media fascinations, such as watching soap operas, talk shows, and sports events and reading novels.

My friend Phil operates a used-book store. He tells me that some customers (mostly women, but some men) come in and buy the light romance novels by the boxload. "It's not unusual to sell a hundred to a customer. Then she comes back two weeks later for more." Such activities can provide a neurochemical reward for the satiation personality, causing an addiction.

The theme of responsibility avoidance can be met through watching television or reading excessively. When individuals begin to develop an addiction to such activities, other responsibilities usually suffer.

A fantasy life with others can contribute to the addiction. By fantasy life, I refer to the obsessive interest in actors, TV hosts, athletes, or authors. Persons who live their unfulfilled dreams through their fantasies usually are searching for adequacy. This apparent temporary escape from reality may seem innocent enough, but it actually lowers self-esteem. The lack of intimacy leaves a void, making people feel trapped and not allowing them to accomplish their goals in life.

Satiation personalities frequently suffer from compulsive overeating, relationship, and worship addictions.

Arousal personalities may become addicted to media that create excitement, such as pornography, video games, sports, or the cop shows on television. The mental or physical excitement stimulates the excitatory neurochemicals and creates an arousal reward.

The arousal personalities addicted to the media may be searching for power. The fantasy of pornography or the identification with sports figures can supplement this need. They derive pleasure from the excitement of video or computer activities. The release of excitatory neurochemicals is a positive reward for the arousal personality.

Media fascination, drug, sex, violence, and risk taking addictions are all similar in their ability to provide a neurochemical reward.

14. Nicotine

Nicotine addiction is similar in many ways to alcohol and drug addiction. Often the nicotine meets pleasure and approval seeking themes of behavior.

Certain people receive antianxiety effects from nicotine, while others get antidepression effects. It depends on baseline neurochemical levels and personality. The pleasure of nicotine is a strong reinforcement to addicted persons.

Nicotine use often begins through approval seeking behavior. Young adults may try cigarettes to get social acceptance among their peers, and they soon become addicted. The approval seeking need often transfers to a pleasure need after the addiction becomes evident.

Nicotine, alcohol, work, and gambling addictions are frequently interrelated. Both personalities, arousal and satiation, are affected.

15. Perfection

Early in my career, I had an administrative assistant who was extremely efficient and excellent at detail work. I was overjoyed because she provided needed skills to operate the clinic efficiently.

After a few weeks, I realized that I was tiptoeing around her, trying not to upset her. She *was* competent, but I couldn't correct her without a defensive argument, such as, "I was only doing my best, you know." Or sometimes, "I'm only human, Dr. Robertson. I give you my best."

At other times she brushed aside suggestions or ideas. The slightest criticism brought out feelings of inadequacy. I finally had to let her go. She was a first-class worker, but she put so much time and energy into everything to make it perfect, she took any changes as a personal insult.

Perfectionism can be an addiction when it provides either decreased or increased excitatory chemical release at the completion of a project. Perfectionists may be seeking less anxiety by doing everything exactly right. In actuality, however, that creates anxiety. But they believe they will be less anxious if they can just do it better the next time. Nevertheless, the temporary excitement of completing a job or task often outweighs the antianxiety effects in some people.

Perfectionism is an attempt to cover up feelings of inadequacy. The need to avoid criticism is so strong that people develop unrealistic expectations to do things perfectly. Eventually, they become their worst critics. They can't do anything perfectly, so they try harder. Their work is never good enough to please themselves. Rewards diminish because perfection can't be achieved. They generally add another addiction to the cycle.

Perfectionism may be a means to gain approval. People want to receive compliments for doing a good job. Perfectionists yearn for approval for being the best. Often compliments (no matter how many their received) can't keep up with their need for approval. Depression then develops.

Most perfectionists are satiation personalities who can also be addicted to alcohol, overeating, relationships, cleaning, worship, or the media.

16. Physical Appearance

Janet was a rather attractive woman with a natural kind of beauty who had enjoyed outdoor activities. She went through a painful divorce a few years ago. Finally she came to our clinic for counseling because of her depression and feelings of inadequacy.

"What do you enjoy doing for fun?" I asked.

"Oh, camping. Hiking. Other kinds of outdoor activities." Then she mentioned that she hadn't done any of them since her divorce.

"Why not?"

"Those things really mess up my hair. And the outdoor exposure dries up my skin and ruins my makeup. Without my makeup, believe me, I look gross."

The divorce had shaken her badly and had created a feeling of physical inadequacy. She tried to cover it up with makeup and just the right clothes. She became compulsive; she admitted that every day she tried on as many as half a dozen outfits before she settled on what to wear.

Persons addicted to physical appearance won't let anyone see them until they are dressed up or made up. Sexual, social, and relationship issues are affected by preoccupation with their physical beauty.

Physical appearance addictions are attempts to attain power and to meet adequacy themes. Their well-developed physique or their beauty provides a feeling of power over others. Since physical beauty is a symbol of self-esteem in most cultures, people develop the addiction at a young age. Often persons focus on their outer beauty because of their feelings of inner inadequacies. They receive temporary relief of this pain, and it goes away when they are alone.

Physical appearance addictions are seen in both arousal and satiation personalities. They often share addictions with perfectionists, exercise addicts, materialists, and workaholics.

FIGURE 13-1
Compulsive Themes of Common Addictions

COMMON ADDICTIONS	COMPULSIVE THEMES						PERSONALITY	
	Adequacy	Approval Seeking	Pleasure	Power	Responsibility Avoidance	Recognition	Satiation	Arousal
1. activity	●	●	●		●	●	●	●
2. alcohol or drugs	●		●		●		●	●
3. approval seeking	●						●	●
4. caffeine							●	●
5. cleaning		●					●	
6. control	●			●			●	●
7. exercise	●	●		●		●		●
8. food	●	●	●	●	●		●	
9. gambling	●		●	●		●		●
10. hypochondria	●			●	●		●	●
11. intelligence	●			●		●	●	
12. material		●	●			●	●	●
13. media fascination	●			●	●		●	●
14. nicotine		●	●				●	●
15. perfection	●	●					●	
16. physical appearance	●			●			●	●
17. religion/worship	●	●		●			●	●
18. rescuing	●						●	●
19. risk taking/excitement		●	●	●		●		●
20. sex	●	●	●	●	●	●	●	●
21. spending	●	●	●				●	●
22. stealing				●				●
23. violence	●	●		●		●		●
24. work	●			●		●	●	●

17. Religion/Worship

Carl was a recent convert to a charismatic movement. Within weeks, he was speaking in tongues and quoting Scriptures. He attended many special services and became an instant leader in the church.

Another new convert, Marvin, was rebounding from cocaine addiction. "Let me tell you something," he said when he gave a public testimony, "I found the 'high' in the church I used to find in drugs!"

Many people applauded. What they didn't understand—and Marvin didn't fully understand about himself at the time—was that he was also addicted to excitement. He had quit cocaine, but he was still addicted to power. He had changed the form of the addiction to the area of worship.

Religion or worship addiction isn't necessarily church related. This addiction can relate to a strong drive for inner peace through various methods. Religious or worship needs can be attained through cults, the occult, social organizations, and fraternal organizations.

Satiation personalities addicted to worship activities are looking for a decrease in excitatory activity. They are generally drawn to liturgical churches or places where they are intellectually stimulated. Usually they feel uncomfortable with charismatic worship. Belonging to groups that accept them for membership alone is important.

Worship addiction as a satiation need is generally related to a feeling of inadequacy and a need for approval. The need to belong and be accepted is usually strong. The ability to become active in churches or organizations meets the need of belonging to a group without risk. Regular attenders are accepted as good persons without anyone needing to know them. There is little personal risk because the acceptance comes from outside (through actions) and not inside (through relationships).

Satiation-worship addiction can also feed into the need for recognition. Some liturgical and highly conservative churches place people in power based upon their level of conservatism, not their ability to serve those in need.

This type of addiction is frequently seen with overeating, romance or relationship, and media fascination addictions.

High-energy cults and occult groups that are frowned upon by most religious people may be rewarding to the arousal personality. Or this personality may be drawn to the emotionally charged Pentecostal or charismatic movement or the intellectually stimulating teaching churches.

The twist in many Pentecostal and charismatic movements is one of superpower. Often the leaders teach converts that they can have anything. They quote clichés such as, "If you believe and pray...," or "If you can believe it, you can receive it." This style of teaching meets the needs of many arousal personalities and can cause a religion addiction.

Feelings of inadequacy may lead people to religion addiction. People who can learn to speak in clichés and quote many Bible verses often get held up as being spiritually mature. Highly energized emotional persons with a religion addiction are often considered solid and mature because of their energy.

Arousal personalities addicted to worship may be vulnerable to drug, sex, and gambling addictions.

Religion addictions interfere with the relationship with God. People are caught up in the religious affairs of the church or group, and their hearts never soften to the Holy Spirit. Often they appear to have tremendous faith, but it's a selfish faith based upon receiving from God, not from giving or serving.

18. Rescuing

Rescuing others can be destructive to all involved. Although a form of control, rescuing is a separate issue. Rescuing attempts to cover up and make excuses for others' actions, which keeps the rescuer from feeling like a failure or from losing the approval of others.

Here's how I often see rescuing in family systems. When children or spouses get involved in negative behavior, rescuers take the blame by believing they have done something wrong or have created the situation that led to the inevitable behavior. Parents feel they failed in ways they can't quite figure out. Why else would their son or daughter use drugs? Children of alcoholic parents know they haven't obeyed or been good enough or they didn't love the parents enough—some inadequacy on their part has driven the parents to drink. Children feel they must be inadequate to meet the needs of their parents who develop addictions.

When persons cover up, deny, or make excuses for others, they are rescuing. Frequent rescuing causes them to deny their own needs, and they become vulnerable to addiction.

Rescuing, relationship addictions, control, overeating, and perfectionism are often seen at the same time. Both arousal and satiation personalities can become addicted to rescuing.

19. Risk Taking/Excitement

Cletus was taking drugs, and he even got into drug dealing. Finally, fed up with his life-style, he decided to quit drugs. Yet within seven months, he was back to using drugs and was starting to deal again. He lived in constant fear of the law cracking down, the wrathful competition of other dealers, and the other drug addicts who wanted to take away his supply.

After another year, Cletus came for help. He made one particularly significant statement: "Quitting drugs was easy. Giving up the 'rush' of the life-style leaves me depressed."

Cletus realized, as so few do, that risk taking and exciting activities can be addicting. Driving fast cars, mountain climbing, parachuting, and white water rafting are examples of risk taking activities. The excitement created by these risks releases excitatory chemicals, which can medicate the depressed person or satisfy the excitement seeker. Most risk takers are arousal personalities.

Risk taking activities can provide a feeling of power over others, situations, or life itself. They provide pleasure, especially for the arousal personality. Risk taking activities also provide for approval and recognition needs. Many people feel admiration and recognition because of their daring and exciting lives.

Risk taking rewards are similar to those of drug, violence, and addictions. The chemical rewards are arousal and excitement oriented.

20. Sex

Clarence was an alcoholic who used to go to bars and end up with a different woman each time. Occasionally he went with prostitutes. His marriage was in bad shape, and his wife threatened divorce, so he stopped drinking.

For a year, Clarence didn't drink, but his marriage didn't get any better. He *demanded* sex at least once a day and sometimes twice. She felt his demands were excessive, while he insisted, "You're my wife. You don't want me playing around, so stop fighting me."

For another year—until his wife convinced him to get help—he continued to develop an addiction to sexual activity. Only later could he say, 'Sex made me feel powerful and adequate, at least temporarily. I had to keep having more of it."

Clarence was a sex addict. There are three types of sex addiction: (1) sexual activity addiction (as with Clarence), (2) romance addiction, and (3) relationship addiction.

Sexual activity addiction is the excessive need for sexual intercourse, with a focus on the number of times performed. Such persons sometimes feel the need for multiple sexual partners because the excitement of the unknown attracts them. The activity may remain with one partner, but the intensity increases, or they ask the partner for unusual or "kinky" forms or give vent to their fantasies such as violence, homosexuality, sadism, or extramarital sex. They often find their partners resist these requests.

Pornography and specifically sexual-related activities may excite them, such as going to topless bars, singles' bars, and nude beaches or even just intensive watching of the opposite sex.

Often this type of addiction is only in their minds, acted out in fantasy thoughts. In a number of instances, I discovered that persons with sex addictions were given strict religious upbringing that taught any exciting activity or variation from simple, missionary-position intercourse with your mate is wrong, including talking, laughing, or having sex with the lights on. With such individuals, the thoughts create the situations even if they don't act upon them. And they also feel guilty.

Frequent, healthy sex isn't a problem; the problem develops when it takes place outside marriage, when the demands aren't acceptable to the marriage partner, or when sex becomes predominant in the person's thoughts.

Sexual activity addiction is a quest for power over other persons.

Our society has increasingly accepted premarital and extramarital activity as normal. That's quite wrong—such activity appeals only to a compulsive and unhealthy society. It is destructive to the individuals it affects. Society has constantly justified and perpetuated sex addictions by making them socially acceptable. Married couples' healthy and rewarding sexual relationships have been destroyed by going along with a social norm.

Sexual activity addictions appeal to the pleasure theme. Sex is fun. Movies and television use sex to enhance pleasure-seeking themes. At sporting events the crowd can admire sexy cheerleaders or baton twirlers. Sex governs much of our society's activities.

Sexual activity is probably the strongest addiction for the person with feelings of inadequacy. When a woman gives herself to a man (or vice versa), he believes that he must be special. He feels desirable, wanted, admired, and excited. Often these emotions create the sexual promiscuity of today's youths, who feel insecure and inadequate. Sex temporarily eliminates that pain.

Sexual activity addiction occurs with people who have approval seeking needs. They feel approved and appreciated when others wish to have sex with them. This is a normal, healthy feeling within marriage. However, even within marriage, if a person doesn't feel approval without sex, there is a problem.

Sexual activity addictions and recognition themes are subtly, but powerfully, related. It has been said, "Power is an aphrodisiac." Individuals often seek sexual relationships with powerful or important people, those in positions of authority or visibility or those who have money, fame, intelligence, a high level of education, or beautiful bodies. Those seeking recognition feel they must be important to be sexually active with such powerful individuals.

Sexual activity addiction is often combined with other addictions that can meet similar neurochemical rewards, such as cocaine use, pornography, and risk taking. Often, the arousal personality is most vulnerable to sexual activity addiction.

Romance addiction involves the same themes and neurochemical rewards as sexual activity addiction. The difference is that the romance addict seeks not intercourse but a feeling of "being sexy" or desirable.

Kathy was a single mother who attended church regularly. "That's one woman who has it all together," others said.

But she didn't have it all together. When Kathy became depressed, her actions changed subtly. At church, she made lengthy eye contact with men, brushed against selected ones, and often left some of the males with an aura of her sensuality.

She wasn't aware of the messages she sent, but she loved the attention she received. She felt inadequate and unwanted. Male attention made her feel desirable.

The romance addict may be either a satiation or an arousal personality. Romance can be active or passive. The active romance is more arousal oriented; the individuals are involved in activities with sexual overtones. They may dress provocatively to attract attention from the opposite sex, whereas their body language and communication may give a different message.

Romance addicts express to vulnerable and insecure people how attractive or intelligent they find them. Secretly, they are searching for vulnerable persons to desire them. They will not actually get involved, usually because they will feel guilty.

Passive romantics are less direct and frequently are satiation personalities. They may do things not normally exhibited by members of their sex. Men may show insincere kindness, interest, humor, and other manipulative characteristics. Some women openly laugh or talk about sex with men; they may give the impression they need a vulnerable man to help them.

Romance addicts *must* be desired and *must* be made to feel good about themselves. If they seek approval and desirability from a spouse, they will probably receive praise. If the romancing goes beyond a spouse or becomes excessive, problems in intimacy will result.

Romance addiction is often related to responsibility avoidance needs and themes. Romance addicts need others to want to have sex with them, but they don't want the responsibility or the consequences that go along with such acts.

This addiction frequently occurs among the religious communities because the pressures and responsibilities of living a good and pure life can be too much of an expectation for many. They obtain relief through romance addiction.

Through romance addiction, persons can temporarily eliminate their feelings of being inadequate. When they feel they are sexy and desirable to others, they believe they must be adequate. Romance addiction frequently occurs in marriage when one spouse is nonsupportive, indifferent, or negative to the other. The spouse who feels inadequate is especially vulnerable to romance addiction.

The need for recognition can be soothed through romance addiction. The feeling that others consider them special and attractive gives them the false sense that they must be important.

The active romance addict may also be addicted to work, action-type worship (such as charismatic services), gambling, and other high-energy addictions. The passive romance addict gets rewards from satiation activities, such as overeating, quiet worship, alcoholism, perfectionism, and cleaning.

Relationship addiction refers to persons who depend on relationships to meet all their needs. Usually they choose one person, but two or three individuals may be involved. Those who are addicted may be physically attacked, emotionally beaten, or sexually abused, or they may be married to alcoholics or others with addictions, but they still look to that relationship for intimacy.

Pam was a relationship addict. She had been married three times. All her adult life she lived with a man or had an extremely close relationship with one.

When she was between relationships, I asked, "Pam, how do you feel?"

"Afraid. Empty." Slowly the words came out, but those first two words best described her feelings.

"How do you feel when you're involved in a relationship?"

A startled look appeared on her face. "Afraid and empty. The same way," she said. Until that moment, Pam had felt that having a relationship with a man brought her security. But because she knew that the relationship wouldn't last, she was afraid and already preparing to feel empty again.

Persons with relationship addictions often stay with their partners, regardless of the cost. They try to change themselves because they need that relationship. Having no relationship is more painful than staying in a bad one, even when they are physically and emotionally abused. Often they spend money and time, buying books and attending lectures to get more information about their spouses' problems. They are always looking for a magic answer to "fix" the situation.

Relationship addicts feel inadequate. Because they aren't better people, they believe, they don't need to be treated better in a relationship. Frequently they marry alcoholics, controlling partners, or emotionally distant people. Although they complain about their situation, they won't make changes. If they do divorce, they repeat their mistakes by marrying personalities just like the previous ones. Compulsive overeating, perfectionism, control, and compulsive cleaning are common among relationship addicts.

Sex addictions, in all their forms, are probably among the most common addictions. Their major impact has been to take away intimacy in marriages.

21. Spending

Compulsive spending is most often associated with antidepression activities. Arousal or satiation personalities who get depressed may try to buy things to feel better about themselves.

Compulsive spending can add to the pleasure theme; just the act of buying stimulates pleasurable chemical releases. And some compulsive spenders buy more for others than for themselves in an attempt to "buy" adequacy and approval.

One fellow I know insists on buying lunch for his coworkers when they go out together. If they decline, he insists, sometimes with anger in his voice. Unconsciously, he tries to create a feeling of success and approval from others.

Alcohol, drug, work, sex, perfection, and cleaning addictions often accompany spending addictions.

22. Stealing

Vanessa was caught shoplifting. When taken to the police station and questioned, she admitted the theft. She also admitted having stolen things several times previously, although she had enough money to buy the items.

"Then why do you steal?" asked a dumbfounded police officer.

FIGURE 13-2
Common Clusters of Addictions According to Personality Type

AROUSAL	SATIATION	AROUSAL & SATIATION
exercise perfection work sex physical appearance	**cleaning** perfection alcohol food worship media fascination	**activity** drug work sex exercise risk taking
gambling drug risk taking sex	**food** control perfection cleaning	**approval seeking** alcohol or drug overeating hypochondria relationship
religion/worship drug sex gambling	**religion/worship** overeating romance or relationship media fascination	**hypochondria** alcohol or drug religion media fascination control
risk taking drug violence sex	**relationship** overeating perfection control cleaning	**control** work alcohol drug perfection
media fascination drug sex violence risk taking	**media fascination** overeating relationship worship	**material** work control sex spending alcohol or drug
violence drug pornography sex risk taking	**intelligence** work perfection approval seeking material	**nicotine** alcohol work gambling
sex activity drug risk taking pornography	**perfection** alcohol overeating relationship cleaning worship media fascination	**physical appearance** perfection exercise material work
romance work worship (active) gambling	**romance** overeating worship (quiet) alcohol perfection cleaning	**spending** alcohol drug work sex perfection cleaning
stealing alcohol drug control sex approval seeking		**work** alcohol drug sex gambling risk taking
		rescuing relationship control overeating perfection

"I do it when I feel low and depressed," she replied. She then explained that stealing brought a feeling of excitement back into her life.

Stealing is an addictive disorder separate from violent crimes. The feeling of getting away with something is more important than obtaining the item. The addiction is created from the release of excitatory chemicals during the stealing episode.

Stealing meets the power need by giving such persons the feeling of control over situations; they love beating the system and not getting caught. This feeling is often a result of the "high" that overcomes depression or temporarily fills voids in their lives.

Stealing is frequently shared with alcohol, drug, control, sex, and approval seeking addictions. The arousal personality is more vulnerable to the addiction than the satiation personality.

23. Violence

Ralph, big for his age and physically strong, was a bully by the time he was in third grade. He didn't outgrow that attitude. Because he came from a wealthy and highly respected family, he got away with some of his behavior.

After he had grown up, Ralph realized that he had felt inadequate all his life. "I didn't measure up," he said. "I wasn't good like the rest of the family."

He seemed to enjoy himself most when he was forcing someone to do something he or she didn't want to do. Eventually he was arrested for kidnapping. Only then was he willing to seek help.

Ralph's need to control others through violence made him feel better about himself. Perpetrators of violence are often seeking the excitement and neurochemical stimulation associated with these activities. Committing violence—controlling others' destinies and intimidating them—can meet the need for power.

Recognition and approval can be related to violence in some cultures. Once these activities become a daily, normal part of behavior, they become acceptable. Persons involved in the highest risks, the most successful criminals, or the most violent ones can receive recognition and approval from this addiction. The media can give them recognition while their careers and their subculture can approve of their taking advantage of the system.

Violent acts also are often attempts to meet or overcome feelings of inadequacy. Feeling that others, who are less deserving than they, have more money or possessions can push them into violence. Their anger toward others' successes is created by disliking who they really are.

Arousal personality needs may be met through violence. Drug, pornography, sex, and risk taking addictions provide similar rewards to those of acts of violence.

24. Work

Working excessively can become an addiction. The neurochemical rewards vary among individuals. Work may decrease stress and provide a form of relaxation to some individuals; for others, it provides an escape from depression. Work becomes an addiction when individuals themselves (or those around them) are affected adversely.

Workaholism may be an attempt to meet the need for power, as defined by the job position or the amount of income. Many companies promote persons because of their loyalty and the number of hours they work. They then help to create a workaholic environment.

The need to feel good about themselves can contribute to developing workaholism. Feelings of inadequacy get temporarily relieved by feeling good about accomplishments and financial rewards for their actions.

Approval is often sought through the work environment. Individuals who receive praise for their work may become workaholics. The need for approval becomes so strong that they may ignore or deny their personal needs or the needs of others.

The need for recognition can be met through workaholism. Most of society looks at what people accomplish or how they earn their living as the symbol of their success. Workaholics put a great number of hours and high levels of energy into being recognized.

Workaholics frequently become addicted to alcohol, drugs, sex, gambling, and risk taking. Arousal and satiation reward center needs can be met through workaholism.

————— ◆ —————

As you read through this chapter, did you identify with any of these addictions? Did you find an illustration that made you think, "Hmm, that's me"?

It's important to know the addiction AND the theme to understand and identify the compulsive behavior. Then you can do something about it.

— 14 —

Breaking the Cycle

Ten basic principles must be followed to break the cycle and recover from addictions.

To break the cycle of addictions, persons have to figure out where they feel most confident. This is the area where they should begin recovery; this is their best entry point.

1. The *spiritual* entry resolves conflicts that create the thoughts that cause the cycle to begin.
2. The *physical* entry changes neurochemistry through diet, exercise, and behavior techniques.
3. The *emotional* entry investigates the compulsive themes and where they developed.

Ultimately, all three areas must be worked on together. Most individuals begin at their entry point and move into the other areas within a short time.

To break the cycle of addictions, persons need to apply the ten principles of recovery.

Ten Principles of Recovery

1. Recovery techniques need to fit the personality

Likes and dislikes are as varied as individual personalities. Some people love escargot and can't eat enough. Others wouldn't touch a dead snail if they were paid to eat it. What persons like in recovery is no different. It's foolish to expect that one program fits all. One of the worst traps persons can fall into is the "right"-way trap.

2. Recovery needs immediate rewards for change to last

It would be wonderful if people didn't require rewards, but realistically, people won't continue to change without feeling good about their actions.

Addictions feel good. They take away pain and treat imbalances.

To ask persons to stop a particular behavior and then say, "Now I want you to try to feel good," is ridiculous. The original conflict—and especially the pain—returns when they stop the addictive behavior. They need a replacement reward that is as strong or stronger than the addiction. If the reward is less, the best they do is transfer to another addiction.

Neurochemical treatment *begins* the process of changing rewards; it doesn't eliminate them.

Any new behavior must satisfy the neurochemical needs in the same way the addiction did.

Bear in mind that a new behavior must be consistent with the compulsive theme and provide a neurochemical reward. If the theme was power and the person had an arousal personality, the new behavior would need to satisfy the power theme and provide a reward for an arousal person. The difference is that the new behavior will need to include intimacy issues—relationships with God, self, and others. As intimacy with God, self, and others develops, the reward center changes and eliminates the power theme.

3. Spiritual health promotes recovery

In my practice and research, I've come to the conclusion that spiritual recovery is ultimately the only way for persons to change their thoughts. Spiritual recovery is an ongoing process that alters the neurochemistry. Persons become addicted when their neurochemistry goes out of balance. It's as if they are no longer able to make choices. At that point, everything goes on automatic.

Spiritual recovery stops the automatic response, and persons once again have choices.

4. Genetic alterations don't signal doom, although they do play an important role

Many individuals assume they can't ever recover because of genetics.

- "My mother was a manic-depressive until the day she died. I guess I'm doomed to be like her."
- "My grandfather was an alcoholic and so was my father. What chance do I have?"
- "My mother and her mother were obese and perfectionists. Why should I expect to be different?

There's more to the picture, however, than inherited genes. If it is true that genetics can't be changed, it is also true that genetics doesn't spell enslavement to addiction. Real addictions come from *experiences* and *chemical changes* in the brain.

The treatment of genetic addictions includes treating neurochemical imbalances and changing perceptions.

Genetic neurochemical imbalances are treatable. And treatable means curable.

5. The social environment and background affects the interpretation of therapy

It's wrong to assume that the same behavior has positive effects for everyone. Exercise may be extremely pleasurable to one, but be uncomfortable to another.

Some people think small groups are the ultimate in therapy, while others won't even try them. Many addicted people have been told how to recover by someone who is in recovery. When they try that method and don't like it, they feel they must be a failure. The truth is, they tried the wrong approach for their personality.

6. Negative behavior can bring about positive rewards

The physiology of the body has no value system. Receiving neurochemical relief is what matters.

The brain doesn't know when a behavior is negative or positive. The way to eliminate negative behavior, then, is to satisfy the needs of the physical body and brain. Only when these needs get met are the spiritual and emotional components able to determine their values and norms.

7. We can rarely trust our emotions

Emotions are a combination of physical, spiritual, and emotional balances. People in addiction see through misperceiving eyes. Selfish desires, needs, and expectations change the reality of what they see.

People use their intellect and emotions to define what is true. When emotions are inaccurate, their self-defined truth will be inaccurate.

Individuals who define truth can only define their perception of truth.

8. Medical disorders can cause physical, emotional, and spiritual imbalances

Medical evaluations are essential to those in recovery. Many compulsive behaviors are due to or complicated by medical consequences.

Addison's disease, or diabetes, and medication can cause depression or other mood changes that can contribute to compulsive behaviors.

9. Hormones affect neurochemistry

Individuals go through cycles in life when their hormones change. Adolescence, middle life, and the senior years are such times. Women's monthly cycles affect their neurochemical makeup, which then affects their emotions and thoughts. These hormonal factors must be considered to understand physical, emotional, and spiritual needs.

10. Diet, activity, and behavior affect neurochemistry

For those who have neurochemical imbalances, a change in diet, activity, or behavior can improve neurochemical levels. But choosing a diet or activity because it feels good, isn't necessarily treating the whole person.

The tendency of those in recovery is to respond to their emotions by doing what feels good. But because of their misperceptions, more often than not, what feels good isn't best for the whole body.

––––––––––––– ♦ –––––––––––––

The ten general principles are necessary to understand the recovery process. Persons need to understand *why* they are making changes in order to make the struggle to change worthwhile.

— 15 —

Spiritual Recovery

Spiritual recovery is essential for recovery from addictions. They way we think about ourselves, others, and life will be affected by spiritual issues. When conflicts exist, chemicals become imbalanced.

Rosa was a client who felt stressed and anxious. She had been in and out of the hospital because of a heart problem. "Slow down," the doctors kept telling her.

Rosa's cardiologist referred her to me. On her first visit, she described feeling alone and unloved: "I suppose my activities are my way of trying to make up for all the unfulfilled things in my life."

The next day I spoke with Jose, her husband, who seemed compassionate and caring. He said, "I've tried to talk to her about the cause of her problems, but she just won't listen."

"Rosa isn't interested in a solution to her problems," I said. "She needs someone to recognize the problems. There's quite a difference." I explained that he could help her best by simply listening to her: "But let her know you're listening. And that you understand. If you don't understand, ask her to clarify for you."

Jose began to listen to Rosa, and he stopped trying to cure her. She did slow down, and her heart problem all but disappeared.

"I still don't understand how it has worked," Rosa reported, "but it has worked. I feel good about it." Because of Jose's willingness to listen, Rosa slowly began to feel loved.

Although neither of them recognized it, they were dealing with spiritual issues. Once they recognized that her need for love and acceptance was a spiritual problem, they also began to notice how it affected her physically.

As both learned, spiritual health is the key to handling spiritual conflicts. But when spiritual conflicts are present, they trigger thoughts that generate emotions that are treated by addictions.

Spiritual health begins with a gift. God gives us the gift of life eternal, and it starts in the present. Like any other gift, we have to accept it. And when we accept it, that is faith.

It's not easy for persons who already feel unworthy to say, "God loves me." One way they come to faith (or believing) is that they first exhaust their efforts at self-improvement. They're still miserable; they can't heal themselves. So they cry out, "I can't do it alone. I need help from a Higher Power."

Crying out is taking that step of faith. It acknowledges a power greater than themselves. Twelve-step programs use the term *Higher Power*. I'm more comfortable referring to God who reveals Himself to us through Jesus Christ.

When Paul wrote to the Romans, he caught this sense of anguish and despair that many addicted persons have to reach before they turn to a greater source of help:

> I do not understand what I do. For what I want to do I do not, but what I hate I do. . . . I know that nothing good lives in me, that is, in my sinful nature. For I have the desire to do what is good, but I cannot carry it out. For what I do is not the good I want to do; no, the evil I do not want to do—this I keep on doing. . . . What a wretched man I am! Who will rescue me from this body of death? Thanks be to God—through Jesus our Lord! (Rom. 7:15, 18–19, 24–25 NIV).

Faith changes lives. Living examples are everywhere.

When I was growing up, I used to hear people say, "God is good for the weak, the poor, the stupid, and the elderly." That was a way of saying God was a crutch, something to lean on, because people couldn't handle life by themselves. I've personally seen too many lives changed for the better to accept that cynical and fallacious thinking.

I've known hundreds of individuals who suffered from addictions and lived in daily emotional pain. They tried everything they knew to cure themselves, including every self-help or mutual-support group around. When they finally said, "Okay, God, I give up," they experienced God's power in their lives.

The power is real, but only to persons who possess it. Individuals who don't accept faith as an integral part of the human condition haven't experienced it, and they don't understand it.

I sometimes say, "I don't understand how heavy airplanes stay in the air, but I fly in them regularly." I don't analyze every plane before I get on it. I trust that I'm going to reach my destination. That's how faith operates.

Faith isn't an option to achieve recovery. *Faith is absolutely essential.*

Some people go to the grave searching for the key to recovery. God hands each of us the key and says, "Believe in Jesus Christ. This opens the door and sets you free."

I think it's important to point out that spirituality isn't measured by church attendance, membership, or baptismal records. Many persons attend church every Sunday with bitter hearts, resentful attitudes, and a lack of peace.

Spirituality isn't based on what people do *not* do, either. I've met those who get praised for their piousness—they appear religious and like to be thought of as good Christians (and maybe they are). They quote Bible verses; sometimes they dress a certain way. In some churches, they have their own vocabulary. I don't want to speak against these people. But if they have faith in the Jesus Christ of the Bible, it's not because of their behavior. They believed, and from their commitment to that belief system, they took on particular forms of behavior.

Belief guides behavior. It doesn't work the other way around.

Developing Spiritual Health

In my practice of helping people as well as in my experience as a believer, I've worked out a progression of steps for those who want full recovery from addiction. By following these steps, persons develop an intimate relationship with God, with themselves, and with others.

The words of Paul, when he explained why he was writing, voice my own feelings:

> My purpose is that they may be encouraged in heart and united in love, so that they may have the full riches of complete understanding, in order that they may know the mystery of God, namely, Christ, in whom are hidden all the treasures of wisdom and knowledge (Col. 2:2–3 NIV).

The following steps develop a functional and vibrant faith.

1. Surrender

Recovery is changing from self-centeredness to Christ-centeredness. The view of life irreversibly alters when this happens. Persons' eyes are opened, and they see reality.

Surrender to God begins with that inner awareness of needing help and realizing only God can provide that quality of help. They make the commitment that says, "As much as I am able, God, I give myself to You."

Surrender isn't a once-for-all experience. It's the starting line. As persons race toward the finish line of life, they keep discovering new areas of surrender—things they need to turn over to God.

Those who surrender to Christ know how to love others and to give themselves freely to others. In the Bible, love is an attitude, not just an emotion. Love means caring enough to do something for others. Love is action. Love works for the good of others.

Once individuals surrender, their values and goals also change. They make this change for themselves and for God, not to be liked or admired. Their lives reflect this new set of values.

Paul wrote of the effects of his surrender to God:

> But what things were gain to me, these I have counted loss for Christ. Yet indeed I also count all things loss for the excellence of the knowledge of Christ Jesus my Lord, for whom I have suffered the loss of all things, and count them as rubbish, that I may gain Christ and be found in Him, not having my own righteousness, which is from the law, but that which is through faith in Christ, the righteousness which is from God by faith (Phil. 3:7–9).

2. Develop Unconditional Love

The steps toward spiritual health move on to unconditional love. This absolute love means accepting themselves and others, regardless of their actions.

Most people—including me—have found it difficult to learn to love others without setting up conditions. Whether spoken or not, so many relationships revolve around the thought, *I'll love you if . . .*

A key to developing unconditional love is understanding that failure is part of everyone's life. If persons fail, they fail. It doesn't change the attitude of those who love them.

God's unconditional love says that God loves us no matter how often we fail. Our unconditional love allows us to love others no matter how often they fail. Our unconditional love allows us to love ourselves no matter how often we fail.

Persons who give up after a setback haven't developed unconditional love. Their lack of love during their failures brings about guilt, anger, and other emotions that paralyze them and prevent them from changing. True unconditional love allows persons the ability to stand up, brush off, and keep moving. They accept the fact that their humanness will cause them to fail.

Those in recovery especially need to learn to love others, even the very people who let them down. Friends, spouses, parents, and children all fail somewhere, sometime. Here's why they fail:

- First, they're human. They make mistakes.
- Second, they have unrealistic expectations placed upon them.

When persons in recovery set up standards for individuals (including themselves), they also set up the basis for failure—demanding more than anyone can deliver.

In 1 John 4:15–21, unconditional love is pictured this way:

If anyone acknowledges that Jesus is the Son of God, God lives in him and he in God. And so we know and rely on the love God has for us. God is love. Whoever lives in love lives in God, and God in him. In this way, love is made complete among us so that we will have confidence on the day of judgment, because in this world we are like him. There is no fear in love. But perfect love drives out fear, because fear has to do with punishment. The one who fears is not made perfect in love. We love because he first loved us. If anyone says, "I love God," yet hates his brother, he is a liar. For anyone who does not love his brother, whom he has seen, cannot love God, whom he has not seen. And he has given us this command: Whoever loves God must also love his brother (NIV).

Persons who focus only on their pain and anger don't develop unconditional love—they can't. They're being controlled by their emotions, and they lack peace within.

Mary struggled with unconditional love. She came for counseling because she said, "My husband is distant, unloving, and insensitive." She admitted, "I've tried everything to get Don to pay attention. Nothing works."

Mary explained that when Don came home after work, he usually asked, "How did things go today?" Then he sat down at the table, ready for his evening meal. But she wanted some kind of affection—a hug, a kiss, or the words "I love you."

Mary went to a meeting for codependent women at our clinic. Another woman asked, "Why are you here?"

After Mary told about her problem with Don, the woman asked, "Does Don listen to you when he asks you how things went?"

"Yes. I have to say that for him. He is an excellent listener."

"Perhaps, Mary, you should listen to the way he loves you, too."

The comment shocked Mary. Then she realized that she had expected him to respond to what she had set up. She wasn't allowing Don to be who he was and to express love by listening to her and really wanting to know about her day. So caught up with her wants, she hadn't considered Don's personality or his "language" of love. Where others would have envied her husband's caring and willingness to listen, Mary had seen only a man who ignored her needs.

Mary behaved conditionally. She was actually saying, "If you love me, this is how you must respond." Conditional love doesn't allow for the other's unique personality response.

Unconditional love begins on the inside. Persons recognize that God loves them and holds up no demands. Because they experience this relationship with God, they can transfer the experience and love others the same way.

It may not be easy. They may need to pray often. They may fail many times, but it's worth working for!

Unconditional love means loving others as they are right *now* instead of deciding what they should or could be. Love doesn't insist that others be more lovable. Love says, "You are wonderful exactly as you are. Even if you never change, I'll still love you."

When others say, "This is what you should be," they make us feel unlovable.

3. Learn Acceptance

God accepts the rich, the poor, the strong, the weak, even you and me. It doesn't matter who they are or how they behave. An attitude of acceptance can disapprove the behavior and still not reject the person.

I can't think of any stronger illustration of acceptance than the life of Jesus. He spent time with the downtrodden and outcast, thus showing His acceptance of them.

After persons know they are accepted by God as they are,
   then they can accept themselves as they are,
      and then they can accept others as they are.

Persons don't change until they accept who they are. Acceptance also recognizes weaknesses, flaws, and inconsistencies—and still doesn't demand change.

I think of William, a young man controlled by sexual dysfunctions. He had been sexually promiscuous and gotten heavily into pornography. He worried about whether he was homosexual. He became so guilt-ridden, he moved away from home and avoided contact with his parents. His parents, aware of his problem, felt that they must have done something to create it. They were also guilt-ridden.

Through Sex Addicts Anonymous, William began to work on the first three steps of the twelve-step program. He struggled with accepting his problem as a problem. One day he called his parents and started telling them about his problem.

"Why don't you come over here, son?" his dad asked.

"You mean, it's all right? You know about my problem, and you still want me to visit?"

"We love you," the father said, his voice breaking.

From that time, William and his parents worked on the problem together. They didn't focus on finding someone to blame. "We just wanted a solution," he shared.

Eventually, William won the sex addiction battle, and he said, "When I knew my folks accepted my condition and still wanted me to be with them, I knew I could make it."

4. Become Self-Disciplined

Most people who don't recover from addictions don't have self-discipline. They may be in control in some areas, but they fail in following through on their spiritual commitments and on changing themselves. Usually not knowing what and how to change, along with a feeling of not being able to do anything, makes them feel powerless. Once they tell themselves, "There's nothing I can do," there is nothing they can do.

They dwell on the situation and refuse to consider that there is help. Most of all, they fail to give God a chance to help them throw off the addiction. Maybe they don't realize that God wants them to be free and to be happy. He doesn't want to punish them or do them harm.

Paul spoke of self-discipline in this way:

Not that I have already obtained all this, or have already been made perfect, but I press on to take hold of that for which Christ Jesus took hold of me. Brothers, I do not consider myself yet to have taken hold of it. But one thing I do: Forgetting what is behind and straining toward what is ahead, I press on toward the goal to win the prize for which God has called me heavenward in Christ Jesus (Phil. 3:12–14 NIV).

Spiritual self-discipline involves letting go of the past, changing unproductive thoughts, and pressing forward.

5. Resolve Spiritual Conflicts

Some readers may think that this chapter is too religious. Or that I'm pushing the spiritual aspect too much. They may not realize that freedom comes *only* after individuals resolve their spiritual conflicts.

6. Listen

Remember Rosa and Jose? He knew the cause, but she didn't want to hear answers. She wanted to hear that he accepted her and loved her.

A vibrant and healthy relationship with God comes through listening. God speaks by displaying His power and awesomeness in nature. God speaks in many ways besides nature. Through the Bible. A poem or an article. When others speak, they may be giving the answers people long to hear.

> Be still, and know that I am God;
> I will be exalted among the nations,
> I will be exalted in the earth (Ps. 46:10).

Simply put, when persons pull themselves away from the noises of life (get quiet), they can hear God. They also learn to hear what others are saying.

The book of Proverbs often mentions the wisdom of listening:

> The way of a fool is right in his own eyes,
> But he who heeds counsel is wise (Prov. 12:15).

> He who answers a matter before he hears it,
> It is folly and shame to him (Prov. 18:13).

7. Share

When persons "talk at" each other, nobody really communicates. Sharing takes the form of talking about strengths and struggles. It's a participation situation; they give and take.

By contrast, I think of a film called *The Subject Was Roses*. A son has just returned home from World War II. He sits at the table with his

FIGURE 15-1
Steps to Developing a Functional Faith

Step 1	Surrender	Change from self-centeredness to Christ-centeredness.
Step 2	Develop unconditional love	Accept yourself and others—regardless of what they do.
Step 3	Learn acceptance	Learn to disapprove the behavior but not reject the person.
Step 4	Become self-disciplined	Let go of the past, change unproductive thoughts, and press forward.
Step 5	Resolve spiritual conflicts	Freedom comes *only* after spiritual conflicts are resolved.
Step 6	Listen	When others speak, they may be giving the answers you long to hear.
Step 7	Share	When individuals share with one another, things change.
Step 8	Change attitudes	Obstacles can be accepted as learning experiences, personal attacks, or challenges.
Step 9	Forgive	Until you are ready to forgive, you won't change.

parents. They talk—but not to each other. All three have problems. The mother is concerned about her health; the father may lose his job; the son doesn't know what he wants to do. It's as if each is in the room alone.

When individuals share with one another, things change. Sharing means listening, of course, but it also means more. It's a way of feeling and participating in the others' good news and hardships. Sharing is reaching out and at least trying to feel what they feel.

Sharing pain, doubts, failures, setbacks, and confusion is healthy. People don't have to tell everyone every problem every day. They don't have to join a group so they can share. Sharing happens whenever individuals interact with others.

It's essential to share with God; it's helpful to share with others.

8. Change Attitudes

The night sky can be beautiful or frightening. It all depends on the viewer's attitude. When individuals look at problems in life as personal attacks, they often get so busy defending themselves, they forget they have options.

Problems beset everyone; they stop only when death comes. How persons handle their struggles in the meantime makes the difference.

Obstacles can be accepted as learning experiences OR personal attacks OR challenges.

Individuals choose for themselves. Whatever they choose, their decisions affect how they behave and the expectations they place on themselves, their children, spouses, friends, peers, and coworkers.

People get disappointed when they set up demands and expectations for others' behavior.

9. Forgive

Others do us wrong. They hurt us. They reject us. (Of course, we are just as guilty in their eyes.) Unfortunately, many focus on their problems and the people who caused them. Over and over and over and over they replay their hurt as they indulge in the blame game:

- "If my father had..."
- "If only my mother had..."
- "She deliberately hurt me by..."
- "Well, remember when you..."
- "I always did this for you, but you never..."

They're filled with anger and resentment. They despise and reject spouses, children, coworkers, bosses, and employees who have done them wrong.

When told they need to forgive, the same individuals have the answers:

- "If you knew how badly she hurt me..."
- "Just as soon as he makes things right..."
- "Why should I forgive? I didn't do anything wrong."
- "Forgiveness? Go talk to my father. He's the one who needs to forgive!"
- "I'm the victim, not the victimizer! Don't talk to me about forgiving!"

These persons are being controlled by negative thoughts. They are the willing victims of torture and pain. That may sound harsh, but it's only to point out that they make no progress. They're stuck in a pain-and-blame situation. Each time they think about being hurt, they hurt even more. Until they are ready to forgive, they won't change.

In the Lord's Prayer, Jesus taught,

> Forgive us our debts, as we also have forgiven our debtors.... For if you forgive men when they sin against you, your heavenly Father will also forgive you. But if you do not forgive men their sins, your Father will not forgive your sins (Matt. 6:12, 14–15 NIV).

He was saying that persons who don't forgive are the ones being hurt. If they can't forgive, they haven't understood what it means to be forgiven by God.

Paul provides the answer. It's a matter of changing attitudes. He instructs his readers to replace an unforgiving spirit with love:

> Therefore, as the elect of God, holy and beloved, put on tender mercies, kindness, humility, meekness, longsuffering; bearing with one another, and forgiving one another, if anyone has a complaint against another; even as Christ forgave you, so you also must do. But above all these things put on love, which is the bond of perfection (Col. 3:12–14).

Changing the thoughts and attitudes so that persons can forgive is the last but crucial step toward spiritual health. But if they focus on being hurt, maligned, misunderstood, and rejected, they are self-centered. They tend to quit an addiction only to trade it for a different one. They're still addicted, even if they transfer to what many would consider a "lesser" addiction. When they strive to become Christ-centered, they can recover from addictions and experience inner peace and happiness.

— 16 —

Who Can Help You

The support system is one of the most important factors in recovery.

Six recovered individuals spoke in a meeting, giving their stories; four of them were female. They had different addictions over varying periods of time, and they conquered their compulsive behavior by different methods. As I listened to them, however, I realized that they mentioned one common element.

"My wife was there for me, all the way," said one.

"Without my three children's support," said a woman in her late fifties, "I don't know how I could have survived."

A woman in her twenties blew a kiss and said, "That's for my mom and dad. They had every reason to hate me, but they stuck by me instead." Tears slipped down her cheeks. "I give thanks to God for them. They cared about me when I wasn't able to care much about myself."

"They loved me unconditionally," one man said of his small support group.

Support system. That's what it came down to for each of them. They fought tough battles, and they won. But none of them said, "I did it alone." They were smart enough to know that they needed help and they got it.

Perhaps even more important, *they set up the support system at the beginning of their recovery.*

Everyone needs support and wants it. Yet those who need it most are often afraid to ask for help. They fear being rejected by those they ask, or they fear that their supporters will tire of them and quit. Or they may choose the wrong supporters or worry about acceptance, especially once they start opening up about who they "really are." Most of them have

161

trouble trusting anyone. This lack of trust is often one of the things that started them on the path of addictive behavior.

People need to feel accepted. People need unconditional love. People need to feel that they are all right in the eyes of others—no matter how badly they mess up.

Although everyone needs support by feeling accepted, accountability is an equally important part of the recovery process. The two should work together so that it's a matter of giving and receiving.

The term *accountability* is confusing to many people; they assume it means constantly reporting on their progress to someone else, like a person on parole. Who likes that? A strong part of us wants the independence and freedom to do what we want when we want. The distinct advantage of acceptance and accountability as parts of support is summarized in Ephesians 4:15 as "speaking the truth in love."

The support system is to speak the truth—not to control—but to provide feedback. Acceptance is belief in persons, whether they are succeeding in their plan or failing miserably. Acceptance is love. Accountability begins with a commitment to change. When persons in recovery commit themselves to certain actions, they need someone to follow up, to encourage them, and to suggest other options for change.

All persons "give account" to a support system of how they have handled their commitment.

A support system can be a group, a fellowship, or one individual; in this chapter a support system refers to any form of human support.

Seven Functions of a Support System

1. A Support System Is an Accountability System

Although I've already mentioned this element, it's so important I want to emphasize it. An essential part of the recovery from addictions is accountability. The disease of addiction plays tricks on the mind, causing it to manipulate and rationalize. Persons don't develop an addiction without these traits, and the same traits hamper recovery, usually without their knowledge.

A true accountability system helps to keep manipulation and rationalization to a minimum. A well-thought-out and selected support person helps those in recovery to stay motivated for the duration of the recovery process.

2. A Support System Provides Reality Checks

Since neurochemical changes affect the way individuals see life, recovery from addictions includes cleaning up some misperceptions. If persons understand life differently from what it truly is, they tend to make changes based on wrong information. A support system provides accurate information for them to develop healthy lives.

For example, when Elizabeth started her recovery, she couldn't ask her husband for help (she did ask her birth family) because she felt he didn't love her. He yelled at her because of her addictive behavior, threatened divorce and, at one time, threw away her prescription pills. Although he was mistakenly trying to help, Elizabeth interpreted that as hatred for her. She needed help outside herself to recognize that her feelings didn't mirror reality.

3. A Support System Allows Persons to Share Freely

A support system makes persons feel comfortable sharing their excitement, failures, or frustrations. Unless they have the opportunity to share, subtle mind games destroy their self-confidence or cause anger and resentment. When they are doing something they don't want to do but have to do, they become frustrated. Change is doing something they don't really want to do.

Most people want their pain to go away, but they don't want to change. Sharing their hurts, failures, and successes keeps them motivated and open. Sharing may be deep or superficial, depending on the personalities involved. Some people share everything, every day, while others share selectively and infrequently. There is no right or wrong way or level of sharing.

4. A Support System Develops Priorities

Often persons become overwhelmed when they look at their problems. They feel they need to change them all—immediately! Support systems help them evaluate what is important and what isn't by setting priorities. They prioritize by two areas: (1) what to change, and (2) when to change.

When to change identifies compulsive themes and addictions. When to change addresses the stages of addictions.

5. A Support System Assists in "Identifying" with Others

Support systems provide caring persons to identify with, persons who allow addicted individuals to feel understood and to know they're not alone. Those who have experienced the same addictions have a common way to identify. As those in recovery speak, they often say, "I've been there. Yes, that's how it was with me, too."

Others provide identification by sharing their own struggles even if

they've never been addicted. A supporter says, "I can't think of any time
when I felt I had to do something, when I had no control. But I can
remember a few times when I wanted to do something and the urge was
so strong..." The supporter is reaching out and saying, "I want to
understand. I identify with your need to be understood."

FIGURE 16-1
Functions of a Support System

Function 1	Accountability	A true accountability system helps to keep manipulation and rationalization to a minimum.
Function 2	Reality checks	A support system provides accurate information.
Function 3	Sharing	Without sharing, subtle mind games can destroy self-confidence or cause anger and resentment.
Function 4	Priorities	A support system helps evaluate what is important and what isn't by setting priorities.
Function 5	Identification	A support system provides caring persons to identify with so that addicted persons know they're not alone.
Function 6	Self-esteem	A support system raises and strengthens self-esteem so that those in recovery feel better about who they are.
Function 7	Family	People who succeed in winning the battle of addictions have support systems within their families.

6. A Support System Raises Self-Esteem

To know that they are understood in itself helps to raise persons'
self-esteem. It's strengthened again when they have a relationship that's
unconditional. Those in recovery can feel better about who they are.

Self-esteem is a person's view of his or her strengths and weaknesses. A person with a healthy self-esteem accepts weakness without
feeling inferior to others. A person with a healthy self-esteem builds up
others and has a purpose in life.

7. A Support System Must Eventually Involve the Family

The people who succeed in winning the battle of addictions have
support systems within their families. Even if it's negative support, it's
support—a fact not often understood.

The difference between an angry, negative support system and a
positive support system is the attitude. Both forms are expressions that
the family want to see recovery take place. Those of the angry, negative
support system believe they must force addicted persons to change or
they themselves have failed. Most of the time, once they get involved in

supporting persons in recovery—especially once they have received instructions on how to be supportive—they shift toward openly positive support.

Persons need to feel accepted and accountable in a positive, loving environment.

Types of Support Groups

Support systems come in different forms, but there must be some human support. Group support, which isn't for everyone, is based more on personality needs and availability. Regardless of the type, the Help Yourself Recovery System for addictions won't work without a support system of some sort. Support groups fall into several majors types.

1. Fellowships

Generally, fellowships follow a twelve-step approach to recovery and are designed for people who have a desire to stop specific addictions. They are the oldest and most popular form of self-help group support available for addictions.

Alcoholics Anonymous is a fellowship dedicated to individuals who want to stop drinking. Some groups are comfortable in expanding their definition to include other drugs.

Each group has a different personality. It is important to look at each group's personality to determine if it perpetuates compulsive themes or assists addicted persons in overcoming themes.

2. Religious Support Groups

A few Christian twelve-step programs exist. They frequently use the Bible and the twelve steps together. Overcomers Outreach is one of the largest and most popular Christian organizations for alcoholics and adult children of alcoholics.

Religious organizations can be valuable support systems. They are free, and they generally offer spiritual training. Often the religious groups are a mixture of people with differing problems. Even so, they are as supportive as those in twelve-step programs and may be appropriate for some individuals.

Persons comfortable in the "generic" groups need not feel guilty for not attending a group specializing in their addictions. All aspects of support can be provided by an accepting and loving group. As with twelve-step fellowships, people must develop accountability and priorities through an individual support person.

Whether specific groups or "generic" groups, they are worthwhile if they fulfill the seven functions of a support system.

Going to worship as a member of a congregation can actually be as effective as participating in a support group. Some individuals don't need much personal interaction. Listening to a minister's sermon and having an occasional conversation with another person who attends the church may be enough for them. Supplementing their support system with an individual is still necessary.

For some, Sunday school is a group support system. They learn about the Bible and human behavior and interact with others. Most churches have Sunday school classes that work through problems in marriage, family, and other areas. These groups can be extremely supportive and bonding. Combined with individual accountability, reality checks, and priority choices, they can provide an excellent support system.

Some churches have prayer and Bible study groups. These groups are usually smaller and more intimate than Sunday school classes. The relationships become more supportive and helping, meeting the needs of individuals who do well in small intimate sharing groups.

Small groups or extended group participation is a new movement in churches today. These church-related groups are often led by laypeople and provide for social needs. They include groups for the elderly, single parents, the recently divorced, and persons with AIDS. Larger, active churches can offer many options for the person seeking support through group participation.

3. Family Systems

When family systems combine with a spiritual support system, persons seeking recovery can achieve the inner peace often missed with other support systems alone.

Family systems are the ultimate in support groups.

An effective family system must follow a few basis concepts. For example, they must be honest with one another, and their honesty must allow them to speak up about frustration and confusion. Most problems in the family system are due to the lack of understanding of the other person's problems and the members take every remark as a personal attack.

A family support system should have some essential qualities.

Families need to provide *accountability*. Often controlling and demanding parents or spouses believe they have provided accountability, but they have actually set standards for others. These same people hide behind religion and rituals to justify their positions. True accountability within a family system comes from an agreed upon and understood set of behavior and rules, developed and agreed to by all members.

Acceptance is another key element. Unless members accept the others where they are, they won't change. Most accept others for what they should be, could be, or have the potential to become. They criticize, manipulate, and control the individuals in a hope that they will get them to that point. Accepting persons where they are and encouraging them through support enable them to make their own changes.

Families must offer *encouragement*. If they don't offer recognition, praise, love, and comfort, persons in recovery seek those qualities outside the family system.

Criticism is destructive. Addicted persons are so self-critical (if they're honest) that they don't need anyone else reminding them of the sixteen million times they have let themselves and others down.

Those who point their fingers tend to justify their actions by calling it constructive criticism. Regardless of what they call it, criticism is criticism. When a sheep wanders away, the shepherd doesn't beat it back into the fold; the shepherd leads it. By contrast, how often do families beat the one wandering rather than offer safety and direction?

Reality must be part of the family system. The family can be the most supportive or the most destructive environment. One reality is that persons within the family are selfish. They are individually seeking what is best for themselves and in their own way. What is best for the family system is important, and consensus from the whole family should determine the best way. If members are part of the solution and not caught up in feeling as if they are part of the cause for the problem, attitudes can change.

Families need *tolerance* of others' differences and personalities. It helps if they can genuinely thank God that the members of their family aren't all alike. The more similar people are, the more difficult their relationship. People within family systems that have two or more members with similar personalities can become dysfunctional rather quickly. When two or more persons in a family have personalities that are similar, conflicts often develop through competition. This competition may be for love, attention, material things, etc. If the persons are manipulative, they will use one another's emotions to meet their personal needs. Power, control, manipulation, and undermining each other often occur.

Families need to set realistic *expectations*. They need to establish clearly understood expectations and mutually agreed upon consequences in case of failure. The family must be consistent in support and in facing consequences of failure. Only when people know what is expected of them, have agreed to it, and consider it to be fair can they know how to be functional family members.

Individuals within families often set their expectations too high for the others to measure up to. These impossible standards come about because of their own inability to understand that everyone has faults and weaknesses. Some members are so busy blaming others for their faults, they become blind to their own weaknesses. All who set goals to change themselves fail at times. Persons who believe they don't fail have an exceptional ability to deceive themselves.

Families that recognize the strengths in others are families that attract other family members.

4. Outpatient Counseling

The greatest elements of outpatient counseling are not diagnostic skills and therapy techniques. The greatest counselors care, accept, and motivate, and they don't criticize or blame.

If the family system, the church, or the self-help support group doesn't provide accountability and acceptance, persons may want to try outpatient counseling.

5. Individual Support Systems

A friend, a minister, a family member, an employee, or an employer may be the best or only support system for some people. Often, individual relationships are more comfortable for persons than groups. If they like and respect the addicted persons, individuals can be supportive; respect is meant as valuing their decision to recover.

When those in recovery choose a support person, they may select the wrong person. The natural choice is someone who accepts the persons as they are, is a friend, and doesn't care if there are any changes. The individual can be supportive in acceptance but fail miserably in the area of accountability.

All people in recovery need a support system. They need to decide on a system that meets their needs.

Which Support System Is Best?

Individual personalities determine which support system is best for them. It doesn't matter whether the system understands the addiction. However, it must possess the qualities of acceptance, belonging, reality checks, and support.

Everyone is different. Every personality is unique. Every indi-

vidual has a different brain chemistry. Support systems must recognize these facts.

———————— ◆ ————————

Because of my research, personal experience, consultation with experts, and thousands of inquiries, I've set up what I sincerely believe is the strongest and most intensive system available outside inpatient or intensive outpatient services.

This system provides neurochemical evaluations, recovery programs, and strong support systems. If you or someone you know in recovery wants more information or you think we can be of help, please contact us: The Robertson Institute, Ltd., 3555 Pierce Road, Saginaw, MI 48604, 517-799-8720.

— 17 —

Developing a Support System

Asking directly for support is essential, whether it's a request to family members, support groups, church groups, fellowships, or individuals.

As I stressed in the previous chapter, persons in recovery need to develop their own support system. The system should be planned for and not just happen. Because addicted persons are vulnerable, they need to choose their support system carefully. And the support people need to be educated about their responsibilities.

Asking for support isn't a choice. Support is necessary for recovery.

When asking for support, those in recovery need to

• define the type of support they want.
• discuss what the support system can provide.
• decide if they want telephone, personal, crisis, or occasional support.

If persons ask for telephone support, they need to clarify whether calls are appropriate whenever *they* choose or only at specific times, such as biweekly checks. If they want crisis calls, they need to consider their supporters' schedules and preferences. They need to ask,

• "May I call at any hour?"
• "Are there times when you don't want me to call?"
• "Do you want to set a time limit on each call (such as thirty minutes or one hour)?"
• "What about your spouse's attitude? Does your spouse object to your getting calls in the middle of the night? Interrupting dinner?"

Persons in recovery also need to discuss and negotiate these issues:

- "What about your visiting me? Do you want to? Do I want you to visit?"
- "If we visit each other, what are the most convenient times?"
- "If I write a journal, may I share portions of it with you? With the whole group? With others?"

By the way, keeping a daily journal can be helpful for persons in recovery. It's a way for them to record their thoughts and frustrations and monitor their progress. When progress seems slow, they can turn to the journal and see how they felt a month, six months, or a year earlier. It often helps them to accept that they are progressing whether or not they feel like it.

Most support systems that fail set expectations too high.

For those in recovery, give consideration to those who stand with you.

- Remember, they have their own lives.
- Remember, they need free time and family time.
- Remember, they may not be available sometimes because of other commitments.
- Remember, they also get frustrated, especially when they expect progress that doesn't happen.

Changing Support Systems

Sometimes persons in recovery need to change support systems. Here are a few viable reasons for change.

1. They Outgrow the Support System

Lyle quit Overeaters Anonymous after eleven months. "No complaints about them," he said. "I love them. They helped me go through rough times. Nothing against them, but they seem to be staying back where I was six or seven months ago. I don't think they can help me in the steps I'm taking now."

2. Their Priorities Shift

Carol Ann found AA exactly what she needed for two months after she stopped drinking. "They introduced me to a Higher Power," she said. "For some, AA provides for all of their spiritual needs. But I'm ready to move actively into church membership."

3. They Don't Fit

Sometimes, and for various reasons, the support system simply doesn't work. It can be a clash of personalities. The support persons themselves may have their own unresolved issues that get triggered. When that happens, it's right to make changes.

———————— ♦ ————————

If the change promotes and encourages the growth of persons in recovery, it's a good change. *But* if those in recovery want to change the support system for unhealthy reasons (or if their supporters suspect the reasons are unhealthy), they need to rethink what they're doing. If they change to avoid pain or confrontation, they're running away. That is denial.

Elmer joined a Christian group that worked with a twelve-step program. The members agreed that if anyone chose to leave, he or she would tell the other members and then come back one more week to "finish up any old business." They agreed that no one would try to talk anyone else into staying.

Elmer was certain he had outgrown the group. As he had agreed, he told them he was quitting. He returned the next week. One quiet member said, "Elmer, I'll miss you a lot if you leave. You've been supportive of me when I've needed you." He then mentioned two occasions when Elmer had been there for him.

After two others told Elmer how much his presence had meant to them, he withdrew his intention to leave. He shared, "I kept thinking, I don't have a purpose here. I don't really support anyone. I just come here for me."

Andrew also chose to leave his group. When he told them he wouldn't be back, someone said, "For your sake, don't quit. You need us more than we need you right now. You don't like some of the things we say to you. If you leave, you may never really hear them."

Fortunately, Andrew didn't leave. Had he gone, he might have remained in denial. (Denial in this case meant that he was not "hearing" what they were trying to tell him.)

Quitting a support group for the wrong reasons can self-destruct the recovery process.

Responsibilities for Those in Recovery

Can you envision yourself standing in front of those individuals you want to support you? Imagine raising your right hand and making a pledge of your commitment. If they agree to be your support system, here are some things you promise them.

Those who want support need to set guidelines for their support system.

1. "I Promise to Be Accountable to You"

The most difficult problem of the support system is having to confront persons about unreached goals. If you make it clear that you want to be held accountable, you not only give them permission to confront but insist that they do.

Help your support system by telling them the most effective methods to get you to listen openly and nondefensively. You may say, "I get defensive when I feel blame or guilt being laid on me." Then tell them how you respond best: "I can open up whenever you use examples that are similar to my own experience."

Regularly update your support system so they can evaluate your accountability. You can do this through having a weekly meeting, sharing your journal, or making telephone calls. The method isn't as important as consistent contact.

2. "I Promise to Explain Specifically the Role I Expect You to Fill for Me"

What do you expect your support system to do? To be? Some individuals expect nothing more than having a sounding board or a passive listener. Others need active responses and suggestions. Whatever you envision your support system to be, say it or write it as clearly as possible. Your support system need to know this before they agree to fulfill the roles you want.

For example, you might say the following:

- "I want you to be my cheerleader." (At times you may feel like giving up. That's when you need encouragement from your support system.)
- "I want you to believe in me." (You need people to believe in you. Change is painful, but a positive support system can lift your spirits.)
- "I want you to tell me the truth even when I don't want to hear it." (A good support system, if asked, help you keep from lying to yourself or ignoring obvious truths you need to accept.)

Small, specific, and achievable goals are more important than big, vague, and unachievable hopes.

3. "I Promise to Share My Problems and Difficulties with You"

Sharing compulsive themes and addictions along with personal frustrations and difficulties is essential. We all cover up what we don't want to be. Share your fears and conflicts with those who genuinely care. They can ease your pain.

4. "I Promise to Share My Goals and Expectations with You"

Many support systems have failed because of unclear expectations and goals. You can prevent problems by honestly sharing goals and expectations. Make them as specific as you can.

Goals are different from expectations. For example, Joe's goals in life might be getting free from addiction and having a healthy relationship with his family. Expectations are the specific ways he will go about making those things happen by exercising three times a week, having family meetings every Saturday, and attending a breakfast devotional every Wednesday morning with men from his church.

Dreams are goals with time limits. Support systems help set the goals and the time limits.

5. "If You Support Me, I Have Expectations for You"

You are saying, "I expect you to accept me and stay with me, no matter what I say or do. But you do not have to approve my behavior." This statement isn't giving you permission to behave badly. It puts acceptance and approval beside each other.

Acceptance means they are committed to you. I recall a friend once saying, "God loves you. That means you can do nothing to make God love you less. Neither can you do anything that will make God love you more."

Approval means supporting your decision or behavior. They are not committing themselves to agree with everything you say or do. Disapproval of your actions can occur, even though the individuals in your support system fully accept you.

———————— ◆ ————————

Your support system can make or break your recovery. Choose carefully.

Tips for Those Who Want to Be Part of a Support System

Supporting persons who are recovering from addictions is a difficult task. The following guidelines can help you decide whether you want to be involved in the support system. Not being part of the support system doesn't mean you are uncaring. If you sincerely feel you lack the needed qualities, say so. The life of another human being is not something to trifle with.

But don't be scared away, either. If you are willing to try to give your best, you may be just what that already hurting person needs.

Those who need to rescue, control, or cling can't support others. (They are too caught up in meeting their own needs.)

Twelve statements appear below. The first four have to do with WHO YOU ARE; numbers five through twelve deal with WHAT YOU DO.

Try to see yourself facing the person in recovery. Imagine yourself raising your right hand and pledging your commitment.

1. "I Am a Stable, Healthy Person, and I Want to Help"

You're not perfect or fully accomplished, but you're balanced, you're together, and you like who you are, even though you're still putting the finishing touches on your life.

If you're balanced and healthy, you

- encourage instead of berate and condemn.
- offer options instead of saying, "This is the *only* way."
- allow others to grow at their own pace.
- understand when they fail because you remember your own failures.
- feel their struggles because you have struggled.
- trust because you have learned to trust God and others.

Persons who need to fix others usually harm those in recovery. Nobody needs "fixing"; everybody needs loving support.

FIGURE 17-1
Characteristics of a Support Person

Characteristics	Mind-Set
1. Stable, healthy, wants to help.	1. "I grow healthier and more balanced each day. I want the same for you."
2. Knows limitations.	2. "I give you my best. When you need more than I can give, I'll see that you find help."
3. Organized, ready.	3. "I do whatever I need to prepare myself to help you; I expect you to accomplish your daily and immediate goals."
4. Not professional counselor.	4. "I'm not a professional therapist; I'm a friend."
5. Accepting.	5. "I'm for you—no matter what."

2. "I Know My Own Limitations"

Often the best support comes when persons in recovery admit that they need something more than you can provide. You may suggest

- talking to a minister.
- consulting someone from their own cultural, ethnic, or racial background.
- seeking professional help, such as a therapist or physician.

When you feel uncomfortable and beyond your depth, be ready to suggest options for them to handle their particular issue.

3. "I Am Organized and Ready"

An effective support person schedules routine times to talk with those in recovery. You discuss such things as

- what they accomplished.
- what they didn't do.
- why they didn't complete what they agreed to.
- ways to make changes.

You may also suggest that they start keeping a journal. Each day they can write down their goals and objectives for that day.

4. "I Am Not a Professional Counselor"

The role of a support person is to provide encouragement, accountability, acceptance, reality checks, and opinions. Limit your "counseling" to being physically and emotionally present and suggesting options. To grow, persons in recovery need to make their own mistakes and achieve their own successes. You don't make decisions for them, but you support *them* when they make choices—even if you think they are unwise choices.

5. "I Accept You Without Conditions"

Many people struggle with feeling accepted. The greatest gift you can offer anyone is unqualified acceptance.

Acceptance means you allow persons to grow by looking at the process more than at their accomplishments. Their achievements or changing behavior can be slow, much slower than their understanding and insight.

6. "I Accept and Reinforce Your Accountability"

Persons in recovery *want* to be accountable to you as their supporter. And as a supporter, it is your responsibility not only to accept this accountability but also to reinforce their decision to be accountable.

Communicate with each other to discover the method that works best with your personalities: loving confrontation? Gentle prodding? Continued confrontation? You can be a better supporter when you know the style of interaction your partner is most comfortable with.

Accountability does not make demands. Accountability encourages, challenges, and suggests alternatives.

7. "I Do Whatever I Can to Build You Up"

The apostle Paul speaks of encouragement and support:

> Therefore encourage one another and build each other up, just as in fact you are doing. Now we ask you, brothers, to respect those who work hard among you, who are over you in the Lord and who admonish you. Hold them in the highest regard in love because of their work. Live in peace with each other. And we urge you, brothers, warn those who are idle, encourage the timid, help the weak, be patient with everyone. Make sure that nobody pays back wrong for wrong, but always try to be kind to each other and to everyone else. Be joyful always; pray continually; give thanks in all circumstances, for this is God's will for you in Christ Jesus (1 Thess. 5:11–18 NIV).

Reread the characteristics listed. Paul commends those who work hard, respect authority, live in peace, encourage the timid, help the weak, are patient, don't seek revenge, are kind, are joyful, pray daily, and are thankful.

You may not have all of these qualities or have them perfected, but if they define the kind of person you are working toward becoming, you may be an excellent support system. These personality traits also help to build self-esteem in others.

8. "I Will Listen—Really Listen—When You Speak"

An effective support person doesn't offer suggestions or come to conclusions without hearing every side of the discussion. Your role isn't to decide who is right—after all, you're not asked to be a judge—but to help those in recovery understand their thoughts and feelings. When they speak, they may not "hear" what they are saying about themselves. If you listen with your full attention, you may be able to point out things they didn't realize they said until you repeat the words. You can help by presenting other viewpoints and suggesting options. You can train yourself to listen to all the information and not get caught up in the crisis.

9. "I Learn, and I Keep on Learning"

You'll never know everything about supporting others, but you can learn much from experience and from caring. To be effective, you need to learn as much as you can about addiction, which includes neurochemistry, rewards, compulsive behavior, and the importance of following plans for diet, activity, and behavior. It's easier to encourage when you know the plan and the reasons behind the plan.

10. "I Help You Set Priorities and Goals"

Persons in recovery may need to be slowed down. Or they may need to be gently nudged. Some individuals in recovery want to attack all their problems at once. Others focus on an unchangeable issue of life, such as a medical problem or a disabling condition. When people have something that can't be changed ever or at that time, support persons can encourage them to accept those things. Understanding when to motivate and in what areas is crucial.

FIGURE 17-2
Responsibilities of a Support Person

Responsibilities	Mind-Set
1. Accepts and reinforces your accountability.	1. "I lovingly nudge you toward your goal of being accountable."
2. Does whatever he or she can to build you up.	2. "I'm here to help you become whatever you want to be."
3. Listens when you speak.	3. "I hear every word—with my heart."
4. Learns and keeps on learning.	4. "I'm always learning new things so that I can offer you a more effective support system."
5. Helps you set priorities and goals.	5. "Let's work together to help you set—and meet—your goals."
6. Is aware of your need for intimacy.	6. "I know the difference between intimacy and sex. I will guard against unhealthy relationships or sexual activity between us."
7. Provides reality checks.	7. "I promise to point you toward reality."

11. "I Am Aware of Your Need for Intimacy"

This statement also implies, "I know the difference between your need for intimacy, your tendency toward romantic attractions, or your pull toward sexual activity."

Whether you're married or single, if the recovering person is of the opposite sex refuse to be the primary support person.

Nothing draws the innocent into sexual relationships more easily than their wanting to help someone else.

Intimacy and sexuality are difficult for many to separate. A certain bond develops when you help and care deeply for another. If you feel the pull to be more than a support person or are getting angry with the response of the recovering person's spouse, do both of them a favor and become a friend, not a support person.

12. "I Provide Reality Checks"

Those in recovery really do need these checks. If you can question their "reality" in a supportive fashion and get them to explain how they came to such a conclusion, you are well on the way to providing the reality check they need.

———————— ◆ ————————

Can you be part of a support system?

Being asked means the recovering person has confidence in you. Consider this responsibility seriously. But also consider it joyfully.

Jesus said, "Whenever you did this for one of the least important of these brothers [or sisters] of mine, you did it for me!" (Matt. 25:40 TEV).

— 18 —

The Stages of Recovery

*The body will go through four phases to recover.
Knowing what phase is going on and what to
expect will help you get ready for the potential
problems in your recovery.*

Consider these examples of the stages of recovery.

Jonathan was addicted to alcohol, nicotine, and food. He discontinued his alcohol consumption because of a problem with his wife and family. During Stage 1 of recovery, he felt some anxiety and anger because of the brain responding to the lack of alcohol.

When he entered the second phase of addiction, the alcohol had affected his neurochemicals, and he began to decrease his compulsive eating. During Stage 2, he followed the diet for his brain and exercised accordingly. It took him twenty-two months to lose the craving for alcohol and sweets.

Next, Jonathan decided to eliminate his smoking. When he gave up cigarettes, he felt the craving develop again for food and alcohol. Essentially, his brain was readapting to life without nicotine.

He repeated his neurochemical test. (See chapter 21.) Then he changed his diet and exercise plans accordingly. In six months, he found himself totally free from his addictions, and he was thinking clearly.

Stage 3 was not an issue for him because he had no genetic addictions. He needed a total of two and one-half years to reach Stage 4, but he said, "It was worth it."

Cindy was a compulsive overeater and perfectionist. She had dieted numerous times with no success. She finally decided to consider neurochemical treatment since she had a family history of overeating.

She began to follow a diet program for her brain, an exercise program, and a behavioral program.

She lost weight within a week; by the end of the first year, she had lost fifty pounds. Cindy noticed a few mood changes but always used the techniques she had learned. She reached Stage 4 within a few weeks after having begun and kept losing weight as a part of feeling good. The process of feeling good about herself will be a lifetime experience.

Kirk is an alcoholic-workaholic who used neurochemical treatment in his recovery. When he eliminated alcohol, he found himself fearful and resentful at first. But he kept faithfully to his exercise, diet, and behavioral plan.

When he entered Stage 2 of recovery within forty days, he noticed severe mood swings. He eliminated his workaholic tendencies and continued the other diet and exercise programs; soon he felt better.

Stage 3 is as far as Kirk has gone. In the ten years he has been working on the genetic issues, he still fights with a negative attitude and frequent bouts of depression. Because of his previous alcoholism, he prefers to fight them rather than consider medication. Although the attitude and depression are clearing, the process is gradual. Kirk sees the light ahead and is progressing, but he realizes that, for him, it's a lifelong journey.

Norma is in Stage 4, the stage of normal neurochemistry. She was a compulsive gambler and romantic.

Problems continue in her life. Conflicts arise. "But I'm in control of my life now," she says. The biggest difference is that her feelings no longer cause her to lose control. She responds to choices, not compulsions.

She also speaks about being able to apologize, love, trust, and confront: "I feel so good about myself." Norma doesn't feel that others use her or ignore her, and she has overcome a sense of worthlessness. She knows her role in life, accepts her responsibilities and, at least most of the time, faces the hassles of life joyfully.

These four individuals illustrate the stages that people go through in recovery. And the brain does go through stages. During this time, it automatically adjusts and readjusts to changes in behavior, diet, and activities. Adjusting and readjusting are parts of the recovery process that can be used to the advantage of those in recovery—

IF they know what is happening in the brain

AND IF they are willing for the change to continue.

When persons strive for recovery, the brain goes through four stages. When I talk about the stages, people inevitably ask, "How long will it take for me to go through all of them?"

"As long as it takes," I sometimes say. "It depends on you and your chemical makeup. Besides, you can feel better *now*, regardless of how long it takes."

I don't like to emphasize how long the stages take. I prefer to point out five factors that make the difference. I put them into questions for people to think about.

Five Factors Affecting Stages of Recovery

1. "How Long Were You Addicted?"

The longer persons have been addicted, the longer the brain takes to recover completely. However, as soon as they start in recovery, they can begin to feel better. They receive rewards. But it still takes time for the neurological changes to occur, and in some cases it may never return to normal, most notably long-term or overdose situations with alcohol or other drugs.

They need to take offensive action to stop the addictive behavior. Going into the battle, they need to say, "I'm going to win!" This offensive management of addiction is doing something to prevent the addiction from returning.

This "doing something," as I point out elsewhere, means setting up a recovery plan and following it. For Cindy, in the opening illustration, it meant exercising daily, attending self-help groups weekly, and meeting with a support person two or three times a week. She chose those activities as her way to break the addiction cycle and to change her brain chemicals.

2. "How Do You Handle Your Thoughts When You Aren't in Control of the Situation?"

What I call defensive management refers to the process of doing something when thinking starts to become obsessive or compulsive about things that triggered the original addiction. Persons must take some kind of defensive action—a stand against the addiction. Initially, it's a hard fight. Through the years it seems to recur less frequently, but I warn persons that they need to set up a lifetime program of self-defense.

3. "How Severe Was Your Addiction?"

The more severe the addiction, the longer recovery takes. The brain adapted itself to the addiction and needs time to recover. The enzymes tend to adapt according to the severity of the addiction, which means they need longer to readjust.

FIGURE 18-1
Factors Affecting Stages of Recovery

Factor 1	Length of addiction.
Factor 2	How uncontrollable thoughts are handled.
Factor 3	Severity of the addiction.
Factor 4	Consistency of the recovery program.
Factor 5	Attainment of spiritual health.

4. "How Consistent Are You Willing to Be in Your Recovery Program?"

The amount of time it takes to recover depends on the consistency of the recovery program. A brain can't be reprogrammed with haphazard, occasional change. *Consistency* is the crucial factor. When thinking, actions, diets, and behavior change consistently, persons can recover fairly quickly.

Some persons think they can move more quickly through these stages by focusing constantly on their recovery. I sometimes say that they then eat, drink, and sleep the recovery process. That's not the answer.

Such action becomes obsessive. A constant focus on the addiction *isn't* a cure; it is a transfer of the addiction to a fear of the addiction. Persons need to be reminded that the brain takes time to change. The process can't be hurried.

5. "Are You Seeking Spiritual Recovery?"

Spiritual recovery is the most vital part of recovery. Thoughts change brain chemistry that creates or adds to the addictive process. Persons must change their thought patterns. If they attain spiritual health, their addiction clears away.

So many individuals want to skip this stage or consider it unnecessary. I list it last, but it's the foundation for the others.

Fighting the Symptoms

Understanding the recovery stages helps persons to know what symptoms to fight and when to fight. Here are four tips they need to bear in mind.

1. Fight One Battle at a Time

Persons who try to fight on all fronts at the same time exhaust themselves. When they understand the recovery process and the phases the brain goes through, they use their energy wisely and efficiently.

2. Stay in Control

In recovery, many persons fear the loss of control when they become depressed or anxious. They feel (or fear) the addiction is beginning to creep up on them again. If they sense it is coming, as well as why and when it is coming, they can prepare themselves. Then they fight with self-confidence.

3. Educate Supporters

People need support to make changes. When supportive individuals understand the stages of recovery, they know what to do. For example, when those in recovery go through rapid mood swings, others should understand that this is a normal phase in the recovery process.

4. Realize that Recovery Is a Process

Some individuals have initial dramatic experiences. After five years of being hooked on marijuana, Darryl went with his parents to a Billy Graham crusade. He said, "I felt something happening inside. I knew that I wanted to be free." At the end of the meeting, he went forward. Someone met him, talked to him, prayed for him, and started him on a Bible study program.

"I'm free!" he said to his parents. "I'll never touch pot again! I'm delivered."

God did something special and wonderful for Darryl. But he still had to go through a recovery process. He had abused his body for five years, and it needed time to move back to being normal. Darryl had a lot of problems until he understood this fact.

When persons use a controlled recovery plan, they make the process easier for themselves. If they try to force the recovery process, they get confused and sometimes fail. If they try to recover without a plan that warns them of the hazardous places, they tend to become negative and angry.

Stages of Recovery

Stage 1: Eliminating Behavior

Most people want their addictions to go away without their having any pain.

Stage 1 begins the day persons stop the behavior.

The most effective way to eliminate addictions is to figure out what thoughts triggered the behavior. Here are questions persons need to ask themselves to track down these thoughts:

- "*When* do I usually do the behavior?"
- "What was I thinking when I felt the need to do the behavior?"
- "Can I see a theme?"
  (This may not be apparent at first. They may have to think about this and observe themselves over a period of a few days. In time, they can begin to realize that they had thoughts of loneliness, rejection, or anger to set them off.)
- "Am I willing to set up a plan for doing an alternative behavior when the emotions develop?"
- "Am I willing to set up a plan to prevent the situations that cause the thoughts that trigger the behavior?"
  (For example, they can ask a friend to come over when they're experiencing feelings of rejection. They may want to keep a journal to record their thoughts and ideas. Just writing them down can help alleviate them.)

These simple questions can assist persons in avoiding the triggers of the unwanted behavior.

Typically, Stage 1 lasts from two to eight weeks. The neurochemicals bounce around, and persons finally begin to feel better. Many individuals feel recovery is going to be simple because they feel good. They experience no cravings, which sets up a false self-confidence.

When that happens, they may not continue to make consistent changes. "I'm all right now," they say. "I've beaten it." They are the ones who tend to relapse in Stage 2.

In the beginning, those in recovery still focus on one thing—the symptom of the addiction, such as drug dependence, workaholism, or compulsive cleaning. They may be free, but it takes time for them to assimilate this and adjust to life without smoking or gambling.

Many people have insisted to me that they can make changes while continuing their addictive behavior. In over ten thousand cases, I've never seen it happen!

Discontinuing the symptom doesn't cure the addiction, but it's a necessary first step. Addictive behavior covers up the real issues—the causes and needs behind compulsive actions. As long as persons focus on the cover-up symptom, the true issues don't and can't surface.

As long as persons continue their addictive behavior, they are not in recovery.

If persons attempt to change their neurochemistry while continuing in their addictions, they're wasting their time and energy. By continuing to drink or use drugs, they won't be able to get a clear picture of reality. The defense system acts like a blindfold, preventing them from seeing the truth about themselves. As soon as they decide to change—and they begin that change by eliminating the addictive behavior—their defenses aren't needed any longer. This brings about an almost automatic change in attitude. It's as if the blindfold has fallen off and they can see.

I've also observed that those in the support system become helpful only when they know that the change has begun. And how do they know? When their friends and loved ones stop overeating, exercising compulsively, or being promiscuous.

Eliminating the behavior isn't the end. The process is just beginning.

In this stage, even though they no longer use cocaine, they still think about it. Thoughts about the high they received or the calmness they felt may fight to control them—for a while. They need an awareness of the battles they face. Old compulsive habits can strike at them through their feelings, yearnings, desires, and mood shifts.

It takes time, but the brain chemistry changes.

The emotional pain in the first stage of recovery can feel devastating.

The first stage of recovery is a lonely time. No matter how committed persons are to recovery, a part of them still doesn't want to give up their addictions. Yet they know they must. Any reason—often the smallest, most insignificant thing—tempts them to return to their addictions. The car not starting one morning, the newspaper not arriving, or the bakery no longer preparing a favorite dessert seems minor to most people. But to those who struggle with addictive habits, it can be just the excuse they need to go backward.

In Stage 1, they feel, but those feelings aren't "real" emotions. Because they haven't been in touch with their real selves for a long time, they don't know the difference. Real emotions are the feelings they would experience if they had a balanced brain. The imbalanced brain causes feelings that seem absolutely "real," but they are a result of the misperception of reality.

Part of the process of Stage 1 is learning to react to true feelings while controlling misperceived ones. When I speak of controlling feelings, I don't mean that persons pretend those emotions don't exist. They acknowledge how they feel, but they refuse to let false emotions turn into actions. They also follow the recovery program that enables them to focus their minds elsewhere.

I give them a basic rule at the beginning: "The longer you focus on a feeling, the more power you give that feeling."

Here's an example of how that works. Sandra gave up her addiction to food, which had been triggered by feelings of rejection. At first it was a good experience—a euphoric feeling. "I did it! I'm free. I don't have to stuff myself every day until I'm actually in physical pain," she proclaimed.

Within ten days, the euphoria vanished. "Nobody really cares," she said. "Everyone stands back, just waiting for me to start overeating again." Actually, her feelings weren't accurate, but she didn't know that.

After two more weeks, Sandra became lonely and fearful. The more she thought about how lonely she felt, the more lonely she became. The voice of her still-confused emotions asserted, "People only tell you what they think you want to hear. They don't mean what they say."

By then Sandra had lost twenty pounds. Despite frequent positive comments such as, "You look good today," and "You've become so thin; sure wish I could get rid of that much weight," she didn't really hear them.

Since she stopped responding to the compliments, the people close to her stopped telling her how good she looked.

"They don't care," she told herself. "If they cared, they'd let me know. They'd say something positive. They'd tell me that I look good or that my new clothes fit nicely."

Sandra's loneliness soon overwhelmed her. That night she overate— the first time in four months. "Nobody cares anyway," she muttered to herself as she heaped her plate full for the fourth time.

What went wrong?

First, Sandra didn't know how to tell which feelings were real.

Second, she stayed with those feelings, letting them fill her mind. The longer she allowed the feelings to go unchecked, the more powerful they became.

Third, she didn't recognize the support of others because of her misperception of reality. Comments such as, "You look good today," were their way of trying to open up a conversation and to offer support. Most people don't know if they should ask individuals directly about their addictions, so they use a safe, superficial phrase as a door opener. Sandra interpreted the comments as indifference and superficiality instead of realizing that others were trying to be supportive.

Fourth, her friends didn't know what to do or say. They were afraid to speak outright about the addiction. Their discomfort convinced her of their lack of concern.

Fifth, as Sandra continued to feel lonely, chemical changes in the brain occurred. Soon she was thinking about her addiction to overeating again: *After all, nobody cares.*

Sandra's story didn't have to end in sadness. She will have a harder time when she decides later that she wants to be free from her compulsion. Unless she and her friends learn about the stages of recovery, she will likely fail again.

The dangerous cycle that emotions such as loneliness create could have been changed. With proper coaching in advance, Sandra would have been able to say to herself, "My friends haven't been addicted. They don't understand how it works or how people like me respond."

If she had been taught how, she could have taken the initiative. She could have gone to one or two friends and shared, "I'm lonely. I feel as if nobody in the whole world cares if I live or die."

Sandra didn't realize that her loneliness was actually a need for support. She had what I call the I'm-feeling-sorry-for-myself blues. *Those are normal reactions.* She could have prevented her sense of loneliness from overpowering her by focusing on being with her friends, sharing her pain and the frustration of addiction. She could have said, "I need you."

Sandra's story illustrates that recovery isn't easy or smooth. The more persons know at the beginning, however, the easier it is for them to go through the recovery stages.

The first stage of recovery is a fearful one. The brain craves the addiction. After all it has used that addictive habit for months (or for years!) to medicate itself. Since the brain no longer gets the relief, pain sets in.

Persons fear the pain. Most individuals will do anything to avoid pain, which is part of the reason they got entrapped in the addiction cycle. When they self-medicate through an addictive behavior, they don't have to face their pain. The mind focuses on the addiction as the way to take away the pain. They feel they've lost something, and that confuses and frightens them. They *need* the addiction. Unless they make behavioral replacements, the neurochemical changes won't take place, and they'll return to their addictions (or different ones).

The reward center is part of this as well. Persons can't just give up the reward provided by addictive habit *unless* they replace it with another reward that will satisfy the same need.

Rewards aren't just for Stage 1; persons must continue having them if they want to stay in recovery. Cravings are the body's way of saying, "I need...I need...I need..."

The emotions and cravings of the first stage have to do with the neurochemical rearrangements. When persons stopped their behavior or their drug, their neurochemistry changed.

During the first stage of recovery, fear is frequent, and rewards are a must.

The rewards may be spiritual, physical, or emotional. That's why I insist on persons implementing a plan that includes exercise, diet, behavioral changes, rewards, and supportive relationships.

In Stage 1, persons must replace addictive rewards with other rewards.

Jeff, a cocaine addict, needed excitatory neurotransmission. He had a theme of power. He particularly enjoyed the social part of his addiction.

After four years, Jeff discontinued his cocaine use. He relied on exercise to replace and stimulate his excitatory neurochemicals. For the first few weeks, he needed to exercise one or two hours every day to feel the release of the excitatory neurochemicals. As part of his plan, he joined a fitness club because the social atmosphere was also important to meet his social needs.

Since the drug had caused a misperception of power, Jeff's recovery included a spiritual element. He joined a group of businessmen who studied the Bible together every morning. Because he was able to talk about his power theme to them, they helped him by centering their Bible studies on this issue.

"Trying to have more power in myself only took me away from God," said Jeff later. "Once I understood that I needed God's power, my attitude changed." Then he quoted meaningful verses he had learned in his studies:

> I can do all things through Christ who strengthens me (Phil. 4:13).

> And He [God] said to me, "My grace is sufficient for you, for My strength is made perfect in weakness." Therefore most gladly I will rather boast in my infirmities, that the power of Christ may rest upon me. . . . For when I am weak, then I am strong (2 Cor. 12:9–10).

Jeff was creative in tailoring his behavioral needs to blend with his activity program. This change in his approach to life included a healing of spiritual, physical, and emotional components.

Stage 2: Experiencing Unpredictability

Normally, four to six months after discontinuing the addiction, Stage 2 begins. (There is a long gap from Stage 1 to Stage 2.) Persons start having neurohormonal effects. That is, the brain releases hormones and changes chemicals, and they often feel confused about the "normal" level of neurochemicals. This inrush of chemicals causes emotions to change without reason. One day persons feel on top of the world; the next day, they're severely depressed but can't identify any event or experience that caused the feeling.

Supportive friends, who don't understand what is going on, tell them, "Just get a grip on yourself. Keep going. Don't let this sidetrack you." They speak as if it's a simple matter of making up one's mind about what to do. They don't realize that those in recovery are depressed because the brain is trying to balance itself.

In Stage 2, although persons no longer have the addiction, the brain doesn't yet know what is normal.

This stage usually lasts from six months to two years. "The longest two years of my life," according to one person.

This stage is filled with emotional turmoil. The best way to describe it is to call it unpredictable. It begins easily enough, often with what we call the honeymoon phase.

The struggles in Stage 1 built up self-confidence. Persons felt good about their ability to handle problems. Many used self-discipline and a strong self-will without needing many internal changes. They even began to brag about their recovery. I've known many who become crusaders for the cause. Sometimes they've become fanatical, going to their old cohorts and trying to change them on the spot. "I just want everyone to know the joyous freedom I've experienced" is a typical assertion.

I hate to see this overconfidence. The honeymoon feeling frequently causes them to stop working on their recovery. The decreased pressure from others and their built-up self-confidence make them lose the motivation for change.

"I'm well. Fully recovered." I've heard those statements many, many times. They actually believe what they say. Unfortunately, they stop following their planned approach to recovery.

Typical comments go like this:

- "Aw, the diet was becoming too restrictive and not helping me much anyway."
- "I'm so busy with my new life, I don't have time to waste on an exercise program."
- "Yeah, I read the Bible every day. Didn't fail once. But you know, after a while, well, it got kind of boring. I mean, I was reading the same stuff over and over."

Persons who make such comments don't understand (or have forgotten) how the recovery plan helps.

Those who stop the program learn that self-will eventually fails. They can't push themselves forever. Since they have no backup or support ready, they generally return to their addictions.

Then denial kicks in. They say, "I'm not really doing it again," or "Just this once. You know, to give myself a little courage."

They blame their friends, their bosses, their financial status, their daily pressures. They can come up with a million reasons why the recovery program didn't work for them.

Sometimes they get into self-blame: "I'm a failure. That's all I've ever been."

I've listened to hundreds of people tell me thousands of stories. They almost never say, "I let myself down because I thought I could do it alone."

They are the problem. Self-discipline wins the victory in the battle of addictions. The difference between self-will and self-discipline is confusing to many in recovery. Self-will is the attempt to discontinue an addictive behavior on their own. It's an attitude of "I can do it; I don't need help." This going-it-alone attitude doesn't usually work because the behavior is physiologically and psychologically stronger, and the addictive behavior is an automatic reaction to stress. Self-discipline, however, involves the actions that bring change. When persons know what to do to recover, self-discipline is the willingness to continue to do it.

Self-discipline is crucial in Stage 2. Neurochemicals became imbalanced through consistent and long-term behavior. The reverse, which is neurochemical health, also comes through consistent, repeated, long-term behavior.

If the brain chemicals bounce back and forth because of an inconstant program, most people don't work on their compulsive themes. And they usually fail.

In Stage 2, the brain is unpredictable, and the emotions are unstable. Follow the plan.

In Stage 2, the brain begins to play tricks on persons. They may experience rejection and fear. They don't recognize support or feel they have rewards. They often think of the addiction as more positive than the recovery. When that happens, transferring to other addictions becomes common.

During this time of confusion in Stage 2, they often grow angry. They lash out at everyone. They develop extremes in their thinking. They may want to quit everything they are doing, trade in the spouse, kids, and job for something new and exciting.

FIGURE 18-2
Stages of Recovery

Stage 1	Eliminating behavior	As long as persons continue their addictive behavior, they are not in recovery.
Stage 2	Experiencing unpredictability	Although persons no longer have the addiction, the brain doesn't yet know what is normal.
Stage 3	Achieving genetic recovery	Neurochemicals haven't changed, but persons have transferred their addictions.
Stage 4	Feeling normal like everybody else	Fully recovered individuals have problems, but they have learned techniques for getting control of their lives.

They also resist change. They may say, "I'm already trying as hard as I can. Now it's time for others to change."

BE WARNED: Persons in Stage 2 tend to believe that they won't be happy unless others change. So they resist changing and wait for others to change first.

Because of the unpredictability of Stage 2, many stop trying. They return to their addictions.

Stage 3: Achieving Neurochemical Recovery

Most people in recovery are in Stage 3 today. Neurochemicals haven't changed, but they have transferred their addictions.

They

- are depressed.
- feel negative.
- are fearful.
- have unrealistic expectations.
- believe others have let them down.
- feel resentful and angry.
- continue to focus on their addictions.
- haven't developed an intimacy with God, others, or themselves.

Persons may feel miserable even after reaching Stage 3. First, they didn't follow the neurochemical recovery techniques. Second, genetic alterations (chemical imbalances acquired from their parents) prevent them from feeling good.

Most people recover completely if they find joy, peace, and fulfillment in their lives and if they use neurochemical techniques.

Others have a genetic component that may require the use of

medication to control their neurochemical alterations. For instance, Leslie had a neurochemical imbalance passed on by her mother. She saw life only through the lenses of depression. She began antidepression medication along with diet, exercise, and behavioral techniques of her recovery program. Over the next two years she tapered the amount of her medicine as the other techniques caught up.

The medication wasn't to control anxiety, depression, or mood swings but to normalize genetically influenced neurochemical makeup. Few people who work hard in recovery require medication. However, in the beginning stages, many people request (sometimes demand!) medication without trying drug-free recovery. When they *want* (rather than *need*) drugs, at least two things are going on: (1) They are still trying to run away from the pain involved in recovery, and (2) they want to continue the addiction experience.

Stage 4: Feeling Normal Like Everybody Else

At Stage 4, fully recovered individuals have problems, but they have learned techniques for getting control of their lives. They have learned to make choices and often say, "I feel normal. I feel like everybody else."

Stage 4 is a process. A person feels better longer each day, and then feels better for more days each month. Eventually, bad days come only when something such as death or some other uncontrollable circumstance occurs. Stage 4 lasts forever.

Part III

---------- ◆ ----------

THE PROGRAM

—19—

Your Systems at Work

Seven environmental areas have a profound influence on your choice of addiction.

The information in this chapter will show you how to build your individualized recovery program. This program gives you rewards through diet, activity, and behavioral changes. At the same time you begin to balance your brain.

BUT FIRST, you need to identify the "systems" that influence you.

You see, seven environmental areas have had a profound influence on your choice of addiction. All or some of these areas are responsible for your initial choice that became automatic through the Pavlovian response: (1) Family systems; (2) Friends and peer influences; (3) Cultural influences; (4) Sex roles; (5) Social values; (6) Racial and ethnic influences; and (7) Religious values.

What to do: 1. Read the information about each system. 2. Answer each question. 3. Record your total.

1. Family Systems

You learned certain forms of behavior from your system, that is, from the way your particular family handled conflict. (This refers to your family of origin.) If you can identify the behavior you were taught, often by silence or negative example, you can grasp why you behave as you do.

Answer yes or no to the following questions.

1. Did your family system use behavior similar to yours to overcome bad or depressed times?   Yes ☐   No ☐

2. Did your family system use similar behavior to celebrate good times?   Yes ☐   No ☐

3. Did your parents ever indicate—even by their approving

197

attitude—that the behavior was part of what being good meant or what they highly respected in an individual? Yes ☐ No ☐

4. Did any of your siblings turn to similar behavior when they celebrated or overcame tough times? Yes ☐ No ☐

5. Did your behavior begin before the age of twelve? Yes ☐ No ☐

Scoring: One "yes" answer reflects some family system conflicts but is normal. Two "yes" answers reflect conflicts significant enough to cause a problem for most people. Three indicate significant conflict. Four "yes" answers would indicate a major conflict caused by the family system.

Answering yes to three or more generally means the family has had a considerable impact in teaching you this form of behavior. The family needs to be educated to provide support for you or other family members.

Your Score _____

2. Friends and Peer Influences

Friends or peers can have a considerable influence on the choice of your addiction. Everyone needs approval and acceptance from friends. Sometimes this need overshadows what is healthy. As a general rule, individuals want approval more than they want personal comfort. Often peer acceptance becomes more important than values.

Answer yes or no to the following questions.

1. Did one or more of your closest friends experience the same addiction? Yes ☐ No ☐

2. Was the addiction or behavior considered to be "cool," respected, positive, or necessary by your friends? Yes ☐ No ☐

3. Did any friends mention or have you observed that the same form of behavior may be a problem for them? Yes ☐ No ☐

4. Did any friends mention or have you observed that their similar behavior caused them a problem with their families or others?
Yes ☐ No ☐

5. Did persons close to you ever mention or have you observed that your behavior was creating a problem for them? Yes ☐ No ☐

Scoring: A "yes" answer to two or more questions indicates that your friends or peers have had a significant influence on your behavior. Your friends need to be educated or replaced if support is desired from them.

Your Score _____

3. Cultural Influences

Cultural influences can affect the development of your addictive disorders. Culture in this sense often means subculture and refers to the attitudes and teachings of the people who live in your community, town, or neighborhood.

Most cultures don't intentionally teach addictions. Members of a community learn them through various unwritten or unspoken rules.

Answer yes or no to the following questions.

1. Does your culture tend to use this same behavior to celebrate events?   Yes ☐   No ☐

2. Does your culture tend to use the behavior to assist in overcoming sadness, conflict, or death?   Yes ☐   No ☐

3. Do many people of your community experience difficulty with the same addiction or behavior?   Yes ☐   No ☐

4. Is it an internally held cultural belief that the behavior or addiction is actually a strength in character?   Yes ☐   No ☐

5. Would it be difficult to admit your addiction to others of the same culture? (You're afraid that if you do, they won't accept it as a problem.)   Yes ☐   No ☐

Scoring: One "yes" answer reflects some cultural influences, but that is normal. Two "yes" answers reflect enough influence to cause a problem for most people. Three "yes" answers indicate significant influence. Four "yes" answers indicate an area of major conflict. If you seek recovery, you may benefit from talking with a recovering person from your cultural background about cultural values.

Your Score _____

4. Sex Roles

Gender or sex-role definitions vary among cultures and racial backgrounds. These unwritten rules are taught through generations, often without verifying the accuracy of such presuppositions. Understanding the impact of sex roles is important for recovery.

Answer yes or no to the following questions.

1. Is the behavior that has become an addiction considered a character strength within your sex?   Yes ☐   No ☐

2. Is the behavior taught to others of the same gender considered a desirable behavior from the previous generation?   Yes ☐   No ☐

3. Is the behavior taught to others of the same sex considered a character strength for the next generation?   Yes ☐   No ☐

4. Can the behavior be viewed as maverick, gutsy, or eccentric by others of the same sex?   Yes ☐   No ☐

5. Is the behavior held in esteem by those of the opposite sex? Yes ☐   No ☐

Scoring: One "yes" answer reflects normal sex-role conflicts. Two "yes" answers reflect conflicts significant enough to cause a problem for most people. Three "yes" answers indicate a significant conflict. Four "yes" answers indicate that this is a major area of conflict for you; gender-role definitions have had an impact on your addiction.

A support person of your same sex may be helpful in identifying the influences that gender-role definitions have had on creating the addiction. Most teachings of this kind are unfounded, passed on, or partial truths. They often hinder recovery.

Your Score _____

5. Social Values

Social value systems can play a role in shaping the type of behavior that becomes an addiction. Your financial status, employment position, intellect, beauty, and other individual social issues can significantly influence your behavior choices.

Answer yes or no to the following questions.

1. Do individuals with similar social backgrounds experience similar behaviors?   Yes ☐   No ☐

2. Have individuals with similar social backgrounds described a problem with the same addiction? Or have you noticed the same addiction in them?   Yes ☐   No ☐

3. Is the behavior considered a character strength by others of similar social backgrounds?   Yes ☐   No ☐

4. Do you believe that those with similar social backgrounds are more prone to developing this same addiction?   Yes ☐   No ☐

5. Is the behavior part of the social norm within the value system of your society?   Yes ☐   No ☐

Scoring: One "yes" answer reflects normal social conflicts. Two "yes" answers reflect social conflicts significant enough to cause a problem for most people. Three indicate significant conflict. Four indicate that this is a major conflict area for you.

If you answered yes to two or more questions, the social value system has influenced your choice of behavior in the addictive process.

Your Score _____

6. Racial and Ethnic Influences

Racial and ethnic backgrounds can cause similar predispositions to developing specific addictions. No race is protected from addictions. Neither is one race more addiction inclined than others. The number of persons addicted and their level of addiction to a specific type vary among races and ethnic backgrounds. The determination of racial influence on your addiction is important.

Answer yes or no to the following questions.

1. Is this a common addiction to people of your race or ethnic background?   Yes ☐   No ☐

2. Is the addiction or behavior held in high esteem or considered a character strength by members of your ethnic background? Yes ☐   No ☐

3. Would it be difficult to admit to the addiction to members of your ethnic background?   Yes ☐   No ☐

4. Does your race or ethnic background have unwritten and unspoken rules that support the behavior that has become an addiction? Yes ☐   No ☐

5. Is it common within the race or ethnic group to have a problem with this form of addiction?   Yes ☐   No ☐

Scoring: One "yes" answer reflects normal influences. Two "yes" answers reflect influences significant enough to cause a problem for most people. Three "yes" answers indicate significant influence. Four "yes" answers indicate a major conflict area.

If you are seeking support in your recovery, you may find it helpful to talk with a recovering person of the same race or ethnic background who has the same addiction.

Your Score _____

7. Religious Values

Religious values have considerable influence on most people's choice of addictive behavior. Religious values may be taught by a church or religious group, family members, or friends. Your values may or may not be correct, but you learned them as absolute truths. Any variation from them likely results in a distancing from your faith.

Answer yes or no to the following questions.

1. Is the behavior considered a lesser sin than others within your religious group?   Yes ☐   No ☐

2. Is the behavior rarely mentioned as a sin or problem?
Yes ☐   No ☐

3. Does the behavior hold less guilt than other behavior your group considers sin or weakness?   Yes ☐   No ☐

4. If your religious peers referred to this behavior, would they consider it a character strength?   Yes ☐   No ☐

5. Is there a relief from guilt when the addiction is compared to other behavior that could have been addicting?   Yes ☐   No ☐

Scoring: One "yes" answer reflects normal religious value conflicts. Two "yes" answers reflect significant enough conflict to cause a problem for most people. Three "yes" answers indicate significant conflict. Four "yes" answers indicate that this is a major conflict area for you. Two or more "yes" answers suggest that religion has a strong influence on your choice of addictions.

This choice is generally the opposite of the other environmental influences. Religious teachings can move people from the popular "big sin" addictions to hidden addictions. People with strong religious values tend to choose romance addictions, compulsive overeating, perfectionism, and control. Religious people may become alcoholic or drug dependent, but such people usually leave their church or religious affiliation when that occurs. Most of the other addictions can be hidden better and don't cause the same level of avoidance in the church.

Your Score _____

Your Total Score _____

If your total score is greater than twenty or any single area is more than three, your life-style and social life are affecting your addiction. You should consider support for change and accountability in your life.

The best kind of support for you would be someone who understands the environmental impact you have experienced. Consider the power of the unwritten rules of family, friends, race, culture, church, and others when you want approval to make changes.

—20—

External and Internal Factors

Stresses outside you and within you can hamper recovery. Identifying these stresses and learning how they affect neurochemical levels is important.

Your External Factors

Many external factors contribute to the development of addictive behavior. These external factors (or stresses) change neurochemical levels so you behave in a certain way to relieve the stress or reward yourself.

Remember these principles:

- If an external conflict causes a depressed feeling, it creates a need (compensatory behavior) for an "upper," an excitatory type of behavior, or it causes (causative behavior) a depressed behavior.
- If an external conflict creates anxiety, it creates a need (compensatory behavior) for a "downer," an antiexcitement behavior, or it causes (causative behavior) an excitement behavior.
- If an external conflict occurs frequently, a Pavlovian response develops, and *you then have the potential for addiction*.

When we talk about external conflict, the five major areas involved are (1) Social, (2) Relationship, (3) Job or school, (4) Physical health, and (5) Financial.

Any or all of these areas can develop external stresses that affect the addictive behavior you choose.

1. Social Factors

Social stressors occur in any number of ways, such as when you seek the approval and acceptance of others or when you have conflicts with friends.

Answer yes or no to the following questions.

1. Do your close friends gossip about others when they aren't around?   Yes ☐   No ☐

2. Is there competition within your circle of friends that makes you feel tense?   Yes ☐   No ☐

3. Do you feel jealous when a particularly close friend spends more time with someone else?   Yes ☐   No ☐

4. Is your most critical friend part of your church, school, or job and social circles? Or is your most critical friend involved in all areas of your life?   Yes ☐   No ☐

5. Do you frequently feel the lack of friendship? Or are you a loner?   Yes ☐   No ☐

Scoring: One "yes" answer reflects the normal level of social conflicts. Two indicate conflicts significant enough to cause a problem for most people. Three "yes" answers suggest significant conflict. Four "yes" answers indicate that this is a major area of conflict for you.

If you answered yes to three or more questions, your particular social system can create stress in your life. If you resort to a particular type of behavior frequently in response to such stress, you could develop an addiction.

Your Score   _____

2. Relationship Factors

Your stressful relationships can lead to compulsive behavior. The need of approval from a spouse, parents, or others significantly affects the choice of addictive behavior.

Answer yes or no to the following questions.

1. Does the relationship increase the level of stress?   Yes ☐   No ☐

2. Do you have frequent conflict in the relationship?
Yes ☐   No ☐

3. Do you turn to recreational activities or seek ways outside the relationship to relieve the stress?   Yes ☐   No ☐

4. Is communication difficult in the relationship?   Yes ☐   No ☐

5. Do you feel "put down," controlled, or ignored in the relationship?   Yes ☐   No ☐

Scoring: One "yes" answer reflects the normal level of relational conflicts. Two indicate conflicts significant enough to cause a problem for most people. Three "yes" answers suggest significant conflict. Four "yes" answers indicate that this is a major area of conflict for you. If you said yes to two or more questions, the conflicts of your relationship may contribute to neurochemical changes and addictions.

Your Score   _____

3. Job or School Factors

Job or school stressors are external factors that can contribute to an addiction. Along with this form of stress comes performance-expectation stress.

Answer yes or no to the following questions.

1. Is your identity at least partially dependent on doing your job or attending school? Yes ☐ No ☐

2. Do you feel inadequate at your job or at school? Yes ☐ No ☐

3. Does a supervisor or teacher insist that you could have better results, "If only you ..."? Yes ☐ No ☐

4. Are you feeling frustrated at not being appreciated for your efforts? Yes ☐ No ☐

5. Are you threatened with a job loss or an inability to continue the educational process? Yes ☐ No ☐

Scoring: One "yes" answer reflects the normal level of conflicts. Two indicate conflicts significant enough to cause a problem for most people. Three "yes" answers suggest significant conflict. Four "yes" answers indicate that this is a major area of conflict for you.

If you answered yes to two or more questions, job or school pressures may contribute to the continuance of your addictive behavior.

Your Score _____

4. Physical Health Factors

Your physical health will be a factor in the choice of addictions and your ability to bounce back from neurochemical alterations. An out-of-balance body can create neurochemical alterations and contribute to the addictive process.

Answer yes or no to the following questions.

1. Do you take daily medication to treat a medical condition?
Yes ☐ No ☐

2. Is your weight outside normal ranges for your body size and type? Yes ☐ No ☐

3. Do you struggle to follow a regular exercise program?
Yes ☐ No ☐

4. If you exercise, do you do it compulsively (feel you *must*) to stay in shape? Yes ☐ No ☐

5. Do you have any physical problems that you need to take care of, or do you need to change your life-style? Yes ☐ No ☐

Scoring: One "yes" answer reflects the normal level of physical health conflicts. Two indicate conflicts significant enough to cause a problem for most people. Three "yes" answers suggest significant conflict. Four "yes" answers indicate that this is a major area of conflict for you. "Yes" answers to two or more questions suggest a physical health component that may keep the brain from becoming healthy.

Your Score _____

5. Financial Factors

The handling of money can cause stress in many individuals. These difficulties, in turn, can create neurochemical alterations. Excesses and deficits of income can alter your neurochemicals and create or contribute to the addictive process.

Answer yes or no to the following questions.

1. Is your income less than your expenses?   Yes ☐   No ☐
2. Does the lack or surplus of money affect your moods?
Yes ☐   No ☐
3. Are people trying to take advantage of your financial situation?
Yes ☐   No ☐
4. Are you considering ways to increase your income?
Yes ☐   No ☐
5. Do you put a lot of energy into managing finances?
Yes ☐   No ☐

Scoring: One "yes" answer reflects the normal level of financial conflicts. Two "yes" answers indicate conflicts significant enough to cause a problem for most people. Three "yes" answers suggest significant conflict. Four "yes" answers indicate that this is a major area of conflict for you.

If you answered yes to three or more questions, you have a financial stress level that is adequate to change your neurochemical levels. Financial stresses could contribute to your behavior.

Your Score _____

Your Internal Factors

If you have had internal conflicts—with your self-esteem and spiritual values—they could have created chemical imbalances in your brain. You chose a form of behavior that lessened your uncomfortable feelings. If your behavior is consistent so that it becomes habitual, you have established a Pavlovian response. You have given yourself to an addictive form of behavior.

1. Self-Esteem

Self-esteem refers to the way you feel about yourself. If you value yourself as a person, you have a high self-esteem level. Many factors determine how you feel about yourself: your self-expectations, your needs, your communication skills, and anything else that can change how you view yourself. When chemicals in the brain are out of balance, you won't be able to view yourself or life realistically; that is, you'll have a distorted perception of the way things are.

This distorted view of life can weaken your emotional stability and affect the level of your self-esteem. Essential to the recovery process is a neurochemical balance and the resolution of your internal (emotional) conflicts.

Answer yes or no to the following questions.

1. Most of the time, do you feel that others are better than you? Yes ☐ No ☐

2. Are your moods unpredictable? Yes ☐ No ☐

3. Do you usually feel angry when others succeed or achieve a goal? Yes ☐ No ☐

4. Do you frequently compare yourself to others? Yes ☐ No ☐

5. Do you feel isolated from most people, wishing you had a few close (or intimate) relationships to provide you with security and comfort? Yes ☐ No ☐

Scoring: One "yes" answer reflects the normal conflicts in the area of self-esteem. Two "yes" answers indicate conflicts significant enough to cause a problem for most people. Three "yes" answers suggest significant conflict. Four "yes" answers indicate that this is a major area of conflict for you.

"Yes" answers to two or more questions indicate that self-esteem and emotional stability affect your neurochemical levels. These changes can cause your behavior to develop into an addiction.

Your Score _____

2. Spiritual Conflicts

Although most people have spiritual conflicts, they are often unaware of them. Spiritual conflicts adversely affect the emotions, the chemicals in the brain, and other factors.

Answer yes or no to the following questions.

1. Do you frequently feel guilty? Yes ☐ No ☐

2. Do you have an undefined purpose in life? (You're just not sure what life is all about and why you are here.) Yes ☐ No ☐

3. Do you feel an inner void and wish you had peace?
Yes ☐ No ☐

4. Do you frequently think God is distant from you?
Yes ☐ No ☐

5. Do you either avoid church attendance or make attendance the extent of your spiritual involvement?   Yes ☐   No ☐

Scoring: One "yes" answer reflects the normal level of spiritual conflicts. Two "yes" answers indicate conflicts significant enough to cause a problem for most people. Three "yes" answers suggest significant conflict. Four "yes" answers indicate that this is a major area of conflict for you.

If you answered yes to two or more questions, spiritual conflicts are definitely contributing to your addiction. They can prevent complete recovery.

Your Score _____
Your Total Score for Internal and External Factors _____

Three in any given category or a total of twenty indicates the need to change the way you view life and yourself.

—21—

YOUR Neurochemical Personality

Your neurochemical personality will determine what type of recovery will work for you and what type of chemicals you prefer.

Arousal or Satiation Personality?

Ken and Les are brothers who grew up in a home with an alcoholic mother and a physically abusive father. Both brothers have problems with addiction. Ken has become addicted to cocaine—an upper. Les is addicted to tranquilizers such as Valium. Why the difference? Because they have different neurochemical personalities.

Ken has an *arousal neurochemical personality* because he moves toward the addictive behavior that gets him stirred, excited, stimulated. Les, however, is a *satiation neurochemical personality*. He seeks the addictive behavior that calms him and gives him peace and a sense of security.

The two brothers illustrate the two basic types of neurochemical reward centers—the arousal and the satiation. The personality type depends on what they respond to in their neurochemical reward center. One type isn't superior to the other; they are just two different ways of responding to life.

The Arousal Personality

The arousal personality is excitement oriented, preferring feelings of excitement or "gas-pedal" neurochemical release. These personalities prefer a fast pace over relaxation and boredom. To relax, such personalities must do something to make them feel good. They may enjoy cross-country skiing, diving, swimming, running, and other action-oriented activities. They are more prone to developing addictions to gambling, sex, risk taking, and drugs. They will be attracted to emotional-oriented churches, exercise programs, and changes that provide release of excitatory neurochemicals. They are afraid of being depressed, being alone, and having nothing to do. Often, if things are going fine, they will create a problem to solve. Anxiety and stress are more comfortable to them than boredom or depression.

The Satiation Personality

The satiation personality is antianxiety oriented and enjoys the feeling of relaxation or "brake-pedal" neurochemical release. The mellowing out and self-reflecting spirit means these personalities enjoy relationship activities more than action-oriented activities. They are prone to food, media fascination (especially TV), relationship, perfection, and control addictions. They are so afraid of anxiety, they often become perfectionists and controllers to ward off change or to stop changes from causing anxiety. For them, boredom is more comfortable than excitement.

———————— ◆ ————————

Obviously, most people have a combination of needs, but they generally show a preference for one or the other. This preference is most evident when they feel out of balance or when things "aren't quite right."

You need to become aware of your neurochemical personality because it helps you to understand four important things:

1. What will work in your recovery.
2. What you will unconsciously resist.
3. Whether your addiction is consistent with your personality.
4. Which specific activities will provide you with a reward or cause you to feel good.

To discover your neurochemical personality, answer the twenty-four questions with yes or no. When you're not certain, use yes if it is generally true. Please answer every question.

1. Do you choose activities that require active participation? Yes ☐ No ☐

2. Do you choose activities in which you passively participate or watch the active participants?   Yes ☐ No ☐

3. Are you comfortable socializing with large groups of people? Yes ☐ No ☐

4. Have you ever had any trouble with the police when you were involved in your preferred activities?   Yes ☐   No ☐

5. Do you enjoy watching movies in which violence plays a part?   Yes ☐   No ☐

6. Do you enjoy gambling?   Yes ☐   No ☐

7. Do you frequently buy lottery tickets or bet on sporting events? Yes ☐   No ☐

8. Do you prefer to drink alcohol or use drugs (including caffeine and nicotine) in social settings?   Yes ☐   No ☐

9. Do you get pleasure from drugs that increase your energy level (including nicotine and caffeine)?   Yes ☐   No ☐

10. Do you feel good when you engage in risk-oriented activities (such as speeding, mountain climbing, hang gliding, racing)? Yes ☐   No ☐

11. When you feel stressed, do sexual activities relax you and lessen the stress?   Yes ☐   No ☐

12. Do you prefer to participate in groups (including religious groups) that have strong beliefs and a lot of emotional involvement? Yes ☐   No ☐

13. Do you prefer intimate, close communications with small groups?   Yes ☐   No ☐

14. Do you usually continue to eat even after you are full? Yes ☐   No ☐

15. Do you eat when you are depressed, anxious, or angry? Yes ☐   No ☐

16. Do you use alcohol or drugs to relax?   Yes ☐   No ☐

17. Do you like drugs that decrease your anxiety (including prescription medications)?   Yes ☐   No ☐

18. Do you try to find ways to avoid conflict?   Yes ☐   No ☐

19. On average, do you watch more than fifteen hours of television a week?   Yes ☐   No ☐

20. Do you attend movies or watch movies on TV at least twice weekly?   Yes ☐   No ☐

21. Do you rent videotapes at least once a week?   Yes ☐   No ☐

22. When depressed, do you participate in sexual activities to increase your energy?   Yes ☐   No ☐

23. Are you a member or do you participate in groups (including religious groups) that have strict ethics, rules, or codes of behavior? Yes ☐   No ☐

24. Do you spend much of your free time alone?   Yes ☐   No ☐

Scoring:
1. Add your "yes" answers for 1 through 12 and put the total here: _____
2. Add your "yes" answers for 13 through 24 and put the total here: _____

If you had more "yes" answers to questions 1 through 12, you are an arousal personality. If you had more "yes" answers to 13 through 24, you are a satiation personality. If you have equal numbers of "yes" answers and "no" answers, read the description of each personality and choose the one you believe describes you most correctly.

I AM A/AN _____ PERSONALITY.

This information is crucial for your recovery. Your choices of social activities, physical activities, diet plans, therapy, and support options relate to your reward center type.

Baseline Neurotransmission Levels

Next, you need to identify your baseline neurotransmission levels as part of the necessary information to set up your recovery program.

I can help you figure out your baseline neurotransmission levels by looking at genetic and generational factors. If your baseline neurotransmission level is caused by genetics or generational levels, your recovery will focus on changing the neurochemical levels. If your addiction changed your baseline neurotransmission level, you will need to adapt your behavior.

Genetic or Generational Influences

The following questions can assist in determining if your addiction has genetic or generational influences.

1. Does/did your biological father have this addiction?
Yes ☐ No ☐
2. Does/did your biological mother have this addiction?
Yes ☐ No ☐
3. Does/did this addiction appear in two or more of your biological grandparents? Yes ☐ No ☐
4. Does/did this addiction appear in two or more of your biological siblings? Yes ☐ No ☐
5. Does/did this addiction appear in one or more of your biological children? Yes ☐ No ☐

Total Yes _____   *Total No* _____

"Yes" answers to two or more questions indicate the presence of generational or genetic influences. Four or more "yes" answers indicate that genetic or generational influences play a primary role in your addictive process. Your recovery will certainly require neurochemical manipulation through various techniques.

Acquired Influences

An acquired imbalance comes from consistent, long-term behavior, doing something such as smoking, drinking, overeating, or gambling. The following questions will assist you in deciding if your addiction is acquired.

1. Have you done this behavior at least three times weekly for at least six months?   Yes ☐   No ☐

2. Have you felt more depressed or in a "low" mood since your addiction began?   Yes ☐   No ☐

3. Have you felt more anxiety or nervousness since your addiction began?   Yes ☐   No ☐

4. When you have stopped your behavior, has your depression increased?   Yes ☐   No ☐

5. When you have stopped your behavior, has your anxiety increased?   Yes ☐   No ☐

Total Yes _____ *Total No* _____

A "yes" answer to two or more questions indicates the addiction or behavior has changed your baseline neurochemical level. It is common to have genetic alterations and acquired alterations at the same time. The genetic influences created the addiction, while the behavior continued to alter them.

The following questions will help in determining whether your baseline neurotransmission level is deficient or excessive.

1. Do you feel generally sad or depressed when you're quiet and inactive?   Yes ☐   No ☐

2. Is your life exciting and vibrant?   Yes ☐   No ☐

3. Do you often make plans that involve exciting opportunities or activities?   Yes ☐   No ☐

4. Do you frequently lack interest or motivation to do things? Yes ☐   No ☐

5. Do you tend to exert too much energy in one or a few areas of your life?   Yes ☐   No ☐

6. When you want to relax, do you usually feel hyper or "wired"? Yes ☐   No ☐

7. Do little things frequently upset you and cause you to feel depressed? Yes ☐ No ☐

8. Do little things frequently upset you and cause you to feel anxious? Yes ☐ No ☐

9. Do your fears and insecurities worsen when you're under stress? Yes ☐ No ☐

10. Do you often find it difficult to focus on issues? Yes ☐ No ☐

Downer Questions

Count the number of "yes" answers from questions 1, 4, 7, 8, and 10. _____

Upper Questions

Count the number of "yes" answers from questions 2, 3, 5, 6, and 9. _____

If you answered yes to more Downer Questions, your neurotransmission is probably deficient, too.

If you answered yes to more Upper Questions, your neurotransmission is probably excessive.

If you answered yes to the same number of Downer and Upper Questions, you probably have no preference in neurotransmission.

———————— ◆ ————————

Genetic and generational alterations require neurochemical corrections to help in behavior changes. Diet, exercise, and behavioral options (coming up later in this book) can help. If you follow them, you can also focus on spiritual and behavioral changes.

If your addiction is acquired, spiritual and behavioral changes may receive the first emphasis, followed by diet and exercise.

If you're serious about recovery, begin these programs within a month.

The most difficult task in developing a recovery plan is figuring out your baseline neurotransmission level. For most individuals, a few simple questions are enough to make this determination.

After you've answered the questions in this section, you may want a neurochemical evaluation if your findings aren't clear. For further information on neurochemical evaluations, write or phone: The Robertson Neurochemical Institute, Ltd., 3555 Pierce Road, Saginaw, MI 48604, (517) 799-8720.

—22—
Identifying Themes

Identifying your major theme of behavior will be the basis for beginning to eliminate the need for compulsive behavior.

Milt was addicted to cocaine, risk taking, and sexual activity. After I started to work with him, he realized that he turned to these activities when he felt inadequate, lonely, or unliked. He also learned that his main theme was a search for power, and he started to consider alternative forms of behavior.

Milt found that he didn't need to feel powerful when his children and wife thought he was a supportive person and a great father. Because he was arousal oriented, he developed a relationship with them through doing exciting things such as boating and horseback riding.

He received a reward from the relationships and soon realized he had a lesser need for power. When he did feel the need for power, he learned that a heavy workout at the gym helped him.

Because he understood his themes—which I will explain next—he knew when the feelings were sneaking up on him. He could deal with them before it was too late.

Milt is now developing a sense of true intimacy, he's growing spiritually, and he knows he can change his themes.

Like Milt, you need to identify your major theme of behavior. This knowledge will be the basis for change. You can then start to eliminate the need for compulsive behavior.

Themes

The following test will help you identify your compulsive themes. Answer each question with yes or no. If you are unsure, select the one that is true most of the time.

1. Adequacy

1. Do you have unrealistic expectations of others?   Yes ☐   No ☐
2. Do you set up unrealistic expectations of yourself?
Yes ☐   No ☐
3. Do you avoid doing things because you fear you will fail or you won't do a good enough job?   Yes ☐   No ☐
4. Do you take negative comments personally?   Yes ☐   No ☐
5. Do you often feel insecure?   Yes ☐   No ☐

2. Approval Seeking

1. Are you comfortable when others express their opinions before you do?   Yes ☐   No ☐
2. Do you dress and behave so that others will be more accepting?
Yes ☐   No ☐
3. Do you fear being disliked?   Yes ☐   No ☐
4. Do you often change (or deny) your beliefs so that others will accept you?   Yes ☐   No ☐
5. Is it easier for you to follow than it is to lead?   Yes ☐   No ☐

3. Pleasure

1. Is it difficult for you to enjoy a quiet evening with friends?
Yes ☐   No ☐
2. Is it common for you to "pay" for entertainment? (This could mean anything from renting videos to paying for sex.)   Yes ☐   No ☐
3. Most of the time, do your family members and friends do what you want?   Yes ☐   No ☐
4. Is having a good time important when free time is available?
Yes ☐   No ☐
5. Do you frequently put off doing important things so you can have fun *now*?   Yes ☐   No ☐

4. Power

1. Do you spend more time working than you think you should?
Yes ☐   No ☐
2. Do you work excessive hours to make more money, even if life is already comfortable?   Yes ☐   No ☐
3. In social situations, do you volunteer opinions on most or all topics?   Yes ☐   No ☐
4. Are you uncomfortable being told what to do?   Yes ☐   No ☐
5. Is it important for you to be in charge and in control of most things?   Yes ☐   No ☐

5. Responsibility

1. Do you tend to procrastinate? Yes ☐ No ☐
2. Do you avoid volunteering your services for organizations or causes because they take up too much time? Yes ☐ No ☐
3. Do you spend more money than you make? Yes ☐ No ☐
4. Is it important to relax, even when a lot of things need to be done? Yes ☐ No ☐
5. Do you get angry or feel anxious when you are told to do something or you are held responsible if something goes wrong? Yes ☐ No ☐

6. Recognition

1. Do you work to get people to respect you? Yes ☐ No ☐
2. Do you agree to serve on committees that make you popular or that have high visibility? Yes ☐ No ☐
3. Do you regularly socialize with people you consider powerful or important? Yes ☐ No ☐
4. Do you buy things on credit to improve your image of being successful? Yes ☐ No ☐
5. At parties, is most of your conversation related to your job? Yes ☐ No ☐

———————◆———————

The element with the greatest number of "yes" answers will indicate your compulsive theme. If several have the same number, discuss the results with someone you trust. Ask for input and insight.

Everyone has themes that govern actions. Understanding your themes is necessary to evaluate the cause behind your addictive personality.

The Law of Compulsive Themes: A theme refers to a psychological need. An addiction is the method used to meet that need. Compulsive themes are the way persons see themselves. Compulsive behavior is the response to such perception.

Addictions

1. Determining Addictions

After you know your major themes, you are ready to work on the addictions you used to meet those themes.

Review the chapter on addictive behavior to be clear about the

addictions present in your life or the ones to which you feel vulnerable.
The following lists may help you in your evaluation.

Circle the addictions currently present; underline those to which
you feel vulnerable.

Power
Activity
Alcohol/drug
Control
Exercise
Gambling
Hypochondria
Intelligence/education
Material
Physical appearance
Rescuing
Risk taking/excitement
Sex
Spending
Stealing
Violence
Work

Pleasure
Activity
Alcohol/drug
Caffeine
Food
Media fascination
Nicotine
Risk taking/excitement
Sex
Violence

Responsibility
Alcohol/drug
Hypochondria
Media fascination
Rescuing
Sex
Stealing

Adequacy
Activity
Alcohol/drug
Approval seeking
Cleaning
Control
Exercise
Food
Hypochondria
Intelligence/education
Material
Media fascination
Perfection
Physical appearance
Religion
Rescuing
Sex
Stealing
Violence
Work

Approval Seeking
Activity
Approval seeking
Cleaning
Exercise
Food
Gambling
Material
Nicotine
Perfection
Religion
Risk taking/excitement
Sex
Spending
Stealing

Violence   Religion
Work   Risk taking/excitement
                                 Sex
Recognition   Spending
Activity   Stealing
Exercise   Violence
Gambling   Work
Material

You may have discovered that you have several addictions within one or two themes. You will address the prominent addictions and themes in the chapter on recovery. Other addictions will lessen as the themes are resolved.

2. Classifying Addictions

Each addiction should then be classified according to whether it satisfies excitatory or inhibitory needs.

An excitatory addiction improves moods or relieves depression. An inhibitory addiction decreases anxiety or causes a "mellowing out." Overall, your addictions will cause your compulsive theme(s) to be excitatory or inhibitory.

MY COMPULSIVE   _____
THEME(S) IS/ARE   _____
                       _____

In the previous chapter, you decided if you had an excitatory (arousal) or inhibitory (satiation) personality. On page 212 you recorded

I AM A/AN _____ PERSONALITY.

Classifying addictions helps in determining the type of effect you seek. If you are out of balance, you will want to increase or decrease your mood level.

In the pages ahead, you will learn how to use this information to decide on YOUR recovery plan—a plan specifically designed for your reward center and addiction.

—23—

Recovery Techniques

After you determine which one of nine neurochemical profiles you are, you can use this information to learn the most effective recovery techniques for you.

We can offer a variety of recovery techniques, but deciding on the most effective one is essential for successful recovery.

Recovery includes

- moving away from the things you do when you are under stress or feel out of balance.
- learning to do the necessary things to maintain neurochemical normalcy.
- identifying your neurochemical profile, which is the result of knowing your neurochemical personality, your compulsive themes, and your neurotransmission levels.

All this works together to tailor a program built around diet, activity, and behavioral changes that lead to recovery.

Identifying Neurochemical Profiles

To discover your most effective method of recovery, you must do the following:

1. Decide if you are an arousal or a satiation personality. (See chapter 21.)

2. Look at your addictions. They decide if your themes are excitatory or inhibitory. (See chapter 22.)

221

3. Know your neurotransmitter level. Knowing the accurate level requires a neurochemical evaluation. However, most people can develop a plan based on estimated neurotransmission levels. (See chapter 21.)

Refer to the questions you answered in chapters 20 and 21:

- Is your neurochemical personality *satiation* or *arousal*?
- Is your compulsive theme *inhibitory* or *excitatory*?
- Is your neurotransmission level *deficient* or *excessive*?

Find the line across the first three columns in Figure 23-1 that matches your findings. The letter in the far right column represents your type of neurochemical profile. For instance, if your neurochemical personality is *arousal*, your compulsive theme is *inhibitory*, and your neurotransmission level is *excessive*, your neurochemical profile is *Type F*.

FIGURE 23-1
Neurochemical Profiles

Neurochemical Personality	Compulsive Theme	Neurotransmission Levels	Neurochemical Profile
satiation	inhibitory	deficient	A
arousal	inhibitory	deficient	B
satiation	excitatory	deficient	C
arousal	excitatory	deficient	D
satiation	inhibitory	excessive	E
arousal	inhibitory	excessive	F
satiation	excitatory	excessive	G
arousal	excitatory	excessive	H

Your neurochemical profile indicates what type of activity, diet, or behavioral techniques may be beneficial to you. The profile assists in determining the rewards likely to be most effective over time.

Type A Neurochemical Profile

If you have a Type A neurochemical profile, you typically have long-term genetic predispositions to compulsive disorders. An investigation into the family history may reveal alcoholism, perfectionism, compulsive overeating, or other compulsive disorders.

The neurochemical profile suggests the neurochemical baseline or enzyme activity or levels that the brain considers normal may actually be *less* than what would produce good feelings since the person describes being depressed or having low energy most of the time.

There appears to be no behavioral compensation for the altered neurochemistry; that is, you aren't doing exciting activities to overcome the depressed neurotransmission levels. In fact, the low neurotransmission levels may be causing the behavior, which can predispose you to transfer to other addictions.

The goal of Type A neurochemical profiles is to transfer to a positive addiction—initially. Eliminating or minimizing compulsive behavior may be difficult at first. After a period of time, you can eliminate or reduce all compulsive behaviors.

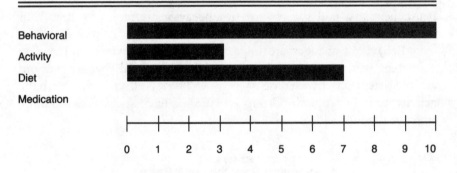

FIGURE 23-2
Recovery Effectiveness Rating
TYPE A PROFILE

Behavioral changes are the most effective way to obtain rewards and remain consistent with neurochemical needs. I suggest that you read the material in the chapter about behavioral changes and then discuss it thoroughly with members of your support system.

The need to belong is essential for you. Without your support system completely behind you, you could hinder the motivation to change. You need support to stay motivated.

Small gatherings or social situations in which you can be self-reflective and receive support would be beneficial. Meditation, Bible studies, self-help, and emotionally supportive activities are probably most acceptable and desirable for you.

You learn spirituality best through a church that emphasizes study. You also interact well with small groups. If forced to share, you may become uncomfortable and stressed.

Activity therapy is beneficial for health, but it's probably more acceptable as a hobby or in a quiet setting than with a large group of people.

Diet therapy can be most beneficial. You will likely follow it closely.

Negative attitude and frustration may be problems in your recovery process. You have a strong tendency to give up. With your Type A profile, you need to accept yourself and others to maintain the energy to recover.

Type B Neurochemical Profile

If you have a Type B neurochemical profile, you probably have used drugs, alcohol, and/or medication or followed a compulsive behavior for a long period. You have adapted to the consistent depression of neurotransmitters by generational, environmental, or outside forces, such as diet, drugs, or long-term, consistent behavioral changes. Your enzymatic system has likely adapted to such changes.

There appears to be no behavioral compensation for such altered neurochemistry, and the rewards for behavior appear to be low. Your behavior is probably a result of the altered neurotransmission.

Behavioral changes are important to obtain rewards and remain consistent with your neurochemical needs. Behavioral changes without any consistent activity/exercise program will be less effective than with the activity/exercise program. Group activities or team sports may be more effective than individual activities.

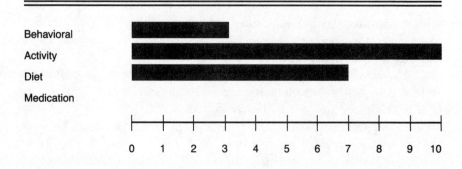

FIGURE 23-3
Recovery Effectiveness Rating
TYPE B PROFILE

You need independence within the group to enjoy the group process. You tend to be more comfortable knowing what is expected of you than just going along with the group. Self-help fellowships and active participation in church activities will be beneficial to you.

Social situations are more comfortable with activities that have some degree of structure. Intellectually or educationally oriented social activities may be most acceptable to you. To be supportive, the family system needs to be aware of the social activities that provide rewards.

You can effectively learn spirituality in a church with a structured environment. Bible studies with intellectual content or emphasis can be helpful. If there is too much emotion involved, you may resist change.

Activity and exercise therapy is essential for your emotional and neurochemical needs as well as for physical health. Activities that make you feel better about yourself while you interact in relationships are extremely valuable. Doing activities with the family, such as skiing or going for walks, can help you build your relational skills.

Diet therapy may be important for a period of time to provide the necessary nutrients for neurotransmitter development.

You tend to have a problem staying with plans you make. Many life-style changes appear to oppose your neurochemical need. *You may be doing what others want, not what you need*. To continue on the road to recovery, you need to develop behavioral changes that are right for your brain, as described in this book.

Type C Neurochemical Profile

If you have a Type C neurochemical profile, you probably have had long-term emotional or physical conflicts that create problems. Resolving guilt and encouraging forgiveness may help you. You can benefit from learning techniques that decrease your stress level.

Your neurochemical profile suggests that you show signs of behavioral compensation that aren't consistent with your reward center. Generally, you do things to try to feel better, but you may do them because of guilt or because others ask you to. It is better for you to engage in activities that satisfy your reward center and help your neurochemical imbalances.

Without resolving your spiritual conflicts, you are likely to transfer to another addiction or compulsion. I encourage you to confront issues and not to avoid them.

You need to make behavioral changes to obtain rewards consistent with your neurochemical needs. You also may respond better to discussing problems with another individual rather than with a group. Activities with a group of people can be good if you are accepting of them and not judgmental.

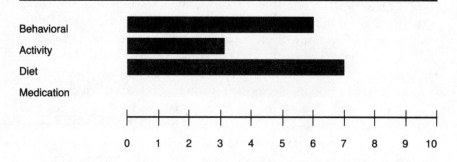

FIGURE 23-4
Recovery Effectiveness Rating
TYPE C PROFILE

You have a strong need to belong to groups, but the discussion could hinder your motivation to change. Don't be tempted to avoid change just because people understand you. Since you need support in relationship, you are particularly vulnerable to transferring to codependency or relationship addictions.

You do best in social situations that remain small, self-reflective, and supportive. Meditation, Bible studies, self-help, and emotionally supportive activities are probably most desirable. Marriage-enrichment or relationship-oriented activities can provide much help.

You can move into spirituality most effectively in churches with an emotional atmosphere and Bible study programs. If negative religious issues exist, consult the minister for help in developing intimacy in relationships.

Activity therapy is beneficial for health, but you'll probably be more open to accept it as a hobby or in quiet settings.

Diet therapy may be most beneficial, and with your Type C profile, you are likely to follow it closely.

Type D Neurochemical Profile

If you have a Type D neurochemical profile, you probably have a genetic predisposition toward a depressed neurotransmission. Your family history may reveal alcoholism, depressive disorders, and compulsive or dysfunctional family systems. Your neurochemical profile describes genetic neurotransmitter alterations that hamper your ability to obtain rewards. You appear to do activities or behavior to treat the chemical imbalances in your brain consistent with your reward center. Essentially,

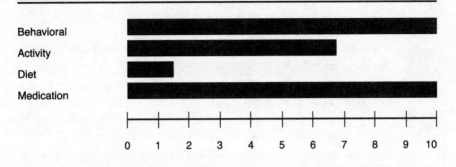

FIGURE 23-5
Recovery Effectiveness Rating
TYPE D PROFILE

your behavioral addiction is a "self-medication" of your neurochemical abnormality. Treatment of the neurochemical abnormality is essential to treat the behavioral issues.

Behavioral changes are essential to obtain rewards and remain consistent with neurochemical needs. Behavioral changes without medical or pharmacological intervention will not be as effective as behavioral changes with medication.

Group discussions in Bible studies or therapy sessions may be more acceptable to you than one-on-one conversation. You will be more comfortable in groups that allow independence; dogmatic or critical groups make you uncomfortable. I encourage self-help fellowships. Become active in a church group. Recovery that deals with dysfunctional family systems may be important.

You will find social situations that include action or directed activities with some degree of structure more comfortable than other types of social settings. Intellectually or educationally oriented social activities can provide support.

Spirituality is most comfortable for you within a structured environment that does not have a strong emotional appeal. I recommend churches that emphasize teaching and study groups.

For emotional, neurochemical, and physical needs, I suggest activity and exercise therapy. You need activities that are healthy and relational. Doing activities with the family, spouse, or children may be very supportive.

Diet therapy is probably not appropriate; however, a healthy diet is a good idea for everyone.

You may need medication and a medical evaluation for neuro-chemical manipulation. If you do need medication, talk with your physician and consider the following guidelines:

1. You have already changed your neurochemicals with alternative methods.
2. Understand your specific goals for the use and effectiveness of medication.
3. Use specific alternative methods to reduce the amount of your medication as soon as possible.
4. If life-threatening situations exist, such as suicidal tendencies or severe depressions, you probably need medication. After you have stabilized, your physician may help you develop goals for discontinuing or reevaluating the use of medication.
5. Ask your physician to help you set goals so that you can eventually discontinue the medication.
6. Don't compromise your recovery by allowing such things as clinical depression or manic-depressive illness. The proper use of medication could enhance your recovery and reduce the chances for a relapse.
7. Using "mood-altering" pharmaceuticals is rarely indicated in any disease in which a chemical dependency condition coexists.

Type E Neurochemical Profile

If you have a Type E neurochemical profile, you probably show a genetic predisposition to enhanced neurotransmission. The family history may reveal alcoholism, anxiety disorders, or other compulsive or dysfunctional family systems. Your neurochemical profile describes genetic neurotransmitter alterations that hamper the ability to obtain rewards.

You appear to do activities or behavior to treat the chemical imbalances in your brain consistent with your reward center. Your behavioral addiction is possibly a "self-medication" of the neurochemical abnormality. Treatment of the neurochemical abnormality may greatly enhance your ability to change behaviors.

Behavioral changes are essential for you to obtain rewards and remain consistent with your neurochemical needs. Behavioral changes with the temporary use of medication may be more effective than behavioral changes alone. Discussing your problems with an individual may be more helpful than working with groups.

You will likely find help in group fellowship or churches that focus on acceptance and belonging. The need to belong is vital, but the discus-

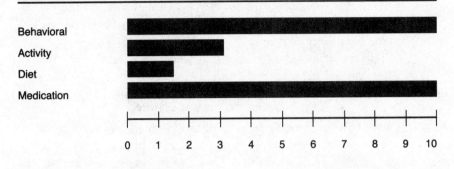

FIGURE 23-6
Recovery Effectiveness Rating
TYPE E PROFILE

sion in a group could lessen or eliminate your motivation to change. The transfer to codependency or relationship addiction is high. You also could benefit from pursuing your dysfunctional family issues.

Small social situations with an emphasis on self-reflection and support are effective. Meditation, Bible studies, self-help, and emotionally supportive activities are probably most desirable. Marriage-enrichment or relationship-oriented activities are important.

Churches that offer discussion-type settings can generally meet your spiritual needs. If you have unresolved negative religious issues, discuss them with a minister.

Activity therapy is beneficial for health but will probably be most acceptable through a hobby or in a quiet setting.

Diet therapy is probably not essential; however, a healthy diet is beneficial to anyone for maximum physical health.

A physician should help you decide whether to use medication. If the physician prescribes medicine, consider the following guidelines:

1. Remember that you tried to alter your neurochemical levels with alternative methods.
2. Before you start, set specific goals for the use of medication.
3. Use specific alternative methods to reduce your medication as soon as possible.
4. In consultation with your physician, set goals to discontinue medication.
5. If you have a life-threatening situation such as suicidal tendencies or severe depression, consult your physician and be ready to take medication. After you have stabilized, the physician may help

you develop goals to discontinue medication or help to reevaluate your use of medication.

6. Don't compromise your recovery because of problems such as clinical depression or manic-depressive illness when the proper use of medication could enhance your recovery or at least reduce the possibility of relapse.

7. The use of mood-altering pharmaceuticals is rarely indicated in any disease in which a chemical dependency condition coexists.

Type F Neurochemical Profile

If you have a Type F neurochemical profile, you are similar to persons who have been involved in long-term physical, spiritual, or emotional conflicts. You need encouragement to resolve your feelings of guilt and to forgive others. Learning techniques to decrease your level of stress may help.

You appear to do activities or behavior to treat the chemical imbalances in your brain not consistent with your reward center. You do better at activities to try to feel better. Do not, however, act because of guilt or because others urge you to. You need the type of activities that satisfy your reward center and balance your neurochemicals.

Without spiritual conflict resolution, you are likely to transfer to another addiction or compulsion. You also need to be encouraged not to avoid issues.

Behavioral changes are important to obtain rewards and remain consistent with neurochemical needs. Behavioral changes without any

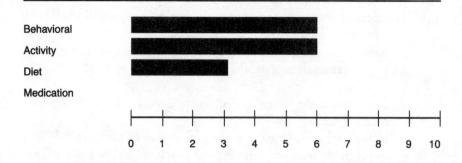

FIGURE 23-7
Recovery Effectiveness Rating
TYPE F PROFILE

consistent activity/exercise program may be less effective for you than if you use only an activity/exercise program.

Group support and participation in church activities may be more effective than individual discussions with your support system. The group would be more effective if it has a purpose and direction. I encourage you to try self-help fellowships and active church involvement. You need support in building relationships. A strong temptation for you is to transfer to codependent or relationship addiction.

Social situations should include action/goal-directed activities with some degree of structure. Intellectually or educationally oriented social activities may be effective.

Your spiritual needs are best met in a teaching, structured environment that doesn't require you to participate through sharing unless you wish to. I recommend a church that emphasizes teaching and study groups.

Activity and exercise therapy is essential to meet your emotional and neurochemical and physical needs. Rewarding and relational activities are vital for you.

Diet therapy may be helpful to assist in the development of neurotransmitters. Some individuals appear to benefit from these precursors, while others receive no benefit. A trial may be helpful to you.

Type G Neurochemical Profile

If you have a Type G neurochemical profile, you probably have used drugs, alcohol, and/or medication or performed a compulsive behavior for a long period. Your profile is similar to that of persons whose neurochemistry has adapted to the consistent excitation of neurotransmitters by environmental, generational, or outside forces, such as diet, drugs, or consistent, long-term behavioral changes. Your enzymatic system may have adapted to such change.

It appears that the chemical changes in your brain are causing your behavior. Rewards for the behavior seem low.

Behavioral changes are important to obtain rewards and remain consistent with your neurochemical needs. Support from an individual is more readily accepted and effective than from groups. Group fellowships or church activities that focus on acceptance and belonging could be beneficial. The need to belong is essential, but the discussion in groups could eliminate your motivation to change.

I suggest you try social situations that remain small, self-reflective, and supportive. Meditation, Bible studies, self-help, and emotionally supportive activities are probably most desirable for you.

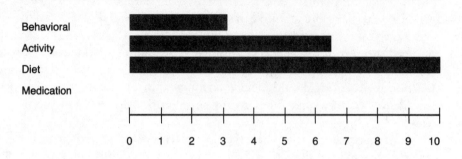

FIGURE 23-8
Recovery Effectiveness Rating

TYPE G PROFILE

Your spiritual needs are best met in a teaching format that allows discussion. I recommend a church that emphasizes Bible study.

Activity therapy is beneficial for your health, but you will probably find it most acceptable in the form of a hobby or in a quiet setting.

Diet therapy may be beneficial. You are more likely to follow a diet program than an activity program.

You tend to have problems with following your plan for any length of time. *You may be doing what others want you to do, not what is best for you.* You need to develop behavioral changes that are right for your brain, as I have described in this book.

Type H Neurochemical Profile

If you have a Type H neurochemical profile, you probably show long-term familial or genetic predispositions to compulsive disorders. Your family history may reveal alcoholism, perfectionism, compulsive overeating, or other compulsive disorders.

Your neurochemical profile indicates that neurochemical baseline levels or enzymatic levels that your brain considers normal are greater than those most people consider normal to have good feelings. That places you in an acceleration type of behavioral need—you constantly search for excitement.

There appears to be no behavioral compensation for such altered neurochemistry, which indicates you are responding to neurochemical abnormality. This situation can predispose you to transferring to another compulsion or addiction. Perhaps your goal in recovery should be to transfer to a positive addiction during the initial phase. Eliminating or minimizing compulsive behavior may be very difficult at first.

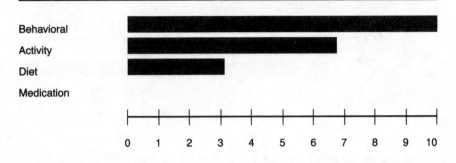

FIGURE 23-9
Recovery Effectiveness Rating

TYPE H PROFILE

Behavioral

Activity

Diet

Medication

0   1   2   3   4   5   6   7   8   9   10

Behavioral changes are essential for you to obtain rewards and remain consistent with your neurochemical needs. Behavioral changes without any consistent activity/exercise program will be less than with the activity/exercise program. Group systems and activities may be more effective support systems than individual interaction. I strongly encourage attendance at self-help fellowships or active church participation.

Social situations should include action/goal-directed activities with some degree of structure. Intellectually or educationally oriented social activities may be most acceptable to you.

Spiritual needs can be met effectively through a high-energy, intellectually stimulating environment that doesn't require you to participate through sharing groups unless you want to. I recommend a church that emphasizes teaching and study groups.

Activity and exercise therapy is essential for your emotional and neurochemical needs and your physical health. Relational high-energy activities are necessary for you to improve your self-esteem and to strengthen relationships.

Diet therapy may be helpful to assist in the development of neurotransmitters. Some individuals appear to benefit from these precursors, while others receive no benefit. A trial may be helpful to you.

You may tend to have a problem following through with your actions because you like to move from one activity or plan to another without completing any of them. I urge you to focus on one activity at a time. If your recovery is to be successful, you need to work at being more self-disciplined.

—24—

Entering Your Three Cycles

Learning your entry point is learning where you feel most confident.

Your Entry Point

To help you decide on your entry point, answer the questions below with yes or no. Try to be as honest as possible.

Physical

1. Do you have a physical disorder that causes you daily discomfort? Yes ☐ No ☐
2. Do you take any medication that affects your mood?
Yes ☐ No ☐
3. Do you spend a considerable amount of time to get relief from your medical disorder? Yes ☐ No ☐
4. Do you have other options to improve a medical problem, such as surgery, physical therapy, or change of diet? Yes ☐ No ☐
5. Is a physician actively involved in of your medical care?
Yes ☐ No ☐

Emotional

1. Do you take medication to change your moods? Yes ☐ No ☐
2. Are you in counseling or therapy? Yes ☐ No ☐
3. Are you aware that your moods vary greatly? Yes ☐ No ☐
4. Do you have a lot of fear, or do you feel very insecure?
Yes ☐ No ☐
5. Do you find it hard to maintain relationships with others?
Yes ☐ No ☐

235

Spiritual

1. Do you feel inadequate?   Yes ☐ No ☐
2. Do you feel you have no purpose in life?   Yes ☐ No ☐
3. Do you lack an understanding of God?   Yes ☐ No ☐
4. Are you afraid of God?   Yes ☐ No ☐
5. Is it hard for you to trust people?   Yes ☐ No ☐

Scoring: Your entry point is your strongest area—the one with the fewest "yes" answers. Change is most effective when persons build on their strengths.

—25—

Diet for a Healthy Brain

*It is important to plan a diet for your brain,
not merely for your body.*

Diet therapy is the most controversial of all therapies mentioned in this book. The conservative medical community denies any beneficial effects, while others claim miraculous effects. I tend to fall somewhere in the middle.

I encourage diet therapy for two reasons. First and probably most important are the behavioral effects. You are adopting a life-style that is more healthy. This doesn't mean a specific diet to alter moods, but a balanced diet that shows you care about yourself. That part is essential and should be accepted by all people. The second aspect is following a specific diet for the brain. Some may benefit tremendously; others may experience no effect. My position is simple. You may wish to try a specific diet based upon the issues discussed in this chapter. If it works for you, use it. If it doesn't work, don't keep spending money and hope it will work. A three-month trial is a reasonable time to see if beneficial effects will be observed.

For those of you interested in a diet for your brain, the rationale is as follows:

Vitamins and minerals help to maintain balance in the brain; they compensate for chemical deficiencies and excesses. *Deficient* levels of enzymes, neurotransmitters, and neurohormones can be *increased* by vitamins and minerals found in certain foods, and *excess* levels can be *decreased* by vitamins and minerals found in other foods.

Before you continue reading, refer to your answers in chapter 20. What is your baseline neurotransmission level? Is it *deficient* (serotonin or adrenergic) or *excessive* (serotonin or adrenergic)? Keep your level in mind as you read about diet and neurotransmission.

Diet and Neurotransmission

The body breaks down proteins into smaller parts called amino acids. Amino acids are essential elements of the diet. They are so important that many diet plans or health food stores list the amino acid levels of common foods. Some people even take amino acid supplements. How you choose to get amino acid will depend on what works for you. You are advised not to combine different types of amino acid products, however, since some kinds of amino acids interfere with other amino acids as well as with vitamins and minerals.

Amino acids are absorbed into the blood from the stomach. They aren't available to your brain until they cross the blood-brain barrier (the gateway to the brain). Since the blood-brain barrier protects the brain from toxic substances in the rest of the body, it selectively allows the passage of certain chemicals to the brain. It also controls the amount of certain chemicals in the brain.

A simple way to understand the blood-brain barrier is to imagine a boat on a river. Persons on the east side of the river can reach the west side only by getting on the boat. Only one boat is available for amino acids, and it has to shuttle many amino acids from one side to the other. The larger and stronger amino acids get on the boat first; only after the larger and stronger ones have reached the other side does the boat return and allow the others to board.

Amino acids come in different sizes and strengths. The ability to bind to the carrier protein (the boat) determines their strength. The amino acids leucine, isoleucine, valine, isovaline, and phenylalanine have a stronger affinity to the carrier protein than tryptophan.

Serotonin is a product of the amino acid tryptophan, a small, weak amino acid. (Tryptophan supplements—other than the tryptophan found naturally in foods—have been removed from the market while their safety is being evaluated. Tryptophanlike substitutes are *not* effective for neurochemical changes.)

Adrenergic neurotransmitters are a product of two strong amino acids—phenylalanine and tyrosine—and includes two neurotransmitters, dopamine and norepinephrine.

Serotonin and adrenergic give their names to two major neurochemical pathways that can lead to excesses or deficiencies in neurotransmission levels: the *serotonergic pathway* and the *adrenergic pathway*.

Serotonergic Pathway

Because tryptophan is a small, weak amino acid, if you eat a lot of protein, tryptophan gets left behind because the larger amino acids are transported first. Tryptophan would thus remain outside the brain, and less of it would be available for making serotonin. This creates a *serotonin deficiency*.

Since carbohydrates are sugars, they don't compete for the same boat as the amino acids. They can use a carbohydrate boat. If you eat carbohydrates with tryptophan, tryptophan can get on the empty amino acid boat instead of competing unsuccessfully with larger and stronger proteins for the amino acid boat.

In order to get more tryptophan to your brain, you need to eat a diet rich in tryptophan and low in other proteins. You may need to supplement your diet with complex carbohydrates.

This same system causes carbohydrate craving when a serotonin deficiency exists in the brain. Your body craves carbohydrates in an attempt to get more tryptophan to cross the blood-brain barrier for conversion to serotonin.

If your serotonin deficiency is *genetic* you may crave carbohydrates. However, you may also crave carbohydrates for other reasons. But consumption of carbohydrates will not effect an increase in serotonin level. Because the serotonin level has not been increased, the craving continues. The result is that you increase your caloric intake in an attempt to satisfy your craving for carbohydrates, and you gain weight.

Weight reduction programs based on restrictive diets are ineffective because most of them are built around eating foods high in proteins and low in carbohydrates. When you begin one of those diets, the boat is full of strong amino acids—which means that tryptophan doesn't get on board. If you continue the restrictive diet, within a few months your brain becomes deficient in serotonin and you begin craving carbohydrates.

This is not simply a problem of willpower—it is a physiological need. Because it is a need, you break your diet. Consequently you gain weight, feel guilty, and finally give up.

To supply tryptophan to the brain, a diet must include tryptophan and complex carbohydrates. (Simple sugars, too quickly absorbed, often create depression and give you that letdown feeling. Complex carbohydrates, which are absorbed more slowly, balance the blood sugar better.)

A good diet, like the one described here, is rich in complex carbohydrates and tryptophan and will come to the aid of the serotonin-deficient brain.

(*Note*: I am not listing amounts to eat. That will vary with individual weights, desire for weight loss, and health factors.)

A Tryptophan-Rich Diet

This is a modified high-protein and complex-carbohydrate diet:

- *Eat* fish, low-fat cheese products, milk products, and turkey with bagels, barley, bread, cereals, corn, crackers, muffins, pasta, potatoes, rice, and rolls.
- *Avoid or use sparingly* beef, cold cuts, lamb, pork, and pork products.
- *Avoid totally* chocolate, coffee, tea, or any other products containing caffeine.

The diet isn't complete yet. The conversion of tryptophan to serotonin requires several substrates (chemicals used in the conversion process). The substrates for tryptophan to serotonin are provided by vitamin and mineral supplements. Several vitamin B products and minerals convert tryptophan. A good multivitamin and mineral supplement will provide all the necessary ingredients for converting tryptophan to serotonin.

Adrenergic Pathway

The adrenergic pathway includes two neurotransmitters, dopamine and norepinephrine, which are converted from two strong amino acids— phenylalanine and tyrosine. These amino acids have no problem passing the blood-brain barrier since they're strong enough to get on the boat. Consequently, a diet program with phenylalanine and tyrosine is less complicated than a diet program with tryptophan.

A high-protein diet increases the amount of phenylalanine and tyrosine available to the brain for conversion to dopamine or norepinephrine.

An Adrenergic-Rich Diet

This is a high-protein and complex-carbohydrate diet:

- *Eat high-protein foods* (listed in order of their content value): cereals, fish, chicken, veal, lean trimmed beef, low-fat milk products, soybeans, whole milk, cold cuts (unless low fat), pork and pork products, and lamb.

• *Eat complex carbohydrates*: cereals, fresh fruits, salads, and vegetables.
• *Avoid* bagels, barley, bread, corn, crackers, muffins, pasta, potatoes, rice, and rolls.

This diet also takes into consideration cholesterol levels, family history, and medical conditions. The conversion of phenylalanine and tyrosine to dopamine and norepinephrine requires substrates. These substrates are found in most diets; however, supplementation can be found in a multivitamin and mineral supplement product.

Diet and Neurochemical Profiles

Refer to your answers in chapter 20. What is your neurochemical profile type? I have divided the diet types into two categories: diets that *enhance* neurotransmission and diets that *inhibit* neurotransmission.

The following diet manipulations will be considered unproven by traditional medical communities. Once again, some people find benefit, while others find no effects. You can try these diet manipulations to determine their effects on you personally. Just because something isn't proven yet doesn't mean it isn't worth trying. However, if mood changes continue to occur and you have tried the following concepts, you may consider a medical or psychiatric evaluation.

Neurochemical profile Types A, B, C, and D benefit from diets that improve neurotransmission. Types A and C usually follow diet plans better than Types B and D.

Neurochemical profile Types E, F, G, and H benefit from diet plans that inhibit neurotransmission. Types E and G are usually willing to follow diet plans, but Types F and H are resistant.

Of course, to be workable, a diet program must take into consideration medical complications. If you have heart disease, diabetes, or other conditions that require a special diet, you would be wise to follow your physician-prescribed diet unless your physician approves the following diet.

Diet to Improve Neurotransmission

The adrenergic-rich diet enhances neurotransmission. Neurochemical profile Types A, B, C, and D can begin with this diet. The diet causes a decrease in depression. Because of the complex nature of neurochemistry, you should review your symptoms to develop a plan tailored more for your needs.

Diet to Decrease Neurotransmission

The tryptophan-rich diet decreases neurotransmission. Neurochemical profile Types E, F, G, and H can begin with this diet and tailor it based upon the symptoms.

Symptoms to Tailor Diet

I'm including a list of symptoms and diet considerations to help in tailoring a diet to fit individual needs. The symptoms described are those most frequently seen that are not influenced by outside factors, such as medical condition, death of a loved one, or loss of a job.

Follow these diets daily.

SYMPTOMS	DIET
1. Anxiety	1. Tryptophan-rich diet
2. Depression	2. Either diet or both
3. Difficulty focusing or concentrating	3. Tryptophan-rich diet
4. Anger	4. Adrenergic-rich diet
5. Difficulty with sleep	5. Tryptophan-rich diet
6. Lack of energy and motivation	6. Adrenergic-rich diet
7. Craving carbohydrates	7. Tryptophan-rich diet

Combining Diets

You may need both diets. Although the diets interfere with each other, you can, with minor adjustments, combine them. Use the adrenergic-rich diet during the day when the tyrosine and phenylalanine are absorbed. Don't eat high-protein foods after six o'clock in the evening. A small amount of food rich in complex carbohydrates and tryptophan makes an appropriate snack at night.

If you take the adrenergic-rich diet early enough, there will be no problem with the tryptophan. Of course, you need to decrease your caloric intake if you add the nighttime snack.

Diets and Moods

You may go through various periods in the day or week when outside influences create stress or depression. This is typical of the temporary neurochemical changes unrelated to baseline levels of neurotransmission. The baseline levels are the *overall* feelings of depression or anxiety you experience with no interference from outside influences. Eating different foods can alter your moods.

1. Foods to Increase Concentration

Often excitatory neurochemical release causes you to have scattered thoughts. The overstimulation of your nervous system causes the multiple firing of nerves, and you have difficulty concentrating. In addition, your thoughts may not seem logical or consistent. Or you have a problem completing tasks. Dietary manipulation can be helpful when lack of concentration is only occasional.

Tryptophan can help in concentration. A turkey sandwich, low-fat milk products, and cheeses, improve concentration by providing a temporary feedback to the adrenergic system.

Concentration can also be affected by depression or other psychological or medical disorders. If poor concentration continues, you may wish to have a medical and neurochemical evaluation.

2. Foods to Decrease Anxiety

The release of excessive amounts of excitatory neurotransmitters causes anxiety. Exercise is usually the most effective method to "burn up" these neurotransmitters. However, a change in diet can also be somewhat beneficial.

Restricting foods that have direct stimulation decreases temporary anxiety conditions. Avoiding red meat, caffeine, and chocolate usually helps. You may also respond to an increase in tryptophan during this time. Turkey, pasta, fish, and lowfat cheese decrease anxiety.

Psychological and medical conditions affect anxiety. If your anxiety persists, you should have medical and neurochemical evaluations done.

3. Foods to Relieve Depression

The type of depression helped by diet is the temporary "down feeling," not the overwhelming chronic type. Increasing the amount of excitatory neurochemicals improves mood. Eat a meal rich in protein and drink a cup of coffee to increase the amount of excitatory neurochemicals. If you feel you need to continue this program daily, I suggest further evaluation. Cereals, fish, chicken, veal, and beef may relieve depression.

4. Foods to Decrease Stress

When you feel stress, avoid coffee, chocolate, and red meat. Since stress causes a release of excitatory neurotransmitters, you don't need more stimulation. Vegetables, fresh fruits, salads, breads, and pasta may decrease stress.

Stress is emotionally, physically, and spiritually destructive. The medical and emotional consequences of stress vary from high blood pressure to anxiety or depression. Handling stress as quickly as possible is important. Temporary relief of the neurochemical alterations prevents or minimizes the medical and psychological consequences.

5. Amino Acid Supplements

Amino acid supplements won't significantly affect baseline neurotransmitters unless you have a dietary or drug-induced deficiency. However, they can have considerable direct effects on moods.

If tyrosine is taken one hour before meals, the stimulating effect can decrease the appetite. Any genetic or baseline neurotransmitter alteration overrides this effect. Compulsive overeating requires balancing the baseline neurotransmitters for appetite suppression to occur.

Phenylalanine comes in *d* and *l* derivatives. The *d* is for persons who experience chronic pain. Taken alone it may not provide much of an effect; however, when it is combined with certain antiinflammatory agents and analgesics, it may prove beneficial.

If you need an adrenergic-rich diet and are underweight, you may prefer *l* phenylalanine. Tyrosine can affect your weight even though it improves your depression.

A healthy diet is important for the brain to change. Otherwise, the brain may want to change, but it won't have the necessary nutrients.

The following list of dietary guidelines will help you in recovery.

Dietary Guidelines

General Guidelines:
1. If a physician has suggested an alternative diet because of a medical or other condition, please follow that advice.
2. If you have any food allergies, use alternative foods.
3. If you have high blood pressure, avoid foods high in sodium.
4. The goal of these diets is not weight reduction but a balanced diet.
5. Your body needs carbohydrates. Complex carbohydrates are more effective than simple sugars (such as sugar or honey).

Specific Guidelines:
1. Eating three meals a day is better than skipping meals.
2. Balance each meal with proteins and fats. If you eat too many

carbohydrates, you can overproduce insulin. After a few hours, this can create carbohydrate craving.

3. Avoid drinking alcoholic beverages.
4. Limit or eliminate your caffeine intake.
5. Trim all visible fat from meat.
6. Decrease the amount of fat you eat. Replace saturated fats with polyunsaturated fats.
7. Decrease the amount of high-cholesterol foods, such as butter, fat, and eggs. (The elderly, young children, and premenopausal women may benefit from eating eggs.)
8. Decrease the amount of processed or refined sugars.
9. Decrease your use of salt and foods high in salt content.
10. Use fresh foods as much as possible.
11. Broil, steam, or bake foods. Avoid frying or immersing foods in fat.

A healthy diet

• follows general guidelines.
• helps your recovery.
• is based on your neurochemical profile.
• assists in altering your neurochemical baseline levels.
• uses food to temporarily improve your moods and emotions.

—26—
Exercising for a Healthy Brain

Neurochemicals can be increased or decreased with exercise, and exercise can be prescribed for its effect on the brain.

Exercise and Activities

Exercise and physical activity can play an important role in the recovery process. Activity and exercise programs are generally suggested to all people. This chapter tries to help the person who doesn't like to exercise or is a compulsive exerciser to maintain a balance. The concepts are based upon your reward center (what you will do) and what you need to do when you feel out of balance. Although it's less controversial than diet therapy, many physicians and psychiatrists may disagree with the activity program based on neurotransmission alterations. We don't know all the answers related to the effect of exercise and activity on neurotransmission, but we do know there is an effect. The most popular and most widely publicized effect is the "runner's high."

The following discussion describes a basis for prescribing activity and exercise for you. Remember that as in all aspects, you may need to vary the activities and exercises to fit your individual needs. The main caution is not to transfer to being an exercise addict if you are an arousal personality.

I believe in prescribing activities in the same way medicine is prescribed. I base my recommendations on the idea of the reward center and neurochemical baselines. As with diet, exercise offers direct, although temporary, results.

247

Exercise and Neurotransmission

I urge exercise for two reasons. First, activity increases or decreases neurochemicals and helps to alter baseline neurochemical levels. Second, when persons feel better, they look better, and they are healthier.

Exercises will depend upon a person's health. Certain medical conditions require physical restrictions; please follow those restrictions. There are other methods to change neurochemistry.

I like to combine a healthy diet with effective exercise programs. These exercises stimulate the cardiovascular system through running, weight lifting, racquetball, basketball, and others; in the activities list, I call these Type E (for *excitatory*) activities. By contrast, Type I (for *inhibitory*) activities are less strenuous but require more concentration (and less cardiovascular involvement); these activities include playing card games, watching quiet movies, woodworking, and doing other hobbies.

At first, cardiovascular exercise or Type E activities burn up excitatory neurochemicals. If they are done daily for thirty to forty-five days, they release endorphins. This reward neurochemical is the one that causes the *runner's high*, a term popularized by long-distance runners who speak of a feeling of peace or a sense of well-being.

Cardiovascular exercise affects brain chemistry. If persons exercise daily for at least two months, they develop an increase in neurotransmission. Running two to three days a week, with a break on alternate days, burns up excitatory neurotransmitters without causing runner's high. (If persons of the excitatory nature get runner's high, they are back on the addictive treadmill.) Following a moderate exercise program would decrease neurotransmission by burning up neurochemicals.

However, some individuals just don't get a reward from cardiovascular exercise or Type E activities. They may respond better to diet therapy or Type I activities. Type I activities can alter neurotransmitters by focusing the thoughts and energy. The relaxing and focusing increase certain neurochemicals. Properly prescribing these activities can enhance or decrease neurotransmission levels.

Exercise/Activity and Neurochemical Profiles

To help you set up your own exercise and activity program, start with filling out an activities list. Refer to your neurochemical profile to help you select your activity program.

Daily routine exercise plans affect neurochemical baseline levels.

Alleviation-of-stress activities are used when persons feel out of balance so they can temporarily relieve their neurochemical imbalances.

Activities List

Complete the activities list to help you decide on the activities and hobbies that you most enjoy. You can also substitute activities that require the same amount of effort.

Each of the activities has an I (or inhibitory) or E (or excitatory) effect. These are the general effects. You may find a particular activity listed as I is actually excitatory to you. If that is the case, consider it an E activity. The same is true if an E activity is actually an I to you.

Check the activities you have participated in and enjoyed.

Activity Program for Type A and Type C Profiles

If you have a Type A or C profile, your goal is to increase certain neurochemical levels through activities. Exercise can be of some help for Type A or C individuals.

Develop an exercise program that consists of I activities from the activities list.

Do a five-minute warm-up, such as walking or stretching.

Do a twenty-minute exercise from the I list.

Do a five-minute cool down, such as walking or stretching.

Schedule

	Sun	Mon	Tue	Wed	Thur	Fri	Sat
Routine	I	I	I	I	I	I	I

To relieve stress, perform E activities.

Routine I Activities (used to change baseline levels)

_____

_____

_____

_____

_____

Stress-Relief E Activities (used to feel better temporarily)

_____

_____

_____

Outdoors

☐ Boating (E)
☐ Camping (I)
☐ Fishing (I)
☐ Hiking (I)
☐ Hunting (I)
☐ Other:

_____

_____

Family

☐ Get-togethers (I)
☐ Picnics (I)
☐ Trips/travel (I)
☐ Walks (I)
☐ Other:

_____

_____

Church

☐ Bible study (I)
☐ Church
  services (I, E)
☐ Get-togethers (I)
☐ Teach or attend
  Sunday school (I)
☐ Other:

_____

_____

Key:
E = Excitatory
I = Inhibitory

Sports

☐ Aerobics (I, E)
☐ Biking (E)
☐ Dancing (E)
☐ Fitness class (E)
☐ Golf (E)
☐ Jogging (E)
☐ Paddleball (E)
☐ Racquetball (E)
☐ Skiing (E)
☐ Swimming (E)
☐ Team sports:

_____

_____

☐ Tennis (E)
☐ Walking (I)
☐ Weight lifting (E)
☐ Other:

_____

_____

Motor Sports

☐ ATV (E)
☐ Dirt bike (E)
☐ Four-wheel/off road
  driving (E)
☐ Motorcycle
  (road) (E)
☐ Snowmobile (E)
☐ Vintage/classic
  cars (I, E)
☐ Other:

_____

_____

Nonphysical (Hobbies)

☐ Attend sporting
  events (I):

_____

_____

☐ Billiards (I)
☐ Cards (I)
☐ Carpentry (I)
☐ Collect things (I)
☐ Computers (I)
☐ Crafts (I):

_____

☐ Creative writing (I)
☐ Go to movies/
  plays/concerts (I)
☐ Landscaping (I)
☐ Music
  ☐ Play (E)
  ☐ Listen (I)
☐ Painting (art) (I)
☐ Puzzles
  ☐ Crosswords (I)
  ☐ Jigsaw (I)
☐ Reading (I)
☐ Table games (I)
☐ Video games (I)
☐ Watch TV (I)
☐ Woodworking (I)
☐ Work on Cars (I)
☐ Other:

_____

_____

Follow the routine schedule to keep in balance. When you feel out of balance, uptight, or anxious, stress-relief activities will alleviate the pressure.

Activity Program for Type F and Type H Profiles

If you have a Type F or H profile, you will benefit at least moderately from an exercise program. The goal is to burn up excitatory neurotransmitters, causing a decrease in neurochemical baseline levels.

Develop an exercise program consisting of routine E activities alternating with routine I activities. Select I and E activities from the activities list.

Do a five-minute warm-up, such as walking or stretching.

Do a twenty-minute exercise from the I list alternating with activities from the E list.

Do a five-minute cool down, such as walking or stretching.

Schedule

	Sun	Mon	Tue	Wed	Thur	Fri	Sat
Routine	I	E	I	E	I	E	I

To relieve stress, perform E or additional activities.

Routine E Activities   Routine I Activities

_____   _____
_____   _____
_____   _____
_____   _____

Stress-Relief E Activities

_____
_____
_____

Follow the routine schedule to keep in balance. When you feel out of balance, uptight, or depressed, stress-relief activities will alleviate the pressure.

Activity Program for Type E and Type G Profiles

If you have a Type E profile, you receive some benefit from the exercise program, but if you are Type G, you receive moderate to high benefits. Feedback systems are used to decrease neurotransmission levels.

Develop an exercise program that consists of *I* activities from the activities list.

Do a twenty-minute exercise from the *I* list.

	Schedule						
	Sun	Mon	Tue	Wed	Thur	Fri	Sat
Routine	I		I		I		I

To relieve stress, perform *I* or additional activities.

Routine *I* Activities (used to change baseline levels)

_____

_____

_____

_____

Stress-Relief *I* Activities (used to feel better temporarily)

_____

_____

_____

_____

Follow the routine schedule to keep in balance. When you feel out of balance, uptight, or depressed, stress-relief activities will alleviate the pressure.

Activity Program for Type B and Type D Profiles

If you have a Type B profile, you will benefit greatly from your activity program. It is an essential part of your recovery.

If you are a Type D, you will benefit moderately from your exercise program. You will use indirect methods to enhance neurotransmission, which results in the runner's high. Even though the exercise program may feel uncomfortable for the first thirty to forty-five days, you will start to feel better. You may need to exert self-discipline in combination with an adrenergic-rich diet for the first two months.

Develop an exercise program that consists of routine *E* activities from the activities list.

Do a five-minute warm-up, such as walking or stretching.

Do a twenty-minute exercise from the *E* list.

Do a five-minute cool down, such as walking or stretching.

Schedule

	Sun	Mon	Tue	Wed	Thur	Fri	Sat
Routine	E	E	E	E	E	E	E

To relieve stress, perform *E* or additional activities.

Routine *E* Activities (used to change baseline levels)

_____

_____

_____

_____

_____

Stress-Relief *E* Activities (used to feel better temporarily)

_____

_____

_____

_____

Follow the routine schedule to keep in balance. When you feel out of balance, uptight, or depressed, stress-relief activities will alleviate the pressure.

The exercise programs listed here are important to follow. They provide neurochemical changes and stress relief and balance. Although some persons resist and don't get much of a reward, I still encourage them to participate in some type of activity or hobby.

Activity Guidelines

1. The goal of an activity is not to make you more muscular or to help you perform better in any specific area. The goal is to promote your health and emotional well-being.

2. It is easier to follow a daily routine than a hit-or-miss approach.

3. If you begin to feel light-headed or uncomfortable while doing your activity, stop. Seek professional advice.

4. If you begin to have more physical or emotional complications after beginning to exercise, consult your physician.

5. Before beginning any exercise program, consult your physician to determine your activity.

FIGURE 26-1
Activities Program

	TYPE OF NEUROCHEMICAL PROFILE							
	A	B	C	D	E	F	G	H
Activities to change baseline levels	I	E	I	E	I	I,E	I	I,E
Activities for temporary stress relief	E	E	E	E	I	E	I	E
Additional activities to relieve objective stress	E	E	E	E	E	E	E	E
Additional activities to relieve subjective stress	E/I	E/I	E/I	E/I	E/I	E/I	E/I	E/I

Key: E = Excitatory; I = Inhibitory

Activity and Stress

These exercise programs affect baseline neurotransmitters. Follow them daily to get the maximum benefit.

Exercise relieves stress by changing neurotransmitters and also prevents stress through neurochemical baseline stabilization.

The type of activity you find to alleviate your stress is highly individualized. However, you should consider two different types of stressful situations.

1. Objective stress refers to stress from situations outside yourself—the kind you can't change, such as taxation, war, inflation, and often company policies. This type of stress creates a neurochemical release. To get relief, a Type *E* workout is generally more effective than Type *I* activities.

2. Subjective stress comes from within. It is that feeling you need to change, but you're afraid to change. Usually it's an unidentified stress and shows through a lack of energy or focus. The cause may be feelings of inadequacy, insecurity, and loneliness. Hobbies or fun activities of Type *I* or Type *E* may help you overcome this type of stress.

Conclusion

Diet and activity programs begin to get the brain ready for behavioral and thought changes. It is important that you follow an activity program. The preceding describes a method to assist you in developing one. If you find alterations to the suggestions work best for you, follow them. It is more important for you to follow an activity and exercise program consistently than to try to do one that doesn't work for you.

Since change can be stressful, you must be in good physical health and have some knowledge of stress-relief techniques. Neurochemicals that are beginning to achieve a better balance also perceive behavioral changes more accurately.

Once you have begun the activity and diet programs, you can then work on behavior and thought changes.

So, please

HELP YOURSELF.

Appendix A

Help Yourself in Ten Steps: Summary and Checklist

Summary. Thoughts change the way you view life. Your conflicting thoughts are generated by unresolved spiritual issues. These thoughts change your neurochemistry, and they create negative emotions. Your addictions have been your body's attempts to resolve the neurochemical changes that were induced by conflicts in the spiritual, psychological, and physical realms.

FIGURE A-1
How Unresolved Issues Change the Way You View Life

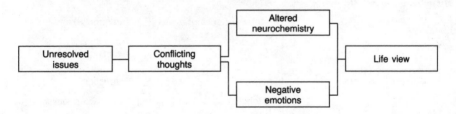

You became addicted to satisfy your compulsive theme—the cause of your addiction. Your brain must be balanced for you to achieve freedom from addiction. Imbalanced brains misperceive information and arrive at inappropriate conclusions.

Proper diet, exercise, activity, and behavioral techniques can make your mind ready to change. True change comes by changing your thoughts through spiritual recovery. The steps to spiritual recovery change your life and enhance your recovery from addiction.

Checklist. Following is a checklist of the main points in *Help Yourself.* The questions and options under each step will serve to focus your attention on what you need to do *for your specific personality* in order to help yourself.

Reference chapters for each subject are given in parentheses.

257

Step 1. Identify Your Entry Point

My entry point (*see chapters 14, 24*) is

- ☐ Emotional
- ☐ Physical
- ☐ Spiritual

Step 2. Identify Your Reward Center

Factors that contribute to the choice and creation of my addictive behavior (*see chapter 10*) are

- ☐ Baseline neurochemical levels
- ☐ External factors
- ☐ Internal factors
- ☐ Neurochemical personality
- ☐ Pavlovian (or conditioned) response
- ☐ Social environment

Step 3. Identify Your Themes and Behavior

My compulsive themes (*see chapters 11, 22*) are

- ☐ Adequacy
- ☐ Approval-Seeking
- ☐ Pleasure
- ☐ Power
- ☐ Recognition
- ☐ Responsibility Avoidance

My addictions (*see chapters 13, 22*) are

- ☐ Activity
- ☐ Alcohol/Drug
- ☐ Approval Seeking
- ☐ Caffeine
- ☐ Cleaning
- ☐ Control
- ☐ Exercise
- ☐ Food
- ☐ Gambling
- ☐ Hypochondria
- ☐ Intelligence/ Education
- ☐ Material
- ☐ Media Fascination
- ☐ Nicotine
- ☐ Perfection
- ☐ Physical Appearance
- ☐ Religion/Worship
- ☐ Rescuing
- ☐ Risk Taking/ Excitement
- ☐ Sex
  - ☐ Sexual Activity
  - ☐ Romance
  - ☐ Relationship
- ☐ Spending
- ☐ Stealing
- ☐ Violence
- ☐ Work

| Generally, my addictions (see chapter 22) are | ☐ Excitatory | ☐ Inhibitory |
| Generally, my major theme (see chapter 22) is | ☐ Excitatory | ☐ Inhibitory |

Step 4. Identify Your Neurochemical Issues

| The cause of my baseline neurotransmission alterations (see chapter 12) is | ☐ Genetic | ☐ Acquired |

Environmental influences (see chapter 19) are

☐ Cultural   ☐ Religious Values
☐ Family Systems   ☐ Sex Roles
☐ Friends/Peers   ☐ Social Values
☐ Racial/Ethnic

External factors (see chapters 10, 20) are

☐ Financial   ☐ Social
☐ Physical Health   ☐ Vocational/Job/School
☐ Relationship

Internal factors (see chapters 10, 20) are	☐ Self-Esteem	☐ Spiritual Conflicts
My neurochemical personality (see chapters 13, 21) is	☐ Arousal	☐ Satiation
My baseline neurotransmission level (see chapter 21) is	☐ Deficient	☐ Excessive

Step 5. Identify Your Neurochemical Profile

My neurochemical profile (see chapters 21, 23) is

☐ Type A   ☐ Type E
☐ Type B   ☐ Type F
☐ Type C   ☐ Type G
☐ Type D   ☐ Type H

Step 6. Get Your Brain Ready to Change

I have an activity and diet program (*see chapters 25, 26*) ☐ Yes ☐ No

Step 7. Identify Stages in Your Recovery

Techniques I need to use in Stage I (*see chapters 11, 18*) are

☐ Change Compulsive Themes
  ☐ Adequacy
  ☐ Approval Seeking
  ☐ Pleasure
  ☐ Power

☐ Recognition
☐ Responsibility Avoidance
☐ Eliminate Addiction
☐ Minimize Emotions of Loneliness and Fear

Techniques I need to use in Stage II (*see chapter 18*) are

☐ Develop Spiritual Health
☐ Resolve Conflicts
☐ Seek Professional Help
☐ Treat Neurochemical Addictions
☐ Use Support System

☐ Managing Unpredictable Emotions
  ☐ Identify the Emotion
  ☐ Offensive Methods
  ☐ Defensive Plan

Step 8. Choose Your Support System

Support systems I plan to use (*see chapter 16*) include

☐ Support Groups
  ☐ Family Systems
  ☐ Fellowships
  ☐ Outpatient Counseling
  ☐ Religious Support Groups

☐ Individuals
  ☐ Employee
  ☐ Employer
  ☐ Family Member
  ☐ Friend
  ☐ Minister

In developing my support system (*see chapters 16, 17*) I have

☐ Asked for Support
☐ Developed Accountability

I have talked with my
support person (*see
chapter 16*) about

- [ ] Acceptance
- [ ] Accountability
- [ ] Cheerleader Needs
- [ ] Goals and Expectations

- [ ] My Problems
- [ ] Reality Checks
- [ ] Role of Support Person

Step 9. Develop Your Spiritual Health

I am learning to (*see
chapter 15*)

- [ ] Change Attitudes Toward Conflicts in Life
- [ ] Develop Acceptance
- [ ] Develop Self-Discipline
- [ ] Develop Unconditional Love

- [ ] Forgive Others
- [ ] Listen to Others, Nature, and God
- [ ] Resolve Spiritual Conflicts
- [ ] Share with Others
- [ ] Surrender to God

Step 10. Accept Your Recovery as a Process

Recovery is a gradual process. It takes time. There is no need for you to hurry or try to force things to happen.

When you make mistakes—and you will make them—accept them, learn from them, and move on.

In accepting the
process, I

- [ ] Give up preconceived notions about addiction and recovery (*see chapters 1–6*)
- [ ] Develop spiritual health that brings with it peace and happiness (*see chapter 14*)
- [ ] Recover completely (*see chapters 7, 8, 9*)

Appendix B

Robertson Model of Behavior

Whenever a concept involving the central nervous system is discussed, it is often necessary to refresh the memory or educate the reader in the whole subject of neuroanatomy, neurophysiology, and neurochemistry. This appendix will help the inquisitive reader understand the principles used in this book. This technical information is not what is helpful to the person, but the practical application of the information presented in this book. The following information summarizes the important aspects of neurochemistry and neurotransmission. Although it is not to be considered complete, since textbooks would be required, it should provide the reader with an adequate understanding of the principles involved and assumptions made.

The definition of addiction in this book is similar to that used by Goodman[1] for practical reasons. He states it as follows: a process whereby a behavior, which can function both to produce pleasure and to provide escape from internal discomfort, is employed in a pattern characterized by (1) recurrent failure to control the behavior (powerlessness) and (2) continuation of the behavior despite significant negative consequences (unmanageability). The older concepts of tolerance and withdrawal are included in this discussion but are not the basis for a behavior becoming an addiction.

NEUROANATOMY

The nervous system is conceptually divided into two major areas, the peripheral nervous system and the central nervous system. The peripheral nervous system is composed of afferent and efferent fibers and is involved in conducting impulses. The afferent, generally the sensory and proprioceptive, fibers carry information to the central nervous system. Within the central nervous system the information is sifted, integrated, and interpreted, and an appropriate message is sent to the effector organ using the efferent or motor fibers. Functionally, the peripheral nervous system is further divided into two additional systems, the somatic or voluntary system and the autonomic or involuntary system. The somatic system controls the activities of the skeletal muscles, allowing the individual to adapt his activities and movements to his environment through his choice. The autonomic nervous system controls the activities of the visceral structures, smooth muscle, heart, and glands. The autonomic system is subdivided into two major divisions, the sympathetic and the parasympathetic. This distinction applies only to the efferent components since corresponding divisions cannot be made on the basis of afferent components. The afferent nerves are included in the autonomic nerve trunk but in most cases serve the somatic as well as the autonomic system.

The central nervous system is the most complex of the biological systems in the body. Fully understanding the integration and operation of over ten billion neurons and an even greater number of glial cells that account for the complicated and varied functions of the central nervous system is beyond our reach. However, medical research has learned much about the basic properties of individual neurons and neurotransmission. The central nervous system is composed of the spinal cord and the brain. The spinal cord acts as a transitional bundle between the central nervous system and the peripheral nervous system. Reflex and autonomic responses don't involve the brain, whereas somatic responses are carried to and interpreted by the brain.

The brain consists of the rhombencephalon, which functions in neural control of vital systems such as the respiratory and cardiovascular systems, controls the state of arousal, and interconnects the cerebellum. The cerebellum is located on the dorsal surface of the lower brainstem and functions in motor control by maintaining equilibrium, processing proprioceptive information, and modulating performance of voluntary movements. The mesencephalon or midbrain functions in auditory and visual activities at the reflex level. The upper part of the brainstem—the diencephalon—involves the thalamus, epithalamus, hypothalamus, and subthalamus. The thalamus is the station for ascending and descending sensory and motor functions. The epithalamus controls the pineal gland and the habenulae, while the hypothalamus controls temperature, water metabolism, and cardiovascular control. It also contains cell bodies of the neurosecretory cells of the posterior pituitary. It becomes especially significant in neurohormonal functions because of this trait. The subthalamus is involved with the extrapyramidal motor system, the red nucleus, and substantia nigra striatum. The telencephalon or cerebral hemispheres of the brain contain the limbic system, consisting of olfactory bulbs, septal nuclei, amygdala, and hippocampus, and the cerebrum containing frontal, parietal, temporal, and occipital lobes. The frontal lobe is associated with motor functions, the parietal with elaboration of thought and somatosensory functions, the temporal with memory and speech, and the occipital with thought and vision.

The brain is connected through several systems. The sensory involves the spinal cord connecting to the lower medulla through second order fibers; the lower medulla to midline to thalamus through the medial lemniscus; and the thalamus to somatosensory cortex through third order fibers. The motor connections are through the pyramidal system, the corticobulbar and corticospinal fibers, and the extrapyramidal system through the telencephalic basal ganglia. The motor connections involve the cerebral cortex, thalamus, basal ganglia, cerebellum, and brainstem nuclei. The central autonomic control or regulatory functions include respiration, cardiovascular, temperature regulation, hunger and thirst, and sexual activities. They are connected to the brainstem and hypothalamus. The limbic system functions with the olfactory system to modulate emotional behavior and is involved in learning and memory through the hippocampus. Essentially, that means it is possible to identify systems involved with sensory functions, motor activity, regulation of autonomic functions, control of respiration, and memory and association. These areas do not act independently but interact with one another to a considerable degree.

NEUROPHYSIOLOGY

Each system is complex and contains a large number of individual cells or neurons. It is well established that communication between neurons—and therefore between various parts of the brain—occurs primarily by chemical synaptic transmission. This communication occurs through electrochemical reactions and neurotransmitter release. Electrochemical reactions involve the individual cell and the level of chemicals within and outside the cell. Within each nerve fiber, anions accumulate immediately inside the cell membrane, while cations accumulate immediately outside the cell membrane. This cation/ anion ratio creates the membrane potential of the cell.

There are two basic ways to develop a membrane potential. The first is active transport of ions through the membrane, creating an imbalance in negative and positive charges on the two sides of the membrane. The second is diffusion of ions through the membrane as a result of a concentration difference between the two sides of the membrane. Active transport involving electrochemical issues occurs through what is known as the sodium-potassium-ATPase pump. A carrier protein will carry sodium to the exterior of the cell and potassium to the interior of the cell, using ATP as the energy source. This creates an imbalance in electrical charges since the anions cannot diffuse through the nerve membrane at all or diffuse very poorly. This sets up a membrane potential of approximately -85 millivolts, which is the resting potential. This potential remains until the membrane is disturbed by factors such as electrical stimulation, application of chemicals to the membrane, heat, cold, mechanical damage to the membrane, or any number of factors that momentarily affect the membrane. Once disrupted, the membrane develops an action potential. The action potential occurs in two separate stages known as depolarization and repolarization. The depolarization causes the nerve fiber to develop a positive charge through diffusion of sodium into the cell. The repolarization, which takes the cell back to the resting potential, occurs almost immediately after depolarization. This chain reaction occurs from one neuron to the other until it reaches the synaptic break in the nerve.

The typical neuron consists of three parts: the soma or the main body of the neuron, the axon (which extends from the soma into the peripheral nerve), and the dendrites (which are projections of the soma into the surrounding areas of the cord). The presynaptic terminals—the ends of nerve fibrils that originate in many other neurons—lie on the surfaces of the dendrites and soma. Some of these terminals are excitatory, and still others are inhibitory. The presynaptic terminals contain the excitatory or inhibitory neurochemicals in vesicles. When the action potential from the presynaptic nerves interacts with the vesicles, they cause a release of the neurotransmitter into the synaptic cleft. Mitochondria within the neuron provide ATP required for synthesis of new neurotransmitters. This transmitter released into the synaptic cleft causes the postsynaptic neuron to change its threshold of excitement. If the neurotransmitter is excitatory in nature, it creates an excitatory postsynaptic potential, causing the resting potential to decrease and an action potential to occur. If the neurotransmitter is inhibitory in nature, it creates a hyperpolarization or an inhibitory postsynaptic potential, causing the resting potential to increase.[2]

The main events in neurochemical transmission include (1) the synthesis of the neurotransmitter and its storage in a synaptic vesicle, (2) the entry of calcium ions into the vesicle and the release of the neurotransmitter into the synaptic cleft, (3) the combination of the neurotransmitter with receptors on the postsynaptic membrane, (4) the depolarization of the postsynaptic membrane causing the response, (5) the inactivation of the neurotransmitter through enzymatic breakdown, removal by diffusion, and reuptake, and (6) the repolarization of the postsynaptic membrane.

It is important to look at neurotransmission more closely to understand neurochemistry and behavior.

Synthesis of neurotransmitters

Five major neurotransmitters will affect the central nervous system, using four pathways. The catecholamine or adrenergic pathway is involved in the biosynthesis of dopamine and norepinephrine. The same pathway continues to cause the development of epinephrine, which is involved significantly in the peripheral nervous system. The amino acids phenylalanine and tyrosine are the main sources of precursors in the development of the catecholamines. Tyrosine is converted to dihydroxyphenylalanine(dopa) through the enzyme tyrosine hydroxylase. This synthesis requires iron and oxygen and tetrahydropteridine cofactor, is the rate limiting step, and is inhibited by excessive amounts of dopa, dopamine, and norepinephrine. Dihydroxyphenylalanine(dopa) is then decarboxylated to dopamine by the enzyme l-aromatic amino acid decarboxylase. This enzyme requires pyridoxal phosphate and is widely available. Dopamine is then taken up into storage vesicles where it is converted to norepinephrine by the enzyme dopamine beta-hydroxylase or is destroyed by monoamine oxidase. For uptake, ATP and magnesium are required. Cofactors for the enzyme are copper and ascorbic acid. Norepinephrine forms a stable complex with ATP and protein in the vesicles. In the adrenal medulla, norepinephrine is N-methylated by phenylethanolamine-N-methyltransferase, requiring adenosylmethionine. The activity of the enzyme is controlled by glucocorticoids.

The serotonergic pathway is involved in the synthesis of 5-hydroxytryptamine (serotonin). The precursor of serotonin is tryptophan, which is converted to 5-hydroxytryptophan by the enzyme tryptophan-5-hydroxylase, which is the rate limiting step. 5-hydroxytryptophan is then converted by aromatic-L-amino acid decarboxylase to 5-hydroxytryptamine. It requires pyridoxal phosphate as a cofactor.

Acetylcholine is another neurotransmitter that is synthesized from choline, requiring choline acetylase and acetyl-co-enzyme A. The major energy source is ATP, and it requires sodium for maximal synthesis.

Gamma-amino-butyric acid is synthesized from the amino acid glutamic acid, requiring the enzyme glutamic acid decarboxylase and pyridoxal phosphate as a cofactor. It is one of the most widely distributed neurotransmitters.

Release of neurotransmitters

The release of neurotransmitters from the vesicle to the synaptic cleft involves the action potential causing a shift in calcium with the resultant exocytosis process occurring. There are numerous hypotheses regarding the modulation of the release of neurotransmitters. One such hypothesis is the presynaptic regulation of norepinephrine release through a negative feedback mechanism. In this hypothesis, the norepinephrine release in response to nerve stimulation triggers a negative feedback mechanism leading to decreased release of further norepinephrine. Another such hypothesis involves the endorphin system that may interact and cause negative feedback to the release of neurotransmitters. Perhaps the most promising is the role of the cyclic nucleotides in synaptic transmission. The two most significant are the cyclic 3', 5'-adenosine monophosphate (cyclic-AMP) and the cyclic $3',5'$ = guanosine monophosphate (cyclic-GMP). Adenosine triphosphate (ATP) is the precursor for cyclic-AMP, while guanosine triphosphate (GTP) is the precursor for cyclic-GMP. ATP is converted to cyclic-AMP through the enzyme adenylate cyclase, and GTP to cyclic-GMP through guanylate cyclase. The metabolism of both is catalyzed by phosphodiesterase. Cyclic-GMP and cyclic-AMP act in opposition to each other.

The regulation of the activity of a family of enzymes known as protein kinases is mediated by these cyclic nucleotides. Activated kinases catalyze phosphorylation of protein. The specificity of the action of these enzymes depends on the nature of the protein kinase and various substrates for these protein kinases in various tissues. The cyclic-AMP system is postulated to function as follows: an action potential stimulates adenylate cyclase; this converts ATP to cyclic-AMP; cyclic-AMP activates protein kinase to catalyze phosphorylation of a specific membrane protein; this protein causes a change in ion permeability of the membrane, resulting in the influx of sodium and/or calcium ions in nerve endings; this causes depolarization; cyclic-AMP is then metabolized by phosphodiesterase, and phosphoprotein phosphatase dephosphorylates the phosphorylated specific protein, causing repolarization. If the enzyme adenylate cyclase is localized within plasma membranes, and it appears to be, it may be the receptor or localized in the receptor. The enzyme appears to have two subcomponents. The first faces the cell exterior that recognizes "first messengers" and specific hormones. The second faces the interior of the cell and causes synthesis of cyclic-AMP from ATP through catalyzing biosynthesis. Cyclic-AMP or cyclic-GMP would be the "second messenger" and activate the protein kinases.

Combination of neurotransmitters with postsynaptic membrane

When a neurotransmitter is released into the synaptic cleft, it will combine with the postsynaptic membrane in a specific receptor site. The number of receptor sites, their affinity, their specificity, and their competition with other chemicals will determine the level of depolarization of the postsynaptic membrane.

Depolarization

Once the neurotransmitter has acted upon the postsynaptic membrane, the influx of sodium and/or calcium causes depolarization and an action potential to develop.

Inactivation

The neurotransmitter will then be inactivated in three methods. The *first* method is reuptake into the vesicles, which is probably the most significant of the methods for norepinephrine. The reuptake of norepinephrine into the nerve terminals involves at least two steps: (1) transport of norepinephrine across the membrane into the neuron (2) binding in the storage vesicle. The transport requires the presence of sodium ions in the cleft, metabolic energy, and continued functioning of sodium, potassium, and ATPase. The binding of the norepinephrine in the vesicle requires magnesium-dependent ATPase activities. The *second* method of inactivation is the enzymatic inactivation of the neurotransmitters. Norepinephrine and dopamine are metabolized through two enzymatic systems. The catechol-O-methyltransferase (COMT) converts norepinephrine to vanillylmandelic acid (VMA) requiring adenosylmethionine and magnesium. The monoamine oxidase (MAO) system deaminates the amines to aldehydes. Aldehyde dehydrogenase then converts the aldehyde to acid requiring NADPH. Dopamine is converted to homovanillic acid (HVA). Aldehyde reductase converts the aldehyde to alcohol requiring NAD. Norepinephrine is converted to methoxy-hydroxyphenylethylglycol (PHPG). Serotonin is metabolized by monoamine oxidase to hydroxyindolacetaldehyde, which is turn is metabolized by aldehyde dehydrogenase to 5 hydroxyindolacetic acid (5HIAA). A significant effect on the serotonin levels can be achieved by inhibiting the reuptake of serotonin as seen with the administration of fluoxetine. Acetylcholine is metabolized by acetylcholinesterase to release choline and an acetylated enzyme. This acetylated enzyme then reacts with water to give acetic acid and the regenerated enzyme. This creates a cycle of regeneration. Gamma-amino-butyric acid enters the Krebs cycle and is converted to succinic acid. *Third,* some of the neurotransmitters are diffused by physical removal by the blood and metabolism in the liver and/or kidney.

Repolarization

Repolarization occurs almost immediately by returning the cell to a resting potential through the sodium-potassium-ATPase pump.

The above information is widely available in medical textbooks, textbooks on neurology, medical physiology textbooks, and various other sources. Individual references are omitted for this reason. This summary of neuroanatomy and neurophysiology is the basis for understanding neurotransmission, the brain, and behavior.

HELP YOURSELF POSITIONS AND ASSUMPTIONS

Various positions are taken in this book. Simple descriptions have been used so that the reader can understand such complex information. It is fully understood that simplicity carries a risk of confusion or misunderstanding but must exist to be functional to the lay audience. The following principles have been discussed in simpler forms in the book. Although the discussion is not exhaustive, it offers validity to the statements in the book. Some assumptions are made based upon present knowledge. The exact mechanism for some of the assumptions will, admittedly, be proven different eventually from what is presented here, but nonetheless should be close enough in concept to make the assumptions realistic.

I. Neurochemicals are altered by thought processes, which alter perceptions

Scientific evidence to describe the exact method by which thoughts alter neurochemistry is not present. However, it is usually an easy concept to accept. Regardless of the part of the brain, whether it be the occipital lobe of the cerebrum, the parietal lobe of the cerebrum, or another area of the brain, that begins the electrochemical response to a thought, the process eventually alters neurotransmission. Any individual who has experienced fear or stress is aware of the excitement, increased wakefulness, diaphoresis, palpitation, and other physiological symptoms caused by neurotransmitter alterations from those precipitating thoughts. Psychiatry has long known that individuals with altered neurotransmission will perceive information differently. Individuals who are clinically depressed often suffer from altered neurotransmission.[3] Antidepressants that affect metabolism or reuptake and/or act as false neurotransmitters can have dramatic effects on these individuals' perceptions. Pharmacotherapy that is specific to alter neurotransmission has been proven to be effective in returning perceptions closer to reality.[4] The obvious and common use of neuroleptics for schizophrenia is one such example. It can be safely assumed that when neurotransmission is altered, perceptions are altered.

II. Neurotransmission can be altered genetically, through the external ingestion of chemicals, and by consistent, repeated behavior

Several psychiatric disorders are known to have some genetic correlations. Schizophrenia, one of the first diseases recognized to have a genetic correlation, is continuing to be investigated as to the exact causes. Recently, a correlation of neurotransmission and receptor sites is being postulated with N-methyl-D-aspartate being implicated.[5] Depression,[6] overeating, and other disorders are also being investigated further for genetic factors. Since there are genetic differences in responses to drug ingestion,[7] and drugs primarily affect neurotransmitters, it is safe to assume that behaviors, which also affect neurotransmission, may have genetic correlations. Alcoholism has a well-documented genetic correlation. One of the first studies showed that sons of alcoholics, who had been adopted by other families, were more than three times as likely to become alcoholic as the adopted sons of nonalcoholics. They were also more likely to become serious alcoholics at an early age.[8] The alteration of neurotransmission by ingestion of chemicals is well documented. In fact, that is the basis for the use of most psychopharmaceuticals. The multiplicity of effects that alcohol causes on the neurochemical systems varies from the endorphins[9] to 5-hydroxytryptamine.[10] The concept of long-term behavior causing neurotransmission alterations is just beginning to be studied. One of the premier studies in this area shows that gambling causes an alteration in the levels of neurotransmitters in pathological gamblers.[11] Recent studies have shown genetic correlations between (1) drug-seeking behaviors and (2) that ethanol, cocaine, and opiates may have at least some common biological determinants.[12] According to the findings of this study, these genotypic patterns of reinforcement in rats and mice appear to correlate highly with patterns of reinforcement from cocaine and opiates. The one common thread among totally different pharmacological and biochemical substances is their effects on neurotransmitters and the reward centers. Once again, the connecting link does not appear to be a specific gene but a specific method by which the brain handles altered neurotransmission. This is an important difference, even if both issues prove to be true. The gene theory on genetic correlation will probably occur between chemically similar substances, whereas the altered neurotransmission theory will connect behaviors and drugs that cause similar alterations in neurotransmission. This would explain more completely relapse and transfer of addiction. Although the mechanisms behind alterations caused by long-term behavior aren't known, the implications are important and need continued investigation. Further discussions regarding the effect of long-term behavior on neurotransmission will appear later in this appendix.

III. Reward centers have a corresponding biochemical component to them

The normal physiology of reward is a combination of neurotransmitters and neuromodulators working in concert to create a feeling of well-being in the person. Consensus in the literature is that intact serotonergic transmission is a prerequisite for "normal" behavior as it relates to reward mechanisms.[13] The enkephalins are also important as hypothalamic neurotransmitters, which are known to stimulate and release neuronal dopamine in the mesocortical regions of the brain. Dopamine or its metabolite, norepinephrine, serves as a substrate for reward sites in the ventral tegmental area and substantia nigra. The inhibitory neurotransmitter gamma-amino-butyric acid suppresses the firing of nigral dopaminergic neurons, preventing overstimulation of the nerve.[14] Factors creating any alterations in the biochemical makeup can change the brain's reward system. Alterations, as we will see later, could include behavior, diet, exercise, or chemical ingestion.

IV. There is a balance in the brain that is physiologically "the most comfortable" for each individual

One of the most essential concepts in this book is that there is a "normal" level of neurotransmission for each individual. Although genetics, life-style, and other components of one's life will cause each person's "normal" to be different from that of others, it is safe to assume an *individual* "normal" exists. This book has used an equation for simplicity's sake, relating neurotransmitter levels to feedback to equal an optimum level, to show a practical approach to this situation. Although the equation seems simple, many interrelated factors make up the equation. The process of feedback, the attempt to bring back to a predetermined level, is seen in the central nervous system. It helps to look at three interactive components—the reward center, intracellular changes, and neurohormonal adaptations—to determine how feedback interacts to maintain a "normal" level. Any alteration in any area will change what "normal" is to the person and subsequently create a change in thoughts and eventually in behavior.

A. Reward center level

We have previously discussed the fine balance of the serotonergic pathway and the enkephalinergic-dopaminergic pathways. The levels of endorphins,[15] enkephalins, dynorphin,[16] and opiate receptor binding sites[17] will also affect the brain's ability to achieve rewards. It appears the brain's reward center has naturally occurring opiatelike substances such as enkephalins and endorphins, which fit opioid receptor sites precisely. When these receptor sites are filled, the individual experiences feelings of well-being or satisfaction. Essentially this means that a reward is a chemical response in the brain. Alterations of these "reward" chemicals could cause the person's response to and desire for a behavior to be altered. This may set up a situation whereby the "psychological" reward and "physiological" normal will differ, thereby causing an alteration in feedback to normalize the physiology, causing dysphoric feelings for the person. Alternatively, the feedback could exist to maintain a euphoria for the person, causing physiological consequences, such as anxiety or clinical depression.

B. Intracellular adaptations

Probably the most exciting and most likely cause of neurotransmission adaptation will occur intracellularly. Several methods can cause adaptation and feedback: (1) adenylate cyclase adaptation, (2) inhibition of the release of neurotransmitters, (3) alterations in the reuptake of neurotransmitters, or (4) alterations in the synthesis of neurotransmitters.

1. Adenylate cyclase adaptation

Earlier in the Appendix we discussed the effects of adenylate cyclase and guanylate cyclase. It is clear that cyclic nucleotide levels can be altered by the exposure of neural tissues to various neurotransmitters.[18] The implications are that excessive amounts of neurotransmitters may cause feedback, hence increasing or decreasing the activity levels of the cyclic nucleotides. This would explain why an increasing amount of excitatory neurotransmitter release may cause a decreased effect after a prolonged period of time. Any thought, behavior, or chemical that would cause an increase in excitatory neurotransmitter release into the synaptic cleft, over a period of time, could cause a decrease in activation of cyclic-AMP by adenylate cyclase, thereby creating less potential for depolarization of the cell. This may explain, in part, why pathological gamblers have increased levels of 3-methoxy-4-hydroxymandelic acid in the urine.[19] A slight variation in the concept may be that the increase in phosphoinositide turnover occurs from excitatory neurotransmitters.[20] And a final variation, although less likely, is the alteration of the calcium ion, acting as a second messenger.[21] Any one of the three, a combination of any, or some yet-to-be-determined method would eventually cause a decrease in the depolarization of the neuron with prolonged excitatory neurotransmitter release. From a practical standpoint we might assume that activities performed regularly that stimulate norepinephrine or dopamine release would cause a decrease in the activity of adenylate cyclase over time. Therefore, a type of "behavioral tolerance" to the euphoria or neurostimulation may be noted. The converse can be expected with inhibitory neurotransmission and guanylate cyclase. Research on inhibitory neurotransmission is extremely difficult because of the wide distribution of gamma-amino-butyric acid in central and peripheral neurons.

2. Inhibition of the release of neurotransmitters

There are numerous hypotheses regarding the modulation of the release of neurotransmitters. One such hypothesis is the presynaptic regulation of norepinephrine release through a negative feedback mechanism. In this hypothesis, the norepinephrine release in response to nerve stimulation triggers a negative feedback mechanism leading to deceased release of further norepinephrine. When amphetamines were administered for long periods of time, the striatal dopamine and other brain monoamines were depleted.[22] This depletion could be caused by decreasing release, causing decreasing biosynthesis of the neurotransmitters in the brain. Another such hypothesis involves the endorphin system that may interact and cause negative feedback to the release of neurotransmitters. Alcohol has been linked to deficits of central neurotransmission. The pineal gland plays an important role in modulating ethanol intake. The beta-endorphin, enkephalin, and dynorphin system is involved in the actions of alcohol and opiates. There is evidence to link ingestive behaviors with the ventral tegmental accumbenshypothalamic axis, whereby the biogenic amines dopamine and serotonin are reciprocally involved.[23] The negative feedback in this situation could be a direct effect of alcohol on the pineal gland or a secondary effect of the endorphin system. It is reasonable to assume some mechanisms exist, when excessive amounts of neurotransmitters are released, to prevent further release from the vesicles.

3. Alterations in the reuptake of neurotransmitters

Perhaps the most widely publicized alterations in the reuptake of neurotransmitters involve cocaine. Cocaine impairs the reuptake of norepinephrine, thereby causing a greater hypersensitivity.[24] This study and others that describe the effects of antidepressant medications, amphetamine and amphetaminelike derivatives, and other psychopharmaceuticals that alter the reuptake of neurotransmitters do not imply that this effect can occur outside chemical intervention. However, these studies do show that any alteration in the reuptake of neurotransmitters can have a profound effect on neurotransmission. Since reuptake involves a fine balance of sodium, potassium, and ATP, it is reasonable to assume that some neurohormonal or feedback effects involving the reuptake of neurotransmitters will be determined in future studies.

4. Alterations in the synthesis of neurotransmitters

Alterations in the synthesis of neurotransmitters fall into two areas. The first is the availability of substrates, cofactors, and precursors that will be utilized in the biosynthesis of neurotransmitters. The second is in the alteration or inhibition of the synthesis of neurotransmitters. The first, which involves the availability of substrates, cofactors, and precursors, is one of the most debated areas in this field. On one side are those who advocate the use of dietary manipulation to alter neurochemistry. On the other are those who believe that dietary manipulation plays little or no role in the synthesis of neurotransmitters. Advocates for the use of dietary manipulation to alter neurotransmission claim fluctuations in the availability to the brain of tryptophan and tyrosine cause major changes in the rates at which neurons synthesize serotonin and the catecholamines, respectively. When plasma levels of these neurons are altered, parallel changes in the amounts of tryptophan and tyrosine that are transported to the brain are observed.[25] Another study assessed the administration of precursors to serotonin on the effect of inducing sleep in newborn infants. A modified formula, containing tryptophan or valine within the range of concentrations found in human milk, was administered to the newborn infants. The study found that infants fed tryptophan entered quiet sleep and active sleep sooner than infants fed valine and spent more time in active sleep and less time alert.[26] Vitamin cofactors have also been implicated in the alteration of moods.[27] In addition, Blum and associates have conducted numerous studies to determine the effect of amino acid supplements on reducing drug hunger and withdrawal from treatment against advice rates of cocaine abusers,[28] improvement of inpatient treatment of the alcoholic as a function of neurotransmitter restoration,[29] and restoration of neurogenetic deficits using neuronutrient adjuncts.[30] With all the research performed on the use of nutrients and supplements to affect behavior, there is still controversy about its beneficial effects. Perhaps this is a situation where unproven and unsubstantiated claims, marketed to the public, as to the effects of amino acids, vitamins, minerals, and other nutrients have tainted the research and conclusions of the investigators. It appears that one group is trying to prove the effectiveness while another is trying to prove the ineffectiveness to satisfy preconceived positions. However, there appear to be some beneficial dietary effects that are inconsistent among the population. The ability to determine who will benefit can be accomplished only through trial and error at this point. It is unwise to make unsubstantiated claims regarding beneficial dietary effects for all.

The other manner in which biosynthesis is altered is through feedback or the interference in and alterations of the activity of enzymes, cofactors, or substrates involved in the biosynthesis of neurotransmitters. It is well established that neurotransmitters have a negative feedback in their own biosynthesis. Dopa, dopamine, and norepinephrine inhibit tyrosine hydroxylase, thereby modulating biosynthesis of the catecholamines.[31] An alteration of the enzyme dopamine beta-hydroxylase is a basis for the use of neuroleptics in the treatment of schizophrenia. The lack of substrates, genetic enzyme alterations, or many other factors can contribute to altered biosynthesis of the neurotransmitters.

C. Neurohormonal effects

The functions of the body are primarily regulated by the nervous system and the endocrine system. The endocrine system, through its effects on adenylate cyclase, protein metabolism, cellular metabolism, and many others, affects the function of the nervous system. Many pharmaceuticals, such as the adrenocortical steroids, cardiovascular regulators, oral contraceptives, and thyroid replacement products, can have profound influences on the central nervous system through their alterations in feedback and release of factors involved in neurotransmission.[32] The hypothalamus-pituitary axes involving the adrenal, thyroid, and pancreas are especially interesting in their effects on neurotransmission and behavior. Norepinephrine probably stimulates the secretion of luteinizing hormone releasing factor, thyrotrophin releasing factor, and growth hormone releasing factor from the hypothalamus. Dopamine appears to stimulate the secretion of prolactin inhibitory factor, while serotonin may inhibit the secretion of prolactin inhibitory factor and thyrotrophin releasing factor. There is also a catecholamine link in the corticotrophin releasing factor. Alterations in these releasing factors cause a varied type of central effects, ranging from depression to rage, and physiological effects from menstruation to sleep regulation.[33] Examples are numerous in the literature where alterations in neurotransmitters affect behavior. Opioids and endogenous opiates, or endorphins, have similar neuropsychiatric responses.[34] These endorphins are likely to have similar effects on the neuroendocrine system as the opiates have been shown to have. For example, opioids have long been known to affect the neurohormonal system exhibited by their inhibition of sexual behavior.[35] If an increase in endorphin, enkephalin, or dynorphin occurs, one can assume similar inhibition of sexual behaviors. Alterations of neurotransmitters that affect neurotransmission will have behavior effects mediated through the neuroendocrine system. Conversely, any alteration to the hormonal system can have profound effects on the nervous system. Premenstrual syndrome, postpartum depression, Addison's disease, hypothyroidism, and a host of other diseases have obvious behavioral symptoms associated with the changing hormonal system. There may be a possible involvement of endorphin imbalance causing dysphoric changes seen in these syndromes. A study, which postulated that the possibility exists for the imbalance of endorphins in premenstrual syndromes and postpartum depression because of the characteristic psychiatric symptomology, reported hormonal changes and the involvement of endorphins in neuroendocrine regulation.[36] Obviously, the complicated link between the endocrine system and the nervous system involves feedback, neurochemical alterations, and the creation of behavioral symptoms.

The concepts described above are extremely complicated and interactive; it is impossible, at this point, to determine their exact integration with one another. However, it is safe to assume the total body is involved in trying to maintain a homeostasis that is "physiologically normal" for that person. This "normal" is not necessarily "psychologically normal" since any single physiological alteration, caused by genetics, generational or environmental reorganization, or present life-style, could alter the body's homeostasis.

V. Exercise may create emotional and physical effects on the body

There is almost universal acceptance that exercise can be beneficial to a person's physiology. Increased cardiovascular perfusion, skeletal muscle toning, and metabolic alterations are among the numerous positive reasons to exercise and are rarely disputed. The issue that is disputed, by a few, is the effect that exercise may have on neurotransmission. Perhaps the interest in this area was piqued by the description of a "high" by marathon runners. Controversy focuses on exercising for mental health. Exercise affects the neurohormonal system and the peripheral nervous system in several ways.[37] Although this study discusses the release of norepinephrine and exercise intolerance in patients with heart failure, it touches on the various factors that may be neurohormonal in nature, affecting neurotransmitters. In another study, the effect of exercise, feedback, and central nervous system involvement is discussed. In this study, the authors conclude the cerebellum is a probable modulating factor in the cardiovascular response. It appears an integration of information from the peripheral afferent fibers, the cerebellum, and the cerebral cortex occurs to result in overall neural control. Exercise training probably modifies the central integration of information and modifies the cardiovascular response to exercise and other stresses.[38]

Perhaps the most interesting review article that suggests exercise has a direct effect on the brain monoamines is one written by Chaouloff. A review of the literature shows that a relationship between exercise and mental health does exist. Physical exercise has been reported to reduce depression symptoms and anxiety and to improve the ability to cope with stress. There appears to be a correlation between endorphins, dopamine, norepinephrine, and serotonin transmission with exercise that can be beneficial to a person's mental health.[39]

It is inaccurate to assume that as much exercise as a person can tolerate is healthy. Fatigue and depression can be seen in overtraining of athletes with an etiology relating to neurotransmission alterations.[40] An increase in 5-hydroxytryptamine synthesis in the brain may be mediated by an increase in the plasma concentration of free tryptophan, thereby causing fatigue during exercise. Glutamine is essential for the proper functioning of cells of the immune system, and a decrease in plasma glutamine concentration postexercise and in overtraining may induce an impairment in immune function. Branched-chain amino acids may be involved in both processes and may be important precursors of nitrogen for the synthesis of glutamine in skeletal muscle or important in the control of glutamine release in muscle. Branched-chain amino acids compete with free tryptophan for entry into the brain. Therefore, a balance of exercise and the level of utilization of branched-chain amino acids and tryptophan appear to be important to prevent fatigue in exercise and depression. Although we are far from knowing the exact amount of exercise or activity appropriate for each person, it is safe to assume there is an appropriate level of exercise for each person. For now, clinical symptoms are the easiest method to determine such levels.

VI. Diet can affect neurotransmission

The section on neurotransmitter synthesis has described numerous studies to support the use of dietary manipulation for management of neurotransmitter levels. In the Preface, it is also stated that the use of dietary manipulation is controversial, and the position is taken to allow a person to try dietary manipulation if desired and then evaluate the specific responses. It is difficult to determine placebo, somatization effects, or behavioral dysfunction in this area. The political climate of professionals versus lay advocates of vitamin and mineral supplementation will probably exist for some time. More complete studies that overcome the major methodologic problems of defining suitable baseline conditions and dealing with large ranges in dose, time course, and severity of symptoms will need to be undertaken to determine the most accurate position.

The assumptions noted are used to develop a model of behavior that is practical but inclusive of the total body and the complex interactions that occur within. Any model of behavior based upon evolving science and research will have assumptions that will prove to be erroneous, in part or total, as research and information continue to be developed. It is most important to evaluate the *concepts* used to develop a model to determine its application to science and longevity. The concepts described here are based upon present research and are reasonable in their approach to compulsive behaviors. They will and must allow for change in the future as research continues, but provide a functional approach to those in need of assistance now. The Robertson Institute is not in and of itself a research institute; the Institute synthesizes information from other researchers, develops a concept, and applies it to the recovery field. Those interested in double-blind, crossover, and controlled studies will be disappointed with the availability of such. However, those looking for information to validate the assumptions made in this book will probably be comfortable with the decision to make the concepts functional and applicable to the individual seeking relief from addiction(s).

Robertson Model of Behavior

The model of behavior described includes all behavior—not just that of individuals suffering from compulsive disorders. Different philosophical and psychological bents can be incorporated in the model.

1. Conflicts produce thoughts

The first assumption made in this model is that conflicts produce thoughts. Specific conflict is not defined since each individual's social, environmental, and personal experiences and personality will determine the perception of conflict. However defined, conflicts produce thoughts. They may be thoughts of anger, fear, guilt, inadequacy, excitement, or any number of others.

2. Inaccurate perceptions produce inaccurate thoughts

Although not a profound statement, it is an often overlooked concept. If a person's perceptions are not accurate, the recovery will not be based upon reality. A person's perceptions will store information in the brain as fact. Recall is based upon past experiences and interpretation of such experiences, which depend on one's perceptions.

3. Neurochemical alterations can be caused by thoughts

Previously, we have discussed the alterations of neurochemicals through thoughts. Exact mechanisms are not necessary to develop the model, although the concept is important. The conflicts or perceptions that have created the thoughts thus create neurochemical alterations.

4. Neurochemical alterations cause emotional responses

It is clear and obvious to anyone involved in the field of psychiatry, psychology, or pharmacology that alterations in neurotransmission create various clinical signs and symptoms. A decrease in norepinephrine, dopamine, or serotonin can cause depression, disturbances in sleep, and other signs indicative of depression. Psychopharmacology is predominantly involved with choosing or developing more specific pharmaceuticals to alter specific neurotransmitters and their resultant effects on neurotransmission. It is recognized that attempting to determine exact neurotransmitter alterations requires laboratory and clinical evaluation. However, a clinical "feeling" that can be related to neurotransmission levels may be determined subjectively by the person. The person who experiences depression without external forces, medical illness, or precipitating factors is more likely to experience symptoms indicative of neurochemical deficits than persons not experiencing depression. The deficits may be in the neurotransmitters, serotonin, norepinephrine, dopamine, or other neuromodulating effects, such as the reward center chemicals. Additionally, it is assumed individuals don't always recognize their depression. That is precisely why the position taken in this book encourages a person to maintain or contact a mental health professional if recovery cannot be achieved through a self-help system.

A neurochemical evaluation that has been referred to in the book is the Institute's proprietary evaluation tool. This tool is based upon a study involving 286 patients recovering from various addictions in an outpatient setting. Questions involving subjective emotional observations were correlated with objective responses to determine a possible neurotransmitter excess or deficit link. The objective questions were developed by using known pharmacological effects of specific psychotropics and/or known symptoms associated with neurotransmitter excesses or deficits. The stronger the correlation between the objective questions, laboratory indices, and/or pharmacological response, the greater the weighing of the question. A correlation was found to a varying degree on 180 of 250 questions. Although the evaluation determines a probable neurotransmitter alteration, it requires clinical verification to be validated. The study found a level of neurotransmission, either increased or decreased, was easier to determine than exact neurotransmitter alterations. Since the model doesn't require the exact alteration, only subjective interpretation of neurotransmission by the person, it becomes a useful piece of information to persons in the recovery field.

5. Emotional responses cause a person to respond with a subsequent behavior

A person's choice of behavior when depressed or anxious is determined by numerous factors. Sociological, environmental, economic, and personal preferences are among the few determinants of the behavior performed in response to emotions. For example, individuals may vary in their response to depression from running to eating to avoidance to sleeping. Responses to anxiety are equally varied. It has been observed by the Institute that individuals will tend to prefer or use certain behavioral themes fairly consistently. This has resulted in classifying certain behaviors as excitatory, others as inhibitory, and some as both. For example, risk taking, crime, and violence, for all practical purposes, are excitatory behaviors. Reading, sewing, and overeating are generally inhibitory or "mellowing out" activities. However, using alcohol, worshiping, or working may be either. The individual's interpretation of how he feels when he "needs" to participate in the activity is significant. This classification of behavior is important to determine if a person is depressed (possible neurotransmission deficits) and is responding through inhibitory activities or is responding through behavioral compensation with excitatory activities.

6. Behavior causes a reward

The Pavlovian experience and the experience of pleasure or relief of pain will determine if originally attempted behavior is repeated. Obviously this reinforcement is very complex and poorly understood. Previously discussed was the impact of endorphins, serotonin, and dopamine on the ability to "feel" a reward. A behavior becomes reinforcing when it creates a reward to the person. Individuals tend to use a certain level of behavior fairly consistently, depending on the emotion they experience. For example, some individuals will tend toward quiet, self-reflective activities when they are stressed, while others tend toward active, gregarious activities. Following observation and study by the institute of over ten thousand patients, Milkman and Sunderwirth's terms[41] of satiation personality and arousal personality were adopted. Although somewhat arbitrarily assigned, they serve as a beginning of categorizing behavioral themes. Milkman and associates use similar terminologies in their hypotheses of drug preference.[42] It is recognized and accounted for that arousal and satiation levels are affected by age and sociocultural factors. A reward is assumed to be a reward when it returns the person to a "feeling" of homeostasis or comfort. The exact mechanism is unknown and may be any one or a number of the mechanisms discussed previously.

7. Behavior can be used to "self-medicate" or it can be a response to neurochemical alterations

Behavioral responses have been divided into two categories. The first is behavior caused by neurochemical alterations. For example, a person showing norepinephrine deficits may exhibit symptoms of vegetative depression. The behavior is altered because of the depression. The second type of behavior is compensatory behavior. In this situation, a person may have norepinephrine deficits but use risk taking or sexual activity to compensate for the depression through seeking excitatory neurochemical stimulation. The determination of whether a behavior is caused by or in response to neurotransmission alterations is important in determining the most appropriate treatment.

8. Neurochemical personalities are helpful to determine compliance, activity, diet, or behavioral changes

The three factors used in this model—the preferred reward (arousal or satiation), the predominant type of behavioral themes utilized (inhibitory or excitatory), and subjective feelings of anxiety or depression (deficient or excessive neurotransmission)—create a combination of nine different subtypes or neurochemical personalities. These have been determined based upon the manner in which a person is classified in the above three areas.

Application of neurochemical personalities

This model furnishes a reasonable way to group addictive persons and their response to therapy. It can assist a person in determining whether behavioral modification techniques should be sought first or whether neurochemical manipulation through dietary, activity, pharmacological, or behavioral adjustments should be first. It is assumed both will be the ultimate; however, modification of behavior while an altered neurotransmission level exists can lead to inaccurate perceptions. Diet can be chosen based upon probable neurotransmitter deficits, although it is extremely difficult to determine an exact diet; a trial and error approach is used with the most logical choice offered first. Additionally, diet may be ineffective in changing neurotransmission levels in some and may be inappropriate. Exercise may be prescribed based upon what a person enjoys, combined with the level of neurotransmission the person appears to have. Exercise may be used to relieve stress or to be an adjunct for neurochemical alteration.

Once again, it is highly variable, but reasonable first choice approaches are offered to the person. Choice of behavior, support groups, and other behavioral modification techniques are applied, based upon rewards, to prevent a person from "feeling out of place or misunderstood." These choices of behavior have been determined by assigning a person a neurochemical personality type and evaluating responses to group therapy, individual therapy, and self-reflective, emotive, experiential, regressive, and cognitive therapy. Patient preference and therapist perceptions of patient response to therapy were then determined. Although still highly subjective and dependent on individual therapist talent, personality, and level of sophistication, it is the beginning of the ability to predetermine patient services.

A behavioral tolerance and withdrawal exist

Of all the concepts presented, the concept of behavioral tolerance is the most theoretical, yet most practical. If behavior causes a release of neurotransmitters and is repeated consistently, will the central nervous system adapt? That is the most entertaining of all the questions asked in the synthesis of this model. Considering that the treatment of compulsive disorders has been reasonably unsuccessful, with high relapse rates and transfer of addiction common,[43] there must be a link that needs to be addressed.

Whether the addiction is wealth,[44] compulsive overeating,[45] sexual addiction,[46] or any of the others, a common characteristic exists: behavior escalates until it gets out of control. Two elements may contribute to this escalation. The first is meeting psychological needs; the second is meeting physiological needs. Drug addiction, tolerance, and withdrawal are clearly psychological[47] and physiological.[48]

Can we extrapolate our experiences to behavior? If behavior causes an alteration in levels of neurotransmission or neurotransmitters, as seen in the urinary metabolites of gamblers,[49] then it is plausible to assume such alterations occur in other behaviors. In a recent article I described the neurobiological effects of sexual addiction.[50] It appears, according to the previous discussions, the central nervous system handles excessive neurotransmission through a modulation system. The method could be cellular, neurohormonal, endorphin related, neurotransmitter synthesis or metabolism, or any combination. Whatever the cause, the result is the same: the "relief" or "reward" sought through the behavior will need to be escalated to bring about the same effect. If the behavior is escalated and a modulating mechanism takes place, the endocrine and nervous systems will become involved. Some changes are immediate, while others respond more slowly. The neurohormonal mechanisms and protein alterations that respond more slowly could be responsible for "unbalanced feelings" after discontinuing the behavior. Many people describe feelings of mood swings that interfere with their recovery several months into their recovery program. Therefore, for them to obtain a "reward" or to feel "normal," the behavior would need to be reinstituted or one with similar neurotransmitter responses substituted. This is a plausible explanation for transfer of addictions or the poor treatment rates seen in addictions.[51] Essentially, this would mean we have never treated addiction, only the responses to addiction. Alcoholism, overeating, or other compulsive behaviors can be primary disorders, at least initially; but they become secondary in time as neurotransmission and brain chemistry adapt. By tailoring diet, activity or exercise, behavior, and rewards to "treat" the individual, compliance improves, brain chemistry is allowed to return to a more "physiological-psychological" homeostasis, addiction recovery rates improve, and relapse rates are lowered.

This model is functional. If persons follow the concepts, not necessarily the details, of the model, they will have potential to overcome their addictions.

NOTES

1. Goodman, A., 1990, Addiction: definition and implications, *Br. J. Addict* 85:621–27.

2. Enna, S. J., and Gallagher, J. P., 1983, Biochemical and electrophysiological characteristics of mammalian GABA receptors, *Int. Rev. Neurobiol.* 24:181–212.

3. Jesberger, J. A., and Richardson, J. A., 1985, Neurochemical aspects of depression, *International Journal of Neuroscience* 27:19–47.

4. Schatzberg, A. F., and Cole, J. O., eds., 1986, *Manual of Clinical Psychopharmacology,* Washington, D.C.: American Psychiatric Press.

5. Etiene, P., and Baudry, M., 1990, Role of excitatory amino acid neurotransmission in synaptic plasticity and pathology, *J. Neural Transm. Suppl.* 29:39–48.

6. Willner, P., 1983, Dopamine and depression, *Brain Research* 283:222–36.

7. Schuster, L., 1990–91, Genetics of responses to drugs of abuse, *Int. J. Addict* 25:57–79.

8. Goodwin, D. W., Schulsinger, F., Hermansen, L., Guze, S. B., and Winokur, G., 1973, Alcohol problems in adoptees raised apart from alcoholic biological parents, *Arch. Gen. Psychiatry* 28:238–43.

9. Genazzani, A. R., et al., 1982, Central deficiency of beta-endorphin in alcohol addicts, *J. Clin. Endocrinology and Metab.* 55:583–86.

10. Ahtee, L., et al., 1974, 5-hydroxytryptamine in the blood platelets of cirrhotic and hypertensive patients, *Experientia* 30:1328–29.

11. Alec, Roy, et al., 1988, Biochemical abnormalities in pathological gamblers, *Arch. Gen. Psychiatry* 45:369.

12. George, F. R., 1991, Is there a common biological basis for reinforcement from alcohol and other drugs? *J. Addict. Dis.* 10:127–39.

13. Hoebel, B. G., 1985, Brain neurotransmitters in food and drug reward, *Am. J. Clin. Nutrition* 42:1133–50.

14. Blum, K., 1984, Psychogenetics of drug seeking behavior, in E. E. Muller and A. R. Genazzani, eds., *Central and Peripheral Endorphins,* New York: Raven Press, pp. 339–56.

15. Hughes, J., 1975, Isolation of an endogenous compound from the brain with pharmacological properties similar to morphine, *Brain Research* 88:285–308.

16. Van Ree, J. M., and De Wied, D., 1985, Neuropeptides and addiction, in K. Blum and L. Manxo, eds., *Neurotoxicology,* New York: Dekker, pp. 135–62.

17. Szara, S., 1982, Opiate receptors and endogenous opiates, *Prod. Neuropsychopharmacolbiol. Psychiatry* 6:3–15.

18. Phillis, J. W., 1977, The role of cyclic nucleotides in the CNS, *Can. J. Neurol. Sci.* 4:151–95.

19. Alec, Roy, et al., 1988, Biochemical abnormalities in pathological gamblers, *Arch. Gen. Psychiatry* 45:309.

20. Smart, T. G., 1989, Excitatory amino acids, *Cell. Mol. Neurobiol.* 9:193–206.

21. Rasmussen, H., Jensen, P., Lake, W., and Goodman, D. B., 1977, Calcium ion as second messenger, *Clin. Endocrinol. (Oxf.)* 5:119–279.

22. Robinson, T. E., and Becker, J. B., 1986, Enduring changes in brain and behavior produced by chronic amphetamine administration, *Brain Research* 396:157–98.

23. Blum, K., and Briggs, A. H., 1989, Ethanol ingestive behavior as a function of central neurotransmission, *Experientia* 45:444–52.

24. Gold, M. S., Washton, A., and Dackis, C. A., 1985, Cocaine abuse neuro-chemistry, phenomenology and treatment, *Nat. Inst. of Drug Abuse Research Mon.* 16:130–50.

25. Wurtman, R. J., 1983, Food consumption, neurotransmitter synthesis, and human behavior, *Experientia Suppl.* 44:356–69.

26. Yogman, M. W., and Zeisel, S. H., 1982–83, Assessing effects of serotonin precursors on newborn behavior, *J. Psychiatry Res.* 17:123–33.

27. Strain, G. W., 1981, Nutrition, brain function and behavior, *Psychiatr. Clin. North Am.* 4:253–68.

28. Blum, K., Allison, D., Trachtenberg, M. C., Williams, R. W., and Loeblich, L. A., 1988, Reduction of both drug hunger and withdrawal against advice rate of cocaine abusers in a 30-day inpatient treatment program by the neuronutrient Tropamine, *Current Therapeutic Research* 43.

29. Blum, K., Trachtenberg, M. C., and Ramsay, J. C., 1988, Improvement of inpatient treatment of the alcoholic as a function of neurotransmitter restoration, *Inter. J. of the Addictions* 23:991–98.

30. Blum, K., and Trachtenberg, M. C., 1988, Neurogenetic deficits caused by alcoholism, *J. Psychoactive Drugs* 20.

31. Bhagat, B. D., 1979, *Mode of Action of Autonomic Drugs,* Graceway, pp. 22–33.

32. Koelle, G. B., 1975, Neurohormonal transmission of the autonomic nervous system, in L. S. Goodman and A. Gilman, eds., *The Pharmacological Basis of Therapeutics,* New York: Macmillan.

33. Christy, N. P., 1975, Diseases of the endocrine system, in P. B. Beeson and W. McDermott, eds., *Textbook of Medicine,* New York: W. B. Saunders.

34. Szara, S., 1982, Opiate receptors and endogenous opiates, *Prod. Neuropsycho-pharmacolbiol. Psychiatry* 6:3–15.

35. Pfaus, J. G., and Gorzaolka, B. B., 1987, Opioids and sexual behavior, *Neurosci. Biobehav. Rev.* 11:1–34.

36. Halvreich, U., and Endicott, J., 1981, Possible involvement of endorphin withdrawal or imbalance in specific premenstrual syndromes and postpartum depression, *Med. Hypotheses* 7:1045–58.

37. Francis, G. S., 1987, Hemodynamic and neurohumoral responses to dynamic exercise, *Circulation* 76:viii–7.

38. Stone, H. L., Dormer, K. J., Foreman, R. D., Thies, R., and Blair, R. W., 1985, Neural regulation of the cardiovascular system during exercise, *Fed. Proc.* 44:2271–78.

39. Chaouloff, F., 1989, Physical exercise and brain monoamines, *Acta Physiol. Scand.* 137:1–13.

40. Parry-Billings, M., Blomstrand, E., McAndrew, N., and Newsholme, E. A., 1990, A communicational link between skeletal muscle, brain, and cells of the immune system, *Int. J. Sports Med.* 11 Suppl. 2:S122–28.

41. Milkman, H., and Sunderwirth, S., *Personal Communication.*

42. Milkman, H., and Frosch, W., 1980, Theory of drug preference, in D. J. Letteri, M. Sayers, and H. W. Person, eds., *Theory on Drug Abuse,* NIDA Research Mono. 30, Rockville, Maryland: NIDA.

43. Khantzian, F., and Shaffer, H., 1981, A contemporary psychoanalytic view of addiction theory and treatment, in J. Lowinson and P. Ruiz, eds., *Substance Abuse,* Baltimore: Williams and Wilkins.

44. Slater, P., 1980, *Wealth Addiction,* New York: Dutton.

45. Billigmeier, S., 1990, *Inner Eating,* Nashville: Oliver-Nelson.

46. Peele, S., and Brodsky, A., 1975, *Love and Addiction,* New York: Taplinger.

47. Drosh, W., and Milkman, H., 1977, Ego functions and drug use, in J. D. Blaine and D. A. Julius, eds., *Psychodynamics of Drug Dependence,* NIDA Research Mono. 12, Rockville, Maryland: NIDA.

48. Wise, R. A., 1984, Neural mechanism of the reinforcing action of cocaine, *NIDA Res. Monosr. Ser.* 50:15–33.

49. Alec, Roy, et al., 1988, Biochemical abnormalities in pathological gamblers, *Arch. Gen. Psychiatry* 45:309.

50. Robertson, J. C., 1990, Sexual addictions as a disease, *American Journal of Preventive Psychiatry and Neurology* 2.

51. Robertson, J. C., 1989, Breaking the cycle of relapse, *Professional Counselor* 3.

Appendix C

Word List

Following are some of the words used in the *Help Yourself System of Recovery*. It may be helpful to refer to this list frequently as you read the text and plan your recovery.

acceptance The admission of reality; the attitude that says, "This is the way it is."

addiction A behavior that is repeated in spite of the consequences to oneself or others.

arousal personality This neurochemical personality type enjoys or is more comfortable with excitatory thoughts, activities, or behavior. (Gambling causes excitement.)

baseline neurotransmission levels The level of neurotransmission that the brain thinks is normal. This level may be different from the level that makes persons feel good. It is then physiologically normal, but it may be different from the emotional or psychological level.

compulsive theme A psychological need met through addictive behavior. (Power is a theme; cocaine use is the addiction.)

defensive management Refers to the process of doing something when thinking starts to become obsessive or compulsive about things that triggered the original addiction.

entry point The area where addicted persons feel the most confident. It can be in the realm of the spiritual, physical, or emotional. This is the area where they begin their recovery.

enzymes Substances in the body that either increase or decrease the action of neurotransmitters.

excitatory An increase in nerve responses caused by a thought, behavior, or activity. (Fear can cause a release of excitatory chemical, and the heart pounds, palms sweat, and concentration increases.)

focal point The area where addicted persons feel the least confident.

inhibitory A decrease in nerve responses caused by a thought, behavior, or activity. (A feeling of inadequacy can cause depression.)

287

neurochemical personality   A person's tendency to enjoy a particular level of neurotransmission. This general characteristic describes persons who receive a reward from addictive behavior.

neurochemical profile   A summary of diet, exercise, and behavioral techniques for a person's brain chemistry that will be healthy for and maximize emotional, physical, and spiritual well-being.

neurochemicals   Chemicals in the brain.

neurochemistry   The study of chemicals in the brain.

neurohormonal   The influence of neurochemicals on the hormonal system; the effects of brain chemicals on a person's hormones.

neurotransmission   The rate at which a nerve carries electrical impulses.

neurotransmitter   A chemical in the brain that controls the rate of neurotransmission or speed of the electrical impulse.

normal   What the physical body tries to maintain. This can be different from what is comfortable emotionally or physiologically.

offensive management   Refers to doing something to prevent the addiction from returning.

reward   The payoff from addictive behavior. It is a good feeling or the lessening of a bad feeling, such as stress.

reward center   The part of the brain that causes a good feeling or lessens a negative one when it is stimulated.

satiation personality   A neurochemical personality that is more comfortable with or prefers a decrease in neurotransmission. (For most people, overeating has a quieting effect.)

spiritual   A view of life that includes purpose and responses to life as well as the understanding of self, God, and others.

spiritual conflicts   Spiritual conflicts occur when a person has disharmony in any of the three areas of unconditional love, acceptance, and self-discipline.

spiritual health   A way of seeing what we are when we grasp the strengths of who we are. Then we can change what we don't want to be. Far too many self-help psychologies ask us to look at what we are and work on what we're not.

spiritual recovery   Unless the family is involved in recovery, the person will not have a spiritual recovery. The person may have a "peaceful coexistence."

theme   General psychological need.

unconditional love   Love without demands.

Bibliography

Dr. Joel C. Robertson

Professional Journal Articles (since 1988)

"Preventing Relapse and Transfer of Addiction, A Neurochemical Approach," *EAP Digest,* Sept./Oct. 1988, Vol. 8, No. 6.

"Interview: Nature of the Beast," *Employee Assistance Magazine,* Oct. 1988, Vol. 1, No. 3.

"Filling the Emptiness: Cocaine Anhedonia," *Professional Counselor,* Jan./Feb. 1989, Vol. 4, No. 3.

"Breaking the Cycle of Relapse," *Professional Counselor,* March/April 1989, Vol. 3, No. 5.

"Interview: Professional Sports and Alcoholism," *Physician and Sports Medicine,* April 1989.

"The Role of Recreation in Treatment: Changing Self-Destructive Behavior," *Adolescent Counselor,* June/July 1989, Vol. 2, No. 2.

"Neurochemistry and the 1990's," *Professional Counselor,* July/Aug. 1989, Vol. 4, No. 1.

"Interview: Sports and Chemical Dependency," *Detroit Magazine,* Sept. 1989.

"Kicking the Habit Around," *Employee Assistance Magazine,* Dec. 1989, Vol. 2, No. 5.

"Sexual Addictions as a Disease: A Neurobehavioral Model," *American Journal of Preventive Psychiatry and Neurology,* May 1990, Vol. 2, No. 3.

"Update on Psychotropics," *Employee Assistance Magazine,* Dec. 1991.

"Prozac, Friend or Foe, to the Recovering Community," *Employee Assistance Magazine,* Dec. 1991.

Special Contracts

"Substance Abuse Treatment Protocols," sponsored in part by the Dept. of Health, Education, and Welfare DHEW #05H00487, 1978.

"Minimal Requirements for Categorization of Substance Abuse

Facilities," sponsored in part by the Dept. of Health, Education, and Welfare DHEW #05H00487, 1978.

Videotapes

"Behavioral Addictions," People Talk Productions, Saginaw, MI, Nov. 1988.

"Cocaine Anhedonia," People Talk Productions, Saginaw, MI, Nov. 1988.

"Corporate Paranoia," People Talk Productions, Saginaw, MI, Sept. 1989.

"On the Cutting Edge," People Talk Productions, Saginaw, MI, Sept. 1990.

"Evaluating Compulsive Behaviors, Using Neurochemical Evaluations," People Talk Productions, Saginaw, MI, Sept. 1990.

Home Recovery Audio Systems

"Dr. Joel Robertson's Home Recovery System—Codependency, The Dependent and You," Robertson Institute, Ltd., Saginaw, MI, Aug. 1990.

"Dr. Joel Robertson's Home Recovery System—Codependency, Resolving Your Inner Conflicts," Robertson Institute, Ltd., Saginaw, MI, Sept. 1990.

"Dr. Joel Robertson's Home Recovery System—Dependency," Robertson Institute, Ltd., Saginaw, MI, Nov. 1990.

"Dr. Joel Robertson's Home Recovery System—Keeping the Weight Off," Robertson Institute, Ltd., Saginaw, MI, scheduled for future release.

Audiocassette Tapes

Over 110 audiocassette tapes are available through the Robertson Neurochemical Institute, Ltd., on compulsive behaviors and life-style adjustment issues.

Taped Television Programs

Over 350 television programs dealing with compulsive disorders and life-style adjustment problems have been provided by Dr. Robertson.

Lectures

Dr. Joel C. Robertson

Treatment Facilities or Programs

College Hospital-Costa Mesa
Costa Mesa, CA
"Dr. Claudia Black and Dr. Joel Robertson Present
    Neurochemistry of Compulsive Disorders"
March 19, 1991

AMA Impaired Health Professionals
Ninth National Conference
Chicago, IL
"Issues in Treatment"
Oct. 29, 1988

National Council on Alcoholism
San Francisco, CA
"Substance Abuse and the Emergency Dept."
Nov. 4, 1978

National Emergency Medical Services Conference
Reno, NV
"Substance Abuse and the Emergency Dept."
Oct. 15, 1979

Great Lakes Student Assistance Conference
Toledo, OH
"Changing Self-Destructive Behavior in Adolescents"
Nov. 13-15, 1988

11th Annual Eastern Regional Conference
Association of Labor-Management Administrators and Consultants on
    Alcoholism
Springfield, MA
"Behavioral Addictions"

June 5, 1989
SECAD-West
Conference on Alcohol and Drug Abuse
Long Beach, CA
"Neurochemistry and Relapse"
May 20, 1989

Advanced Cocaine Seminar
Professional Counselor Magazine
Presenting C. C. Nukols and Dr. Joel Robertson
Kansas City, MO
April 6-7, 1989

North American Congress on Employee Assistance Programs
EAP Magazine
Annual Conference
New York, NY
"Behavioral Addictions: A Neurochemical View"
Aug. 8, 1989

1989 National Alcoholism Forum and Medical Scientific Conference
    on Alcoholism
Atlanta, GA
"Alcohol and Other Drugs: Recent Knowledge/State of the Art"
"Behavioral Addictions—A Neurochemical Approach"
April 28, 1989

First National Healing Our Youth Conference
Edmonton, Alberta, Canada
"Understanding Adolescents' Accelerating Behaviors and
    Misperceptions"
Keynote-Plenary Session
Sept. 17, 1990

Oklahoma Drug and Alcohol Professional Counselor Association
Oklahoma City, OK
"Latest in Research in Brain Neurochemistry"
"Advances in Cocaine Treatment"
Oct. 25, 1990

Edgehill Newport
Newport, RI
"Individual Differences in Neurochemistry"
Oct. 3, 1988

Woodhill Treatment Center
Asheville, NC
"Cocaine: The Addiction Challenge of the 90's"
Sept. 8, 1989

Four Winds Hospital
Katonah, NY
"Neurochemistry and Relapse"
Dec. 22, 1989

O'Connor Hospital
San Jose, CA
"Neurochemistry and Addictions"
Sept. 15, 1989

Lifeline
Chicago, IL
"Neurochemistry and Compulsive Disorders"
Sept. 22, 1989

Lifeline
Detroit, MI
"Neurochemistry and Compulsive Disorders"
Sept. 25, 1989

Williamsburg Recovery Center
Traverse City, MI
"Neurochemistry and Compulsive Disorders"
June 12-13, 1989

Association of Labor-Management Administrators and Consultants on
    Alcoholism
Greater Detroit Chapter
Dearborn, MI
"Current Trends in Cocaine and Alcohol Addiction"
March 9, 1988

National Association of Alcohol and Drug Abuse Counselors
    National Convention
Orlando, FL
"Cocaine Anhedonia"
"Behavioral Addictions"
Film Festival
June 26, 1988

Southeastern Conference on Alcohol Dependency
Atlanta, GA

"Cocaine Anhedonia"
"Behavioral Addictions"
Film Festival
Dec. 1, 1988

Midwest Conference for Alcohol and Other Addictions
Cleveland, OH
"Cocaine Anhedonia"
"Behavioral Addictions"
Film Festival
Aug. 24, 1988

Midwest Addictions Institute
Dearborn, MI
"Cocaine Anhedonia"
"Behavioral Addictions"
Film Festival
Oct. 19, 1988

North America Congress
National Convention
Montreal, Quebec, Canada
"Cocaine Anhedonia"
"Behavioral Addictions"
Film Festival
Aug. 16, 1988

Texas Commission on Alcohol and Drug Abuse in cooperation
    with the University of Texas at Austin
32nd Annual Institute of Alcohol and Drug Studies
Austin, TX
"Neurochemistry of Relapse"
"Cocaine Anhedonia"
July 24, 1989

Interventions
Chicago, IL
"Understanding Accelerating Behavior in Adolescents"
Sept. 14, 1990

Department of the Defense
United States Army
Southern Command
Panama City, Panama
"Understanding Addictions"

"Steroidal Abuse"
Nov. 6-9, 1989

California Association of Alcoholism and Drug Abuse Counselors
Annual Meeting
Santa Cruz, CA
"Behavioral Addictions"—Luncheon Keynote Address
Sept. 23, 1988

The Salvation Army
Starting Point and Turning Point Substance Abuse Services
Grand Rapids, MI
"Neurochemistry and Addictions"
Jan. 9, 1987

National Student Assistance Conference
Arlington, VA
"Acceleration Syndrome"
June 6, 1990

Rivervalley Recovery Center
Medical Staff
Grand Rapids, MI
"Detoxification and Management of the Chemically Dependent Patient"
June 18–20, 1988

Square Lake Counseling Centers
Bloomfield Hills, MI
"Neurochemistry and Addictions"
Sept. 6-8, 1988

Veterans Administration
Saginaw, MI
"Nutritional Aspects of Patients in Substance Abuse Treatment
     Programs"
Dec. 16, 1983

St. Mary's Hospital/Delta College
Advanced EMT Program
Saginaw, MI
"Alcoholism and Drug Abuse"
May 7, 1984

Midland Hospital Center
Nursing Dept.
Midland, MI
"Substance Abuse and Nursing Care"

Sept. 12, 1982
Rivervalley Recovery Center
Treatment Staff
Grand Rapids, MI
"Neurochemistry and Addictions"
June, July, Aug., 1988

Medical or Hospital Staff Inservice

Huron Memorial Hospital
Bad Axe, MI
"Therapy for Acute Intoxication"
May 11, 1984

Huron Memorial Hospital
Bad Axe, MI
"Differential Diagnosis of Psychotropic Drugs"
"Managing Behavioral Emergencies"
Jan. 25, 1985

Saginaw Cooperative Hospitals, Inc.
Department of Family Practice
Saginaw, MI
"Identification and Treatment of the Overdosed Patient"
July 10, 1985

Bay Osteopathic Hospital
BOH Medical Intern Program
Bay City, MI
"Neurochemistry and Behavior"
Sept. 12, Nov. 21, Dec. 5, 1988

Lake Superior State College
National Alcoholism Conference
Sault Ste. Marie, MI
"Over the Counter Drugs and Their Abuse"
Sept. 24, 1979

American Red Cross
Advanced, Emergency Medical Services
Bay City, MI
"Drugs and Their Abuse"
Nov. 21, 1983

American Lung Association of Michigan
Saginaw Chapter

Saginaw, MI
"Nicotine Addiction and Lung Disease"
Nov. 8, 1984

Veterans Administration
Dietetic and Medical Services
Saginaw, MI
"Pharmacological Considerations of Substance Abuse"
Dec. 5, 1986

Veterans Administration
Dietetic and Medical Services
Saginaw, MI
"Nutritional Considerations in Substance Abuse Recovery"
Dec. 4, 1984

Veterans Administration
Dietetic and Medical Services
Saginaw, MI
"Substance Abuse and Counseling"
Feb. 3, 1988

Delta College
Allied Health Division
"Substance Abuse: The Medical Problem"
Sept. 25, 1981

Delta College
Allied Health Division
"Pharmacology of Drugs"
Jan. 3, 1982

Veterans Administration
Saginaw VA Hospital
Saginaw, MI
"Eating Disorders and Addictions"
Jan. 22, 1988

Bay Psychological Associates
Bay City, MI
"Neurochemistry and Addictions"
Sept. 29, 1981

Saginaw Black Nurses Association
Saginaw, MI
"Cultural and Ethnic Issues in Addictions"
Nov. 1, 1983

St. Mary's Hospital
Emergency Medical Services
"Alcoholism and Drug Abuse"
June 2, 1981

Bay Medical Education
Bay City, MI
"Pharmaceutical Protocols in Substance Abuse Patient Management"
Oct. 21, 1981

Bay Medical Education
Emergency Medical Services
Bay City, MI
"Overdose"
March 27, 1982

Saginaw Cooperative Hospitals, Inc.
Behavioral Science Division
Saginaw, MI
"The Neurochemical Basis of Behavior: Pharmacology of Drugs of
    Abuse"
Dec. 4, 1988

Saginaw Cooperative Hospitals, Inc.
Behavioral Science Division
Saginaw, MI
"Sociological Aspects of Chemical Dependency"
Dec. 11, 1988

UAW Region 1-D Winter Institute
Black Lake, MI
"Recognition and Management of the Substance Abuse Person"
March 6, 1978

UAW Region 1-D Winter Institute
Black Lake, MI
"Substance Abuse Programs"
June 2, 1979

St. Mary's Medical Center
4th Annual Pediatric Conference
Saginaw, MI
"Substance Abuse in the Pediatric Population"
Oct. 18, 1988

Rivervalley Recovery Center Medical Staff
Grand Rapids, MI

"Effective Detoxification"
Oct. 11, 1988

AMA Program to Improve Health Care in Jails
Michigan State Medical Society
Saginaw, MI
"Chemical Dependency: Alcohol and Drug Abuse"
Nov. 25, 1980

Saginaw Valley State College
Department of Psychology
Saginaw, MI
"Compulsive Behavior"
March 20, 1984

Bay Medical Center
Nursing Staff
Bay City, MI
"Addictions and Recovery"
Sept. 22, 1982

Bay Medical Education
Thumb Pharmacy Association
Bad Axe, MI
"Pharmaceutical Protocols in Substance Abuse and Patient Management"
July 21, 1982

Michigan Non-Profit Homes Association
Lansing, MI
Annual Conference
"Psychotropics and the Elderly"
"Addictions and the Elderly"
Sept. 19, 1985

Corporate Presentations

Delta College
Health Fair 1980
Bay City, MI
"Understanding Addictions"
March 10, 1980

Chevrolet-Pontiac-Canada Group
General Motors Corporation
Regional Meeting
Detroit, MI

"Cocaine Addiction and Therapy"
Oct. 24, 1986

United Airlines
Medical Coordinators
Chicago, IL
"Cocaine and Its Effects"
April 24, 1989

Chevrolet-Pontiac-Canada Group
General Motors Corporation
Flint Area Employee Assistance Representatives
Flint, MI
"New Advances in Chemical Dependency Treatment"
Nov. 13, 1986

GM-UAW Employee Assistance Program Workshop
New Orleans, LA
"Cost Effective Alternatives to Inpatient Chemical Dependency
    Treatment"—Plenary Session
Jan. 6, 1987

UAW Region 1-D Conference
Grand Rapids, MI
"Substance Abuse and Recovery Techniques"
Dec. 5, 1978

Consumer Power Company
North Central Region
Midland, MI
"Employees and Their Problems"
Sept. 1, 1988

UAW Local 362
Bay City, MI
"The Medical Consequences of Alcohol"
Nov. 5, 1981

GM-UAW Employee Assistance Program Workshop
New Orleans, LA
"Neurochemical Basis of Behavior: Alternatives to Inpatient
    Chemical Dependency Treatment"—Workshops
Jan. 7, 1987

AFL-CIO Community Services Counseling Program
Bay City, MI
"Substance Abuse and Prevention"

March 18, 1986

Little Caesars National Convention
San Diego, CA
"Neurochemistry and Personal Stress-Developing a Lifestyle to
    Maximize Your Potential"
March 6, 1989

Little Caesars National Convention
San Diego, CA
"Drugs in the Workplace—Identification and Employer's Rights"
March 7, 1989

Memberships

Substance Abuse Curriculum Advisory Committee
Delta College
Bay City, MI
April 1980–April 1983

National Council on Alcoholism
May 1975–May 1984

Michigan Alcohol and Addiction Association
May 1975–May 1984

National Institute on Alcohol Abuse and Alcoholism
May 1975–May 1982

National Institute on Drug Abuse
May 1975–May 1982

Alcohol and Drug Problems Association
May 1975–May 1982

Association of Labor Management and Associates
May 1975–May 1991

National Neuroscience and Addiction Research Foundation
Kansas City, MO
Dec. 1, 1989–present

Commission on Ministerial Health
Lutheran Church-Missouri Synod
Ann Arbor, MI
Oct. 7, 1988–Nov. 5, 1989

Bay Osteopathic Hospital
Consulting, Medical Staff
1979–1988